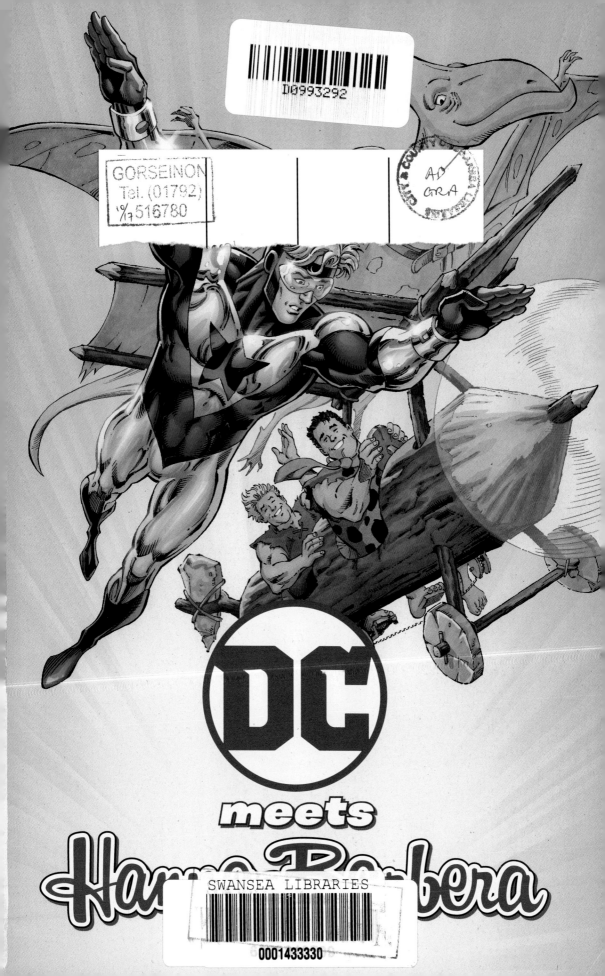

DC
meets
Hanna-Barbera

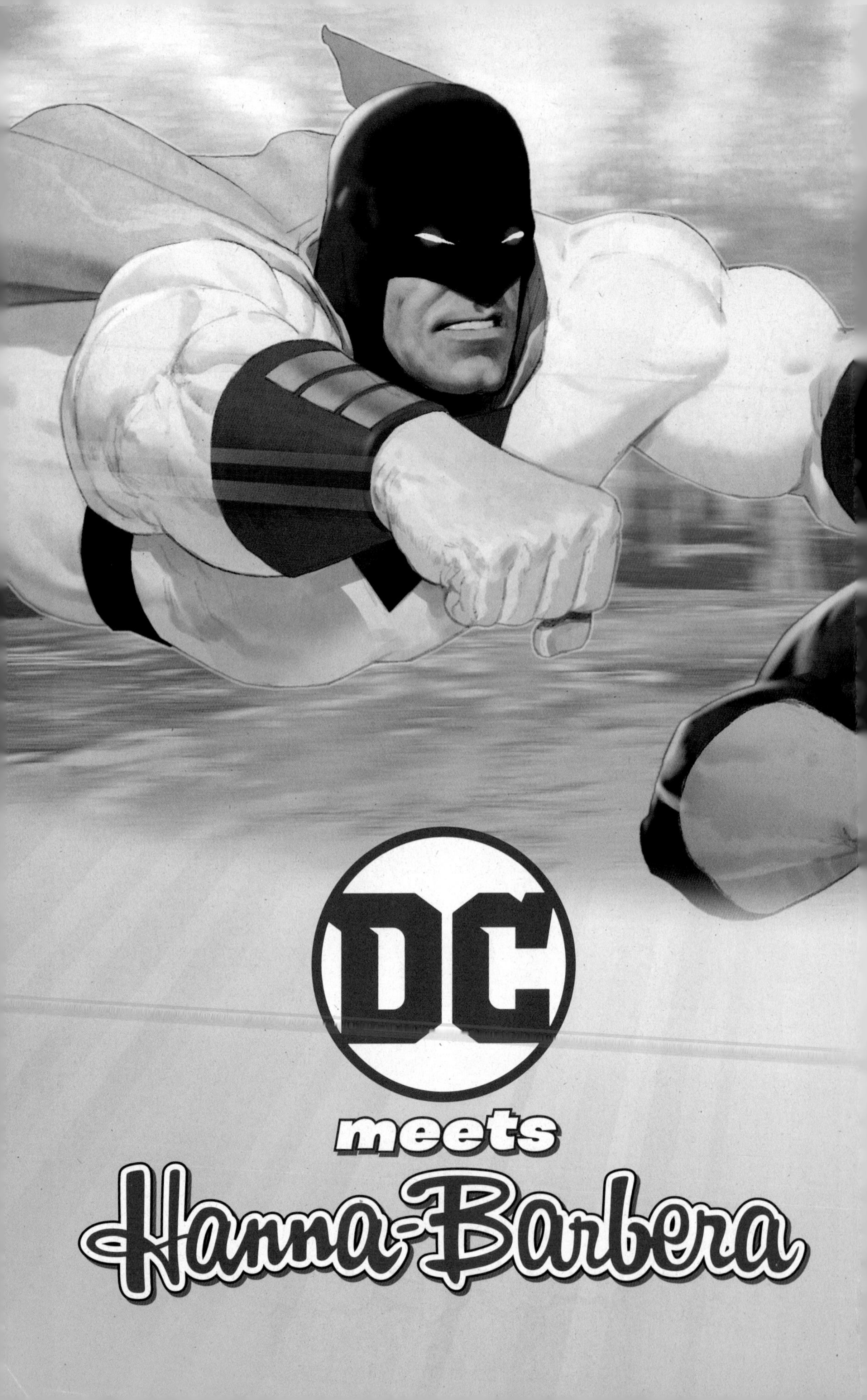
DC
meets
Hanna-Barbera

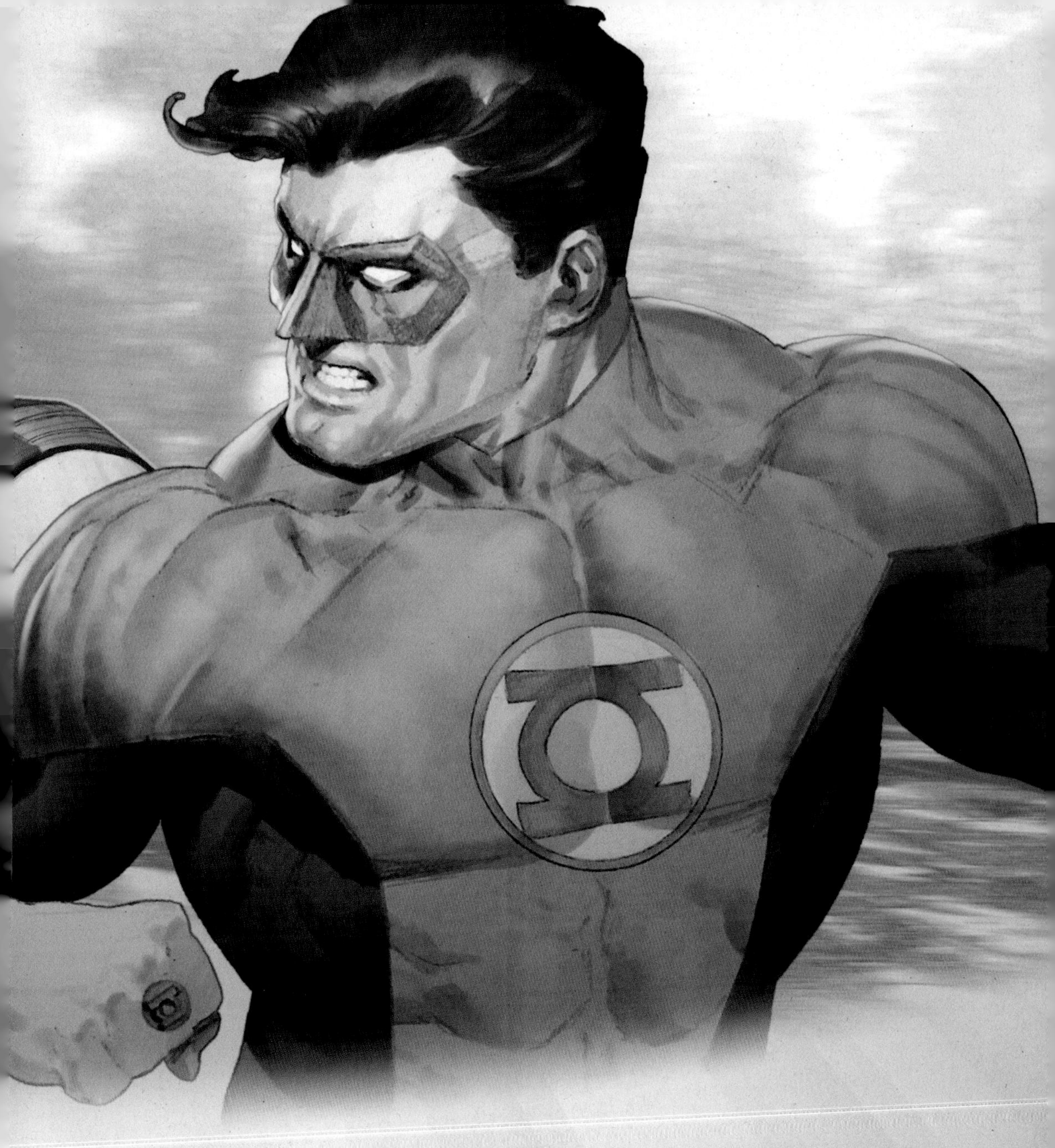

MARK RUSSELL
JAMES TYNION IV
CHRISTOPHER SEBELA
MARC ANDREYKO
JEFF PARKER
TONY BEDARD
JIMMY PALMIOTTI
AMANDA CONNER
HOWARD CHAYKIN
DAN DiDIO
writers

RICK LEONARDI
SCOTT HANNA
ARIEL OLIVETTI
STEVE LIEBER
BEN CALDWELL
MARK MORALES
PIER BRITO
HOWARD CHAYKIN
PHIL WINSLADE
HOWARD PORTER
artists

STEVE BUCCELLATO
ARIEL OLIVETTI
VERONICA GANDINI
JEREMY LAWSON
ALEX SINCLAIR
WIL QUINTANA
CHRIS CHUCKRY
colorists

DAVE SHARPE
A LARGER WORLD STUDIOS
MICHAEL HEISLER
PAT BROSSEAU
NICK J. NAPOLITANO
letterers

ARIEL OLIVETTI collection cover artist

BOOSTER GOLD created by **DAN JURGENS** *ADAM STRANGE created by* **GARDNER FOX**

MARIE JAVINS
EDDIE BERGANZA   *Editors – Original Series*
BRITTANY HOLZHERR   *Associate Editor – Original Series*
ANDREW MARINO   *Assistant Editor – Original Series*
JEB WOODARD   *Group Editor – Collected Editions*
LIZ ERICKSON   *Editor – Collected Edition*
STEVE COOK   *Design Director – Books*
CURTIS KING JR.   *Publication Design*
BOB HARRAS   *Senior VP – Editor-in-Chief, DC Comics*

DIANE NELSON   *President*
DAN DiDIO   *Publisher*
JIM LEE   *Publisher*
GEOFF JOHNS   *President & Chief Creative Officer*
AMIT DESAI   *Executive VP – Business & Marketing Strategy,*
                            Direct to Consumer & Global Franchise Management
SAM ADES   *Senior VP – Direct to Consumer*
BOBBIE CHASE   *VP – Talent Development*
MARK CHIARELLO   *Senior VP – Art, Design & Collected Editions*
JOHN CUNNINGHAM   *Senior VP – Sales & Trade Marketing*
ANNE DePIES   *Senior VP – Business Strategy, Finance & Administration*
DON FALLETTI   *VP – Manufacturing Operations*
LAWRENCE GANEM   *VP – Editorial Administration & Talent Relations*
ALISON GILL   *Senior VP – Manufacturing & Operations*
HANK KANALZ   *Senior VP – Editorial Strategy & Administration*
JAY KOGAN   *VP – Legal Affairs*
THOMAS LOFTUS   *VP – Business Affairs*
JACK MAHAN   *VP – Business Affairs*
NICK J. NAPOLITANO   *VP – Manufacturing Administration*
EDDIE SCANNELL   *VP – Consumer Marketing*
COURTNEY SIMMONS   *Senior VP – Publicity & Communications*
JIM (SKI) SOKOLOWSKI   *VP – Comic Book Specialty Sales & Trade Marketing*
NANCY SPEARS   *VP – Mass, Book, Digital Sales & Trade Marketing*

DC MEETS HANNA-BARBERA

Published by DC Comics. Compilation and all new material Copyright © 2017 DC Comics and Hanna-Barbera. All Rights Reserved. Originally published in single magazine form in BOOSTER GOLD/THE FLINTSTONES SPECIAL #1, GREEN LANTERN/SPACE GHOST SPECIAL #1, ADAM STRANGE/FUTURE QUEST SPECIAL #1, SUICIDE SQUAD/BANANA SPLITS SPECIAL #1. Copyright © 2017 DC Comics and Hanna-Barbera. All Rights Reserved. The stories, characters and incidents featured in this publication are entirely fictional. DC Comics does not read or accept unsolicited submissions of ideas, stories or artwork.

DCC039919

 Copyright © 2017 Hanna-Barbera.
SPACE GHOST, THE FLINTSTONES,
BANANA SPLITS and JONNY QUEST and all related
characters and elements © & ™ Hanna-Barbera.
WB SHIELD: ™ & © WBEI. (s17)
DC Comics
2900 West Alameda Ave., Burbank, CA 91505
Printed by Solisco Printers,
Scott, QC, Canada. 8/18/17. First Printing.
ISBN: 978-1-4012-7604-1

Library of Congress Cataloging-in-Publication Data is available.

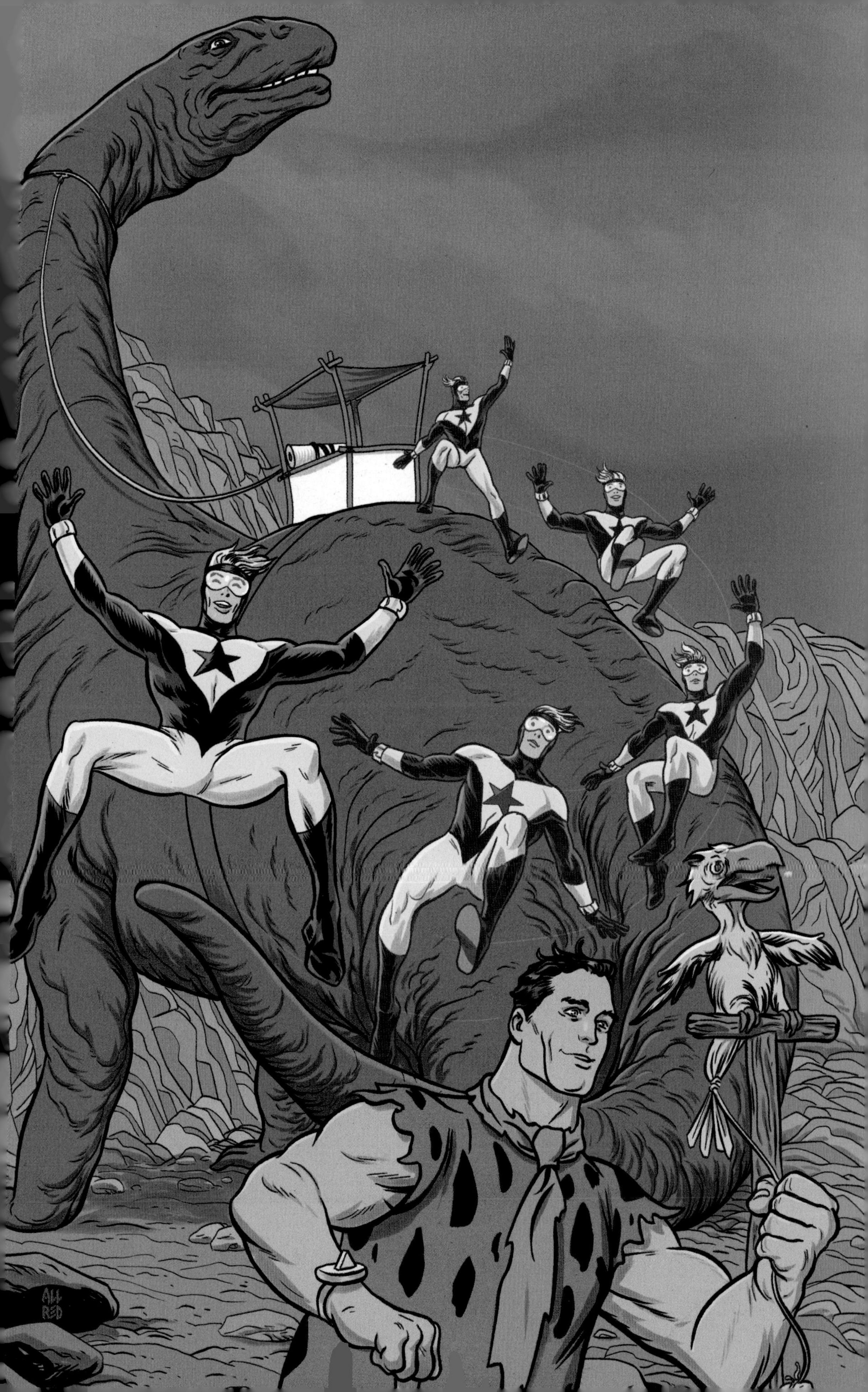
ALL
RED

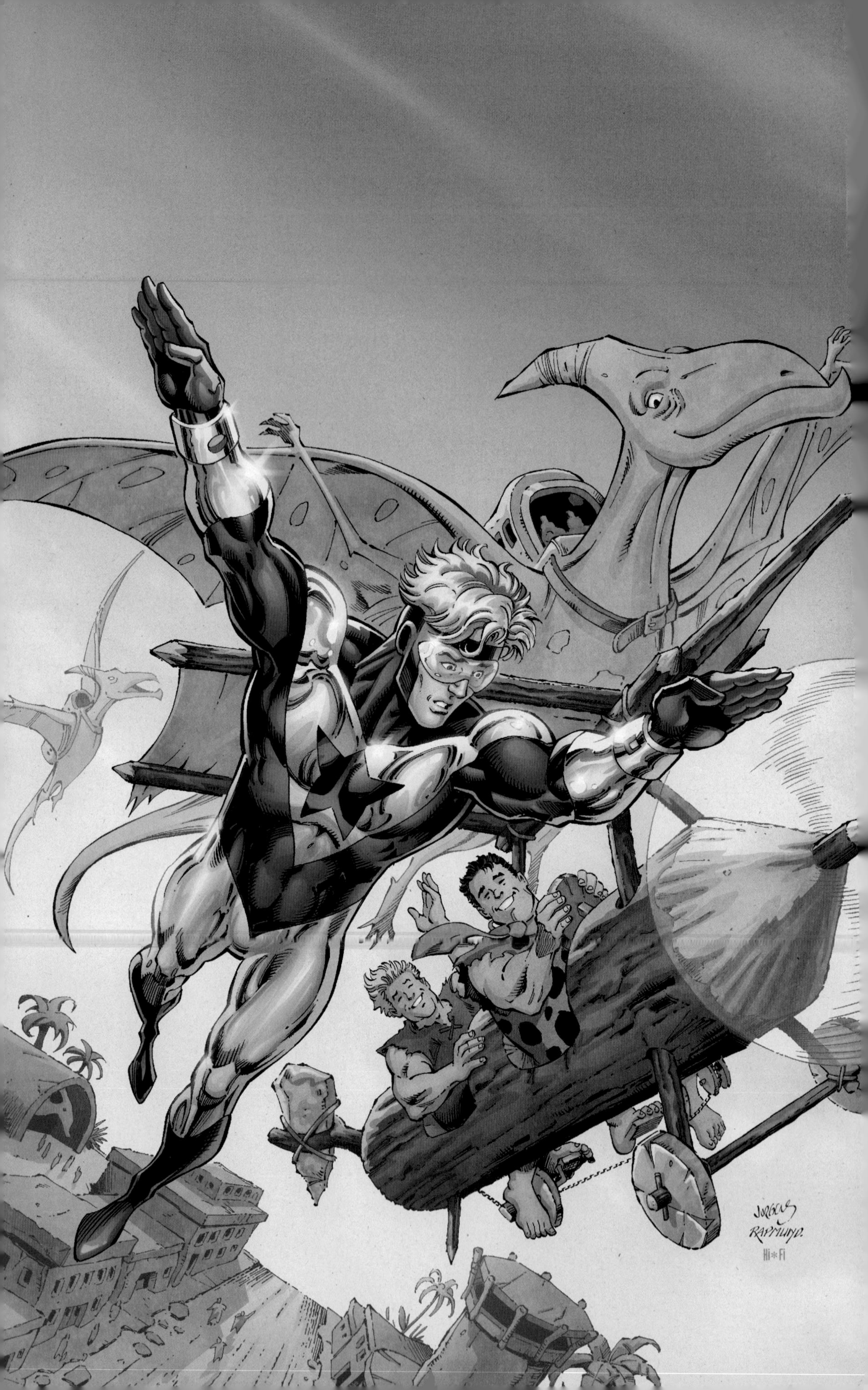
JURGENS
RAPMUND.
HI*FI

WHICH DO YOU THINK IS SEXIER, *SKEETS?* THE BLUE GOGGLES, OR THE GOLD ONES?

I THINK THEY'RE BOTH NICE.

I WANT EVERYTHING TO BE PERFECT TONIGHT. THAT'S WHY I'M TAKING *AMY* TO THE FINEST RESTAURANT IN TOWN.

YOU'RE A SOFT TOUCH, SIR.

DAMN DODO KEEPS EATING MY SOCKS!

PERHAPS YOU SHOULD BE MORE JUDICIOUS IN THE SOUVENIRS YOU KEEP FROM YOUR TIME TRAVELS, SIR.

SQUAGGLE!

MAYBE... DAMN, I THINK I LEFT MY GOOD SWEATER IN MEDIEVAL FRANCE. *OH MY PEACH!* LOOK, SKEETS! *IT'S MY HIGH SCHOOL YEARBOOK!*

TONIGHT'S YOUR NIGHT, YOU HANDSOME CHEETAH.

NORTH GOT SWASHBUCK CLASS OF 240

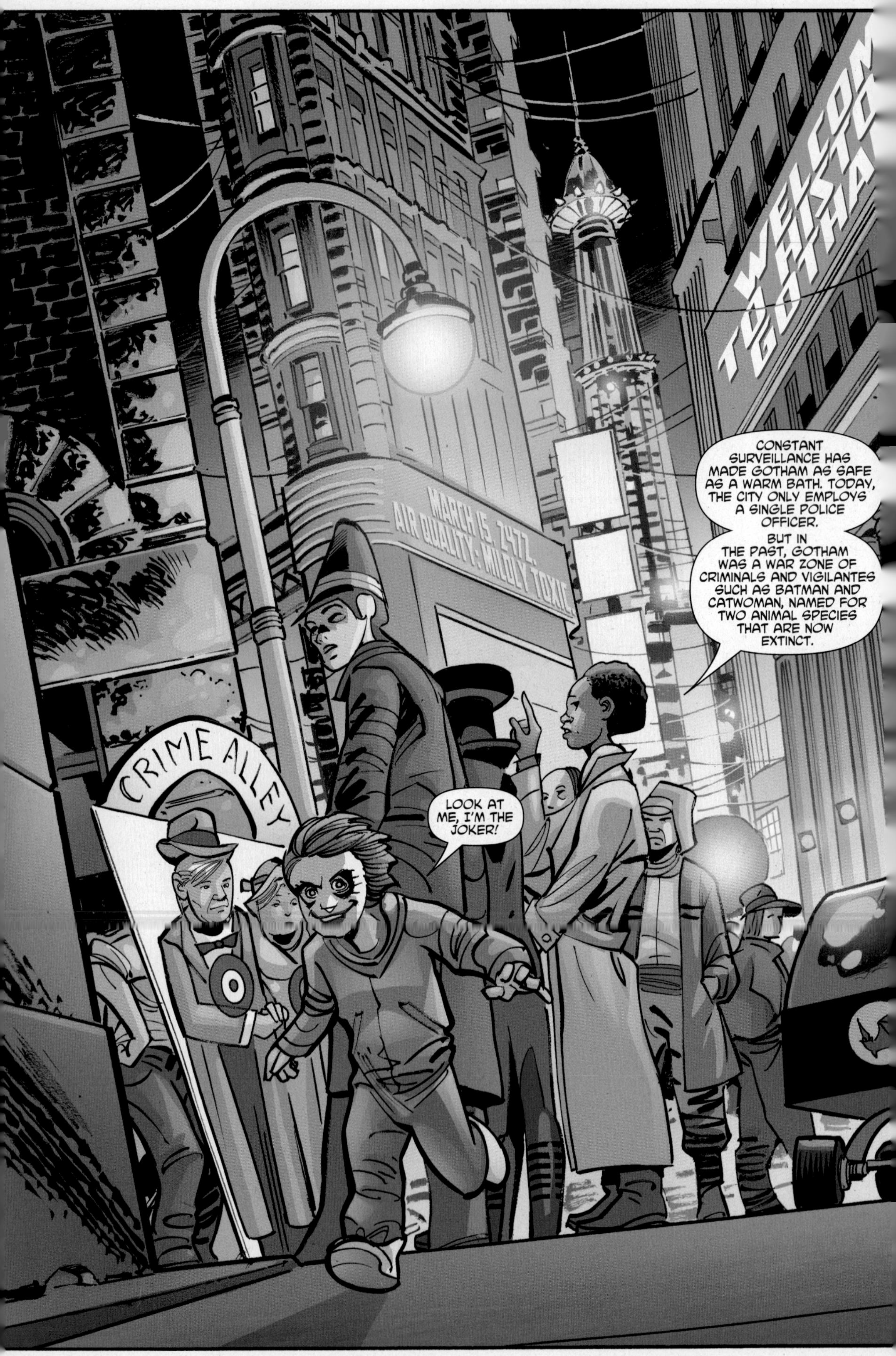
WELCOM
TO HISTO
GOTHA
MARCH 15, 2472.
AIR QUALITY: MILDLY TOXIC.
CONSTANT SURVEILLANCE HAS MADE GOTHAM AS SAFE AS A WARM BATH. TODAY, THE CITY ONLY EMPLOYS A SINGLE POLICE OFFICER.
BUT IN THE PAST, GOTHAM WAS A WAR ZONE OF CRIMINALS AND VIGILANTES SUCH AS BATMAN AND CATWOMAN, NAMED FOR TWO ANIMAL SPECIES THAT ARE NOW EXTINCT.
CRIME ALLEY
LOOK AT ME, I'M THE JOKER!

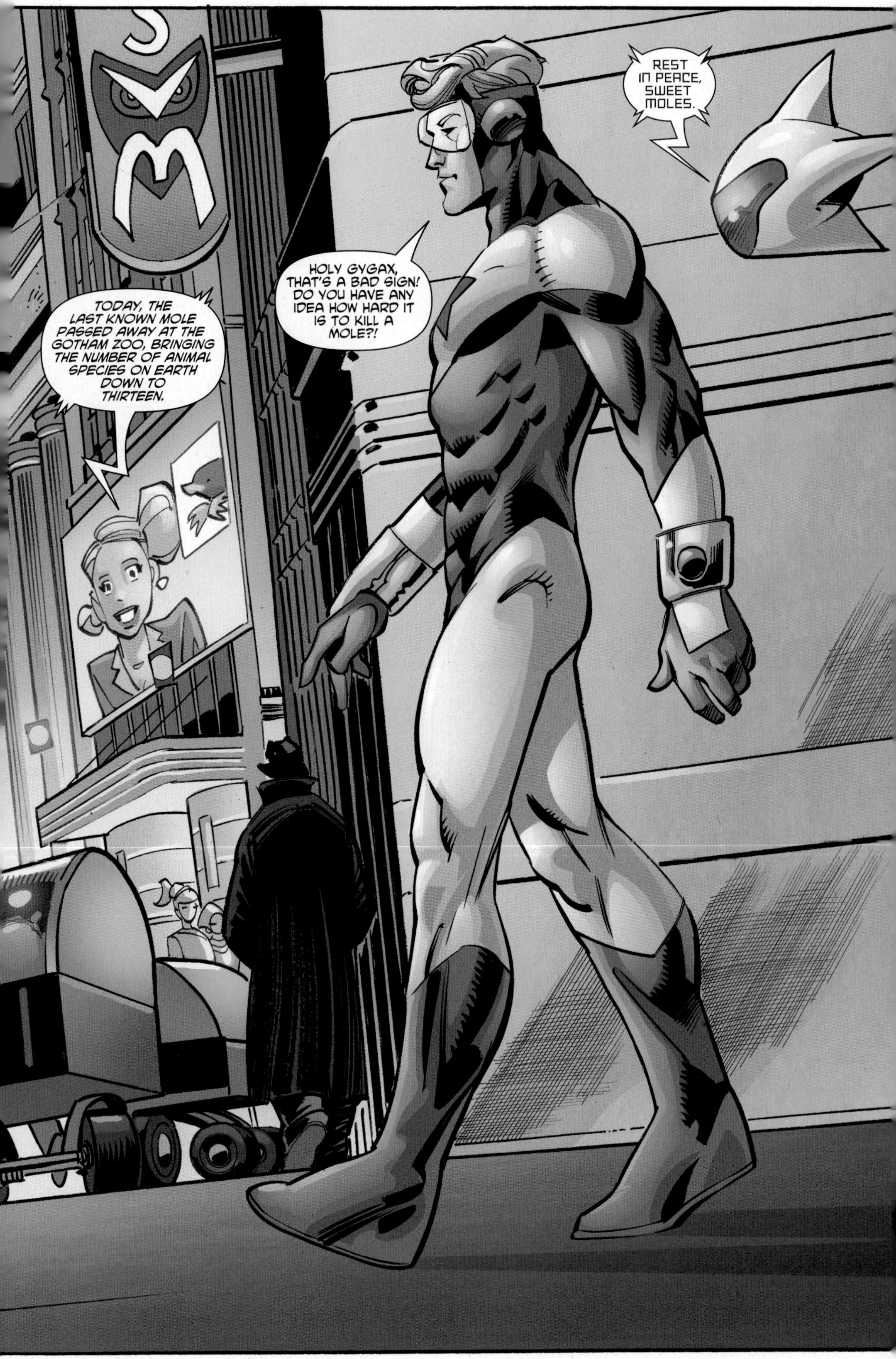
TODAY, THE LAST KNOWN MOLE PASSED AWAY AT THE GOTHAM ZOO, BRINGING THE NUMBER OF ANIMAL SPECIES ON EARTH DOWN TO THIRTEEN.
HOLY GYGAX, THAT'S A BAD SIGN! DO YOU HAVE ANY IDEA HOW HARD IT IS TO KILL A MOLE?!
REST IN PEACE, SWEET MOLES.

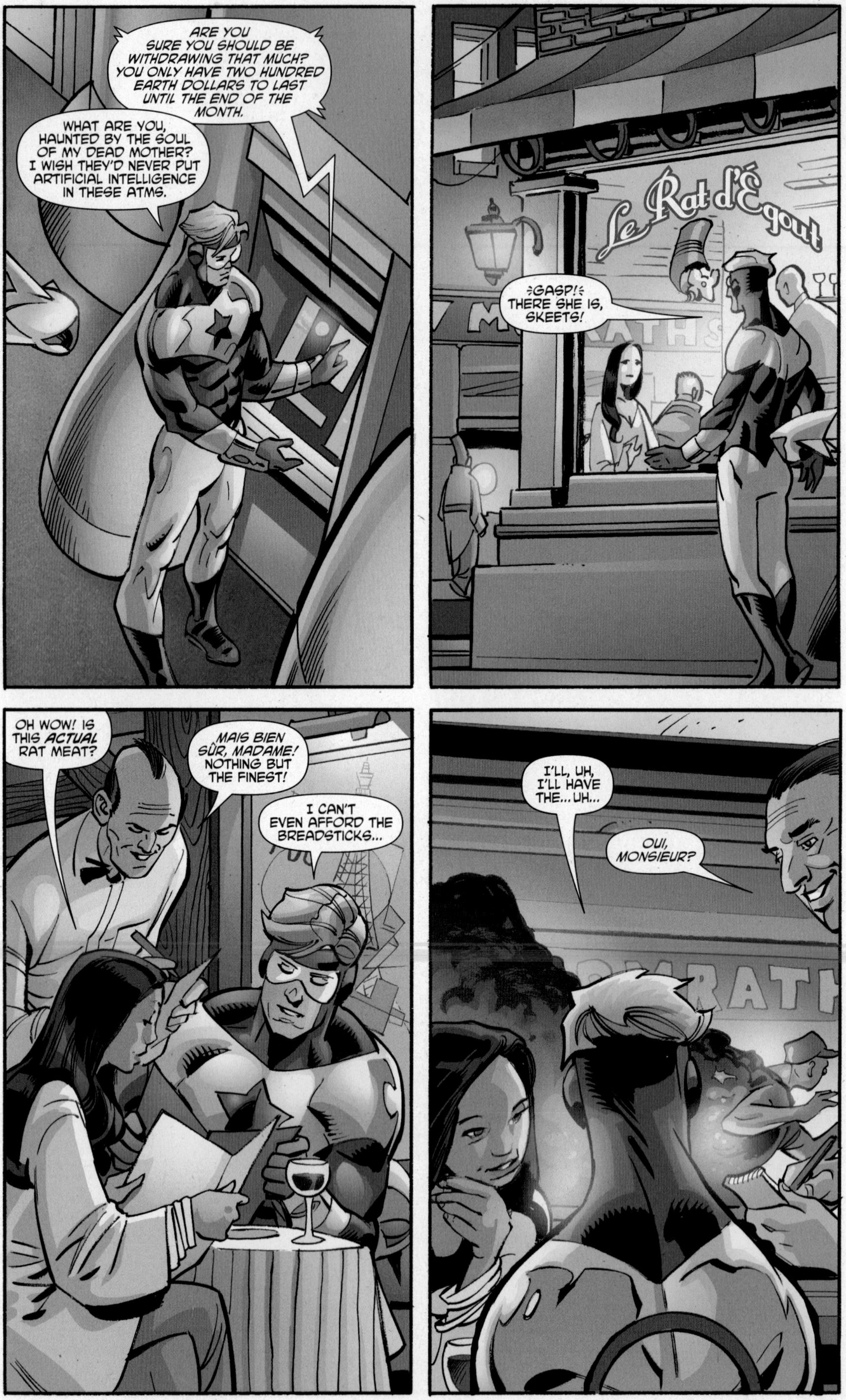
ARE YOU SURE YOU SHOULD BE WITHDRAWING THAT MUCH? YOU ONLY HAVE TWO HUNDRED EARTH DOLLARS TO LAST UNTIL THE END OF THE MONTH.
WHAT ARE YOU, HAUNTED BY THE SOUL OF MY DEAD MOTHER? I WISH THEY'D NEVER PUT ARTIFICIAL INTELLIGENCE IN THESE ATMS.
Le Rat d'Égout
GASP! THERE SHE IS, SKEETS!
OH WOW! IS THIS *ACTUAL* RAT MEAT?
MAIS BIEN SÛR, MADAME! NOTHING BUT THE FINEST!
I CAN'T EVEN AFFORD THE BREADSTICKS...
I'LL, UH, I'LL HAVE THE... UH...
OUI, MONSIEUR?

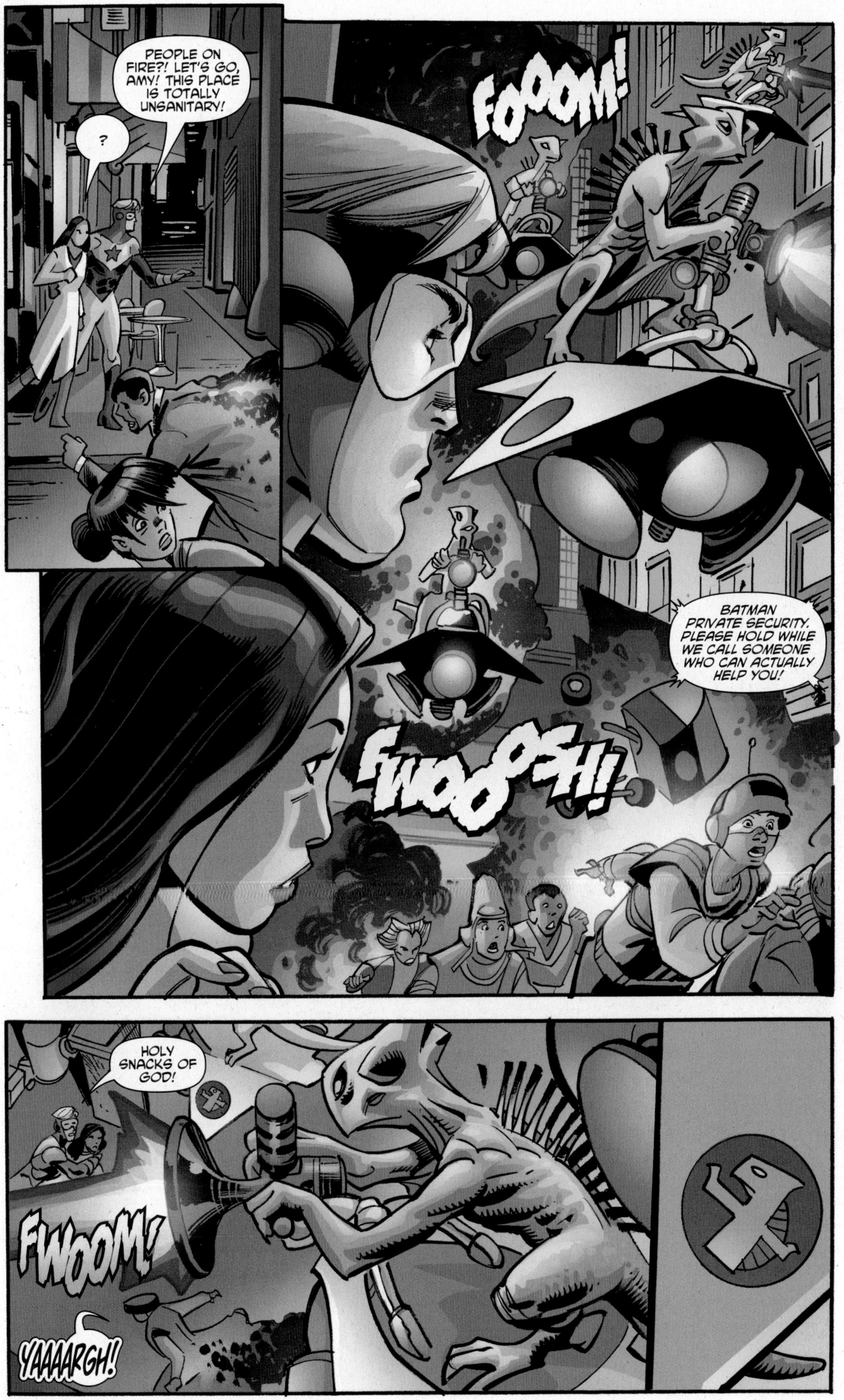
PEOPLE ON FIRE?! LET'S GO, AMY! THIS PLACE IS TOTALLY UNSANITARY!
?
FOOOM!
BATMAN PRIVATE SECURITY. PLEASE HOLD WHILE WE CALL SOMEONE WHO CAN ACTUALLY HELP YOU!
FWOOOSH!!
HOLY SNACKS OF GOD!
FWOOM!
YAAAARGH!

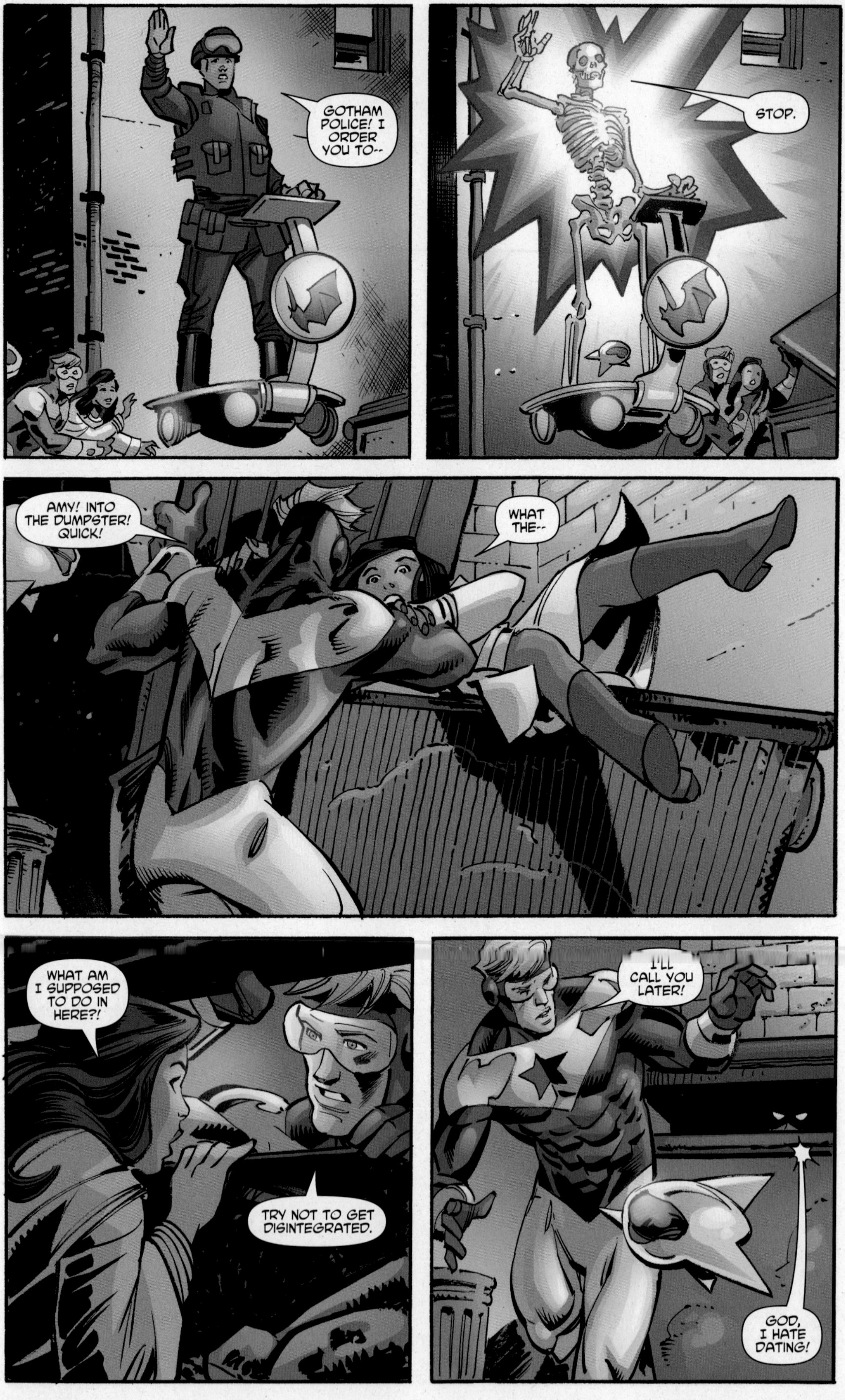
GOTHAM POLICE! I ORDER YOU TO--
STOP.
AMY! INTO THE DUMPSTER! QUICK!
WHAT THE--
WHAT AM I SUPPOSED TO DO IN HERE?!
TRY NOT TO GET DISINTEGRATED.
I'LL CALL YOU LATER!
GOD, I HATE DATING!

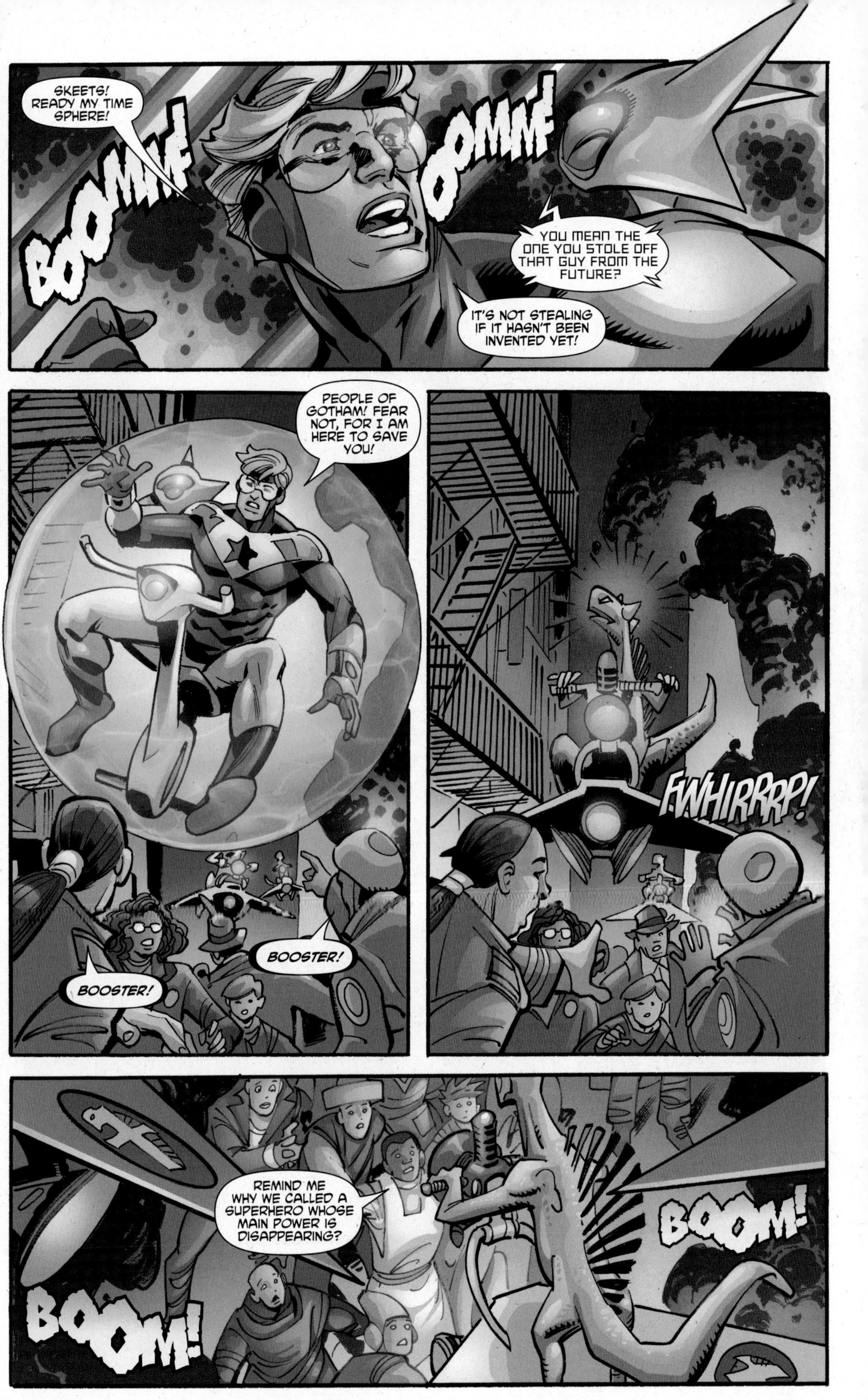
SKEETS! READY MY TIME SPHERE!
BOOMMF
BOOMMF
YOU MEAN THE ONE YOU STOLE OFF THAT GUY FROM THE FUTURE?
IT'S NOT STEALING IF IT HASN'T BEEN INVENTED YET!
PEOPLE OF GOTHAM! FEAR NOT, FOR I AM HERE TO SAVE YOU!
BOOSTER!
BOOSTER!
FWHIRRRP!
REMIND ME WHY WE CALLED A SUPERHERO WHOSE MAIN POWER IS DISAPPEARING?
BOOM!
BOOM!

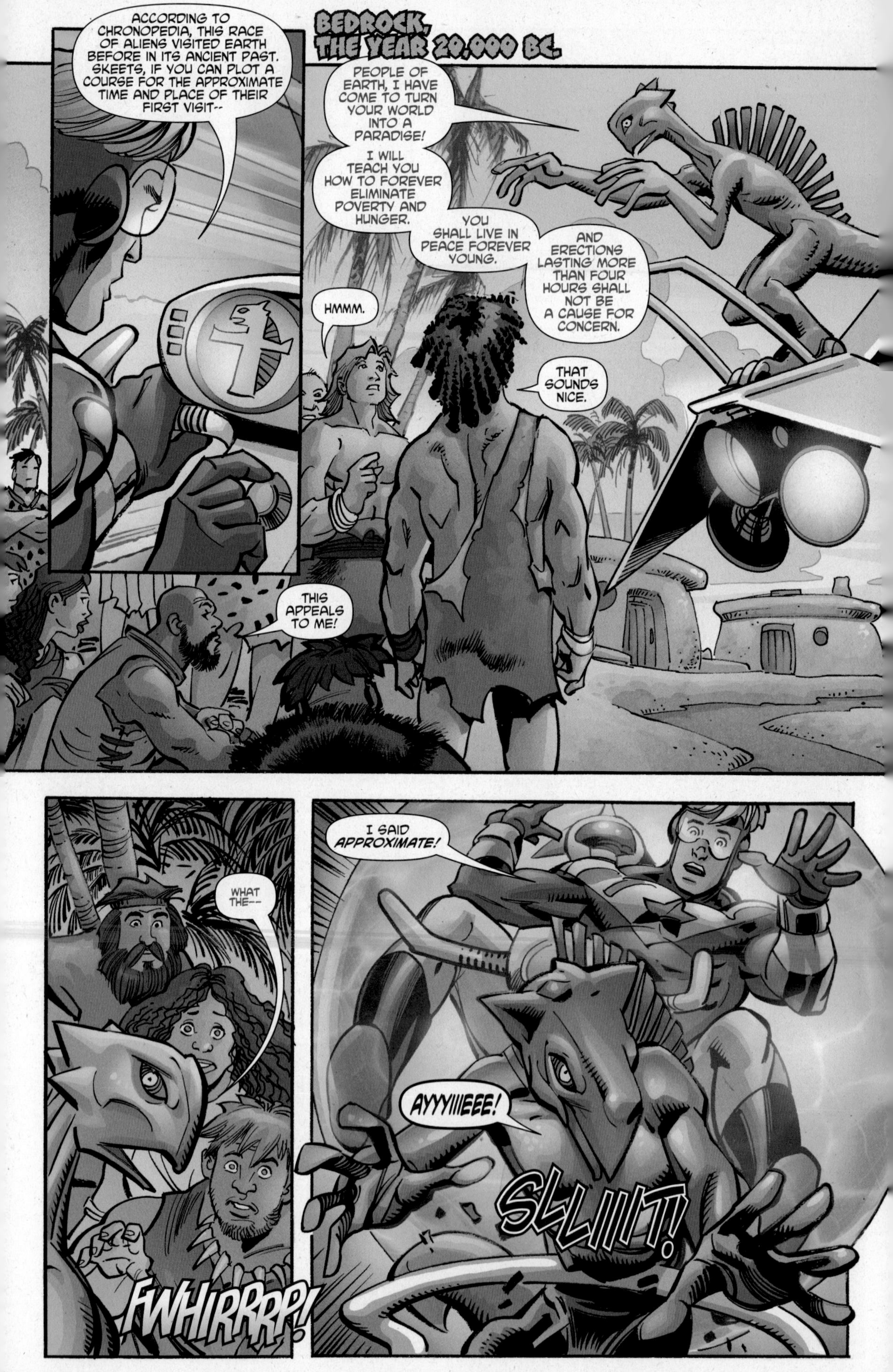
ACCORDING TO CHRONOPEDIA, THIS RACE OF ALIENS VISITED EARTH BEFORE IN ITS ANCIENT PAST. SKEETS, IF YOU CAN PLOT A COURSE FOR THE APPROXIMATE TIME AND PLACE OF THEIR FIRST VISIT--
BEDROCK, THE YEAR 20,000 BC.
PEOPLE OF EARTH, I HAVE COME TO TURN YOUR WORLD INTO A PARADISE!
I WILL TEACH YOU HOW TO FOREVER ELIMINATE POVERTY AND HUNGER.
YOU SHALL LIVE IN PEACE FOREVER YOUNG.
AND ERECTIONS LASTING MORE THAN FOUR HOURS SHALL NOT BE A CAUSE FOR CONCERN.
HMMM.
THAT SOUNDS NICE.
THIS APPEALS TO ME!
WHAT THE--
FWHIRRRP!
I SAID *APPROXIMATE!*
AYYYIIIEEE!
SLLIIIT!

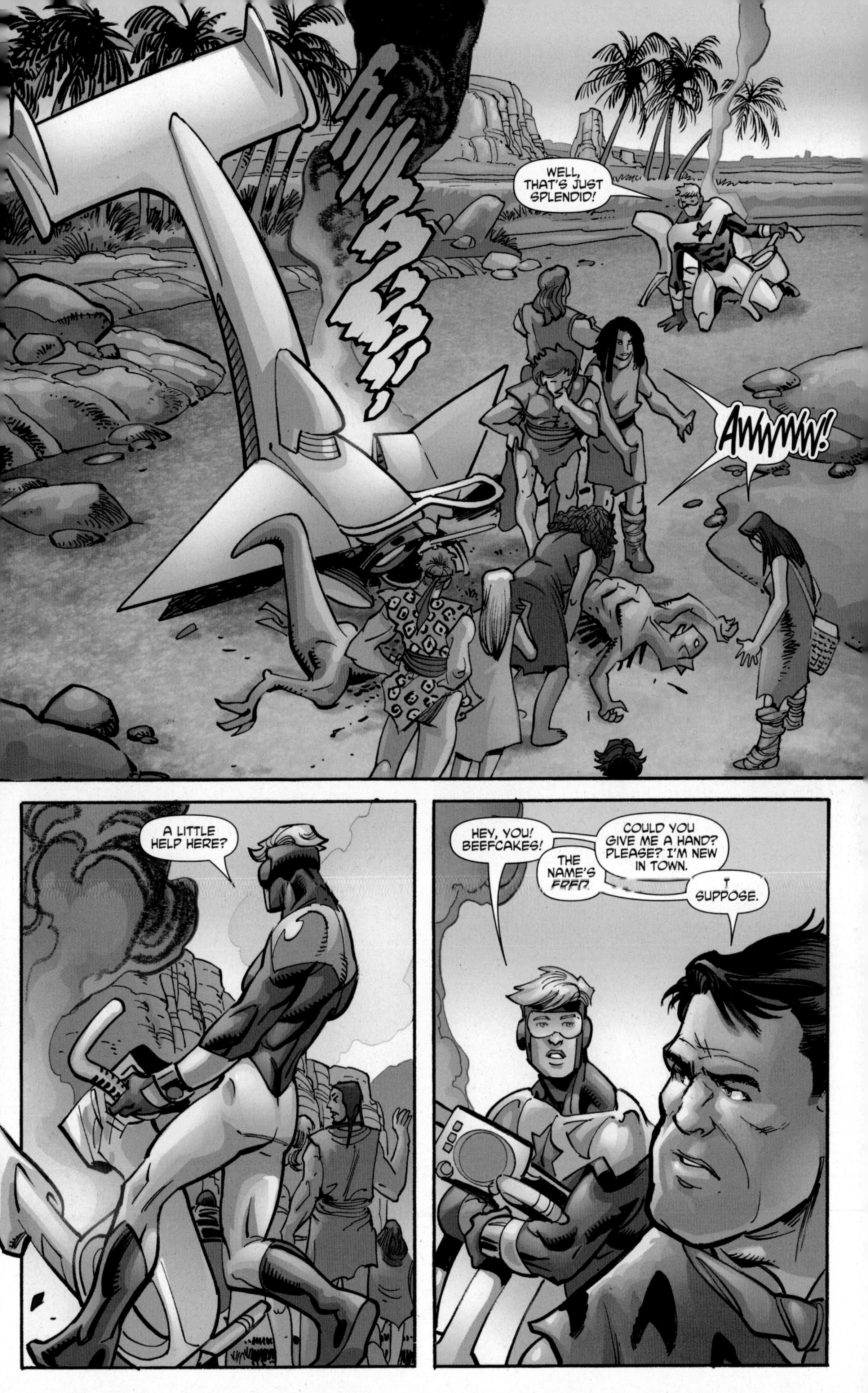
WELL, THAT'S JUST SPLENDID!
AWWWW!
A LITTLE HELP HERE?
HEY, YOU! BEEFCAKES!
COULD YOU GIVE ME A HAND? PLEASE? I'M NEW IN TOWN.
THE NAME'S FRED.
I SUPPOSE.

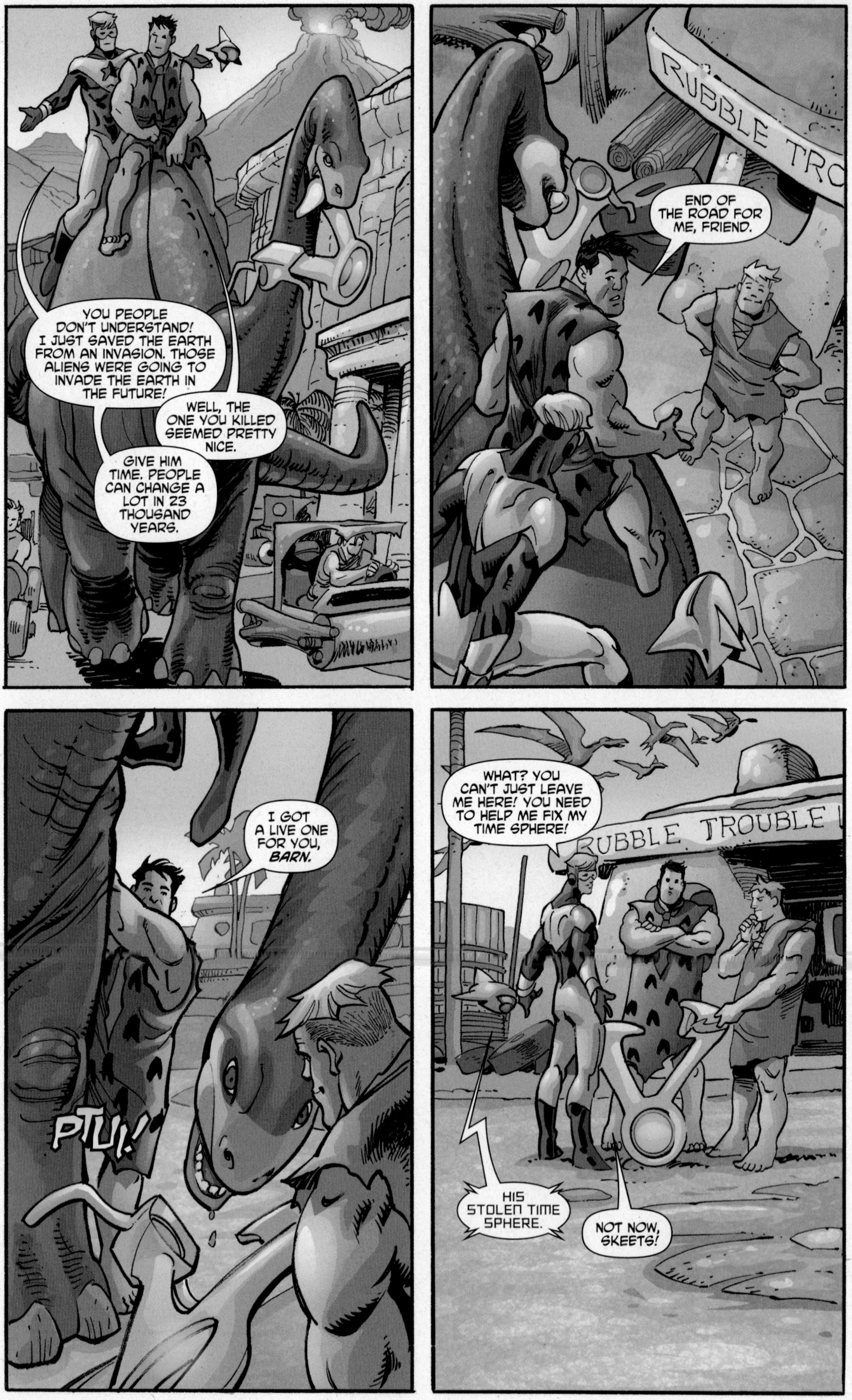
YOU PEOPLE DON'T UNDERSTAND! I JUST SAVED THE EARTH FROM AN INVASION. THOSE ALIENS WERE GOING TO INVADE THE EARTH IN THE FUTURE!
WELL, THE ONE YOU KILLED SEEMED PRETTY NICE.
GIVE HIM TIME. PEOPLE CAN CHANGE A LOT IN 23 THOUSAND YEARS.
RUBBLE TRO
END OF THE ROAD FOR ME, FRIEND.
I GOT A LIVE ONE FOR YOU, BARN.
PTUI!
RUBBLE TROUBLE
WHAT? YOU CAN'T JUST LEAVE ME HERE! YOU NEED TO HELP ME FIX MY TIME SPHERE!
HIS STOLEN TIME SPHERE.
NOT NOW, SKEETS!

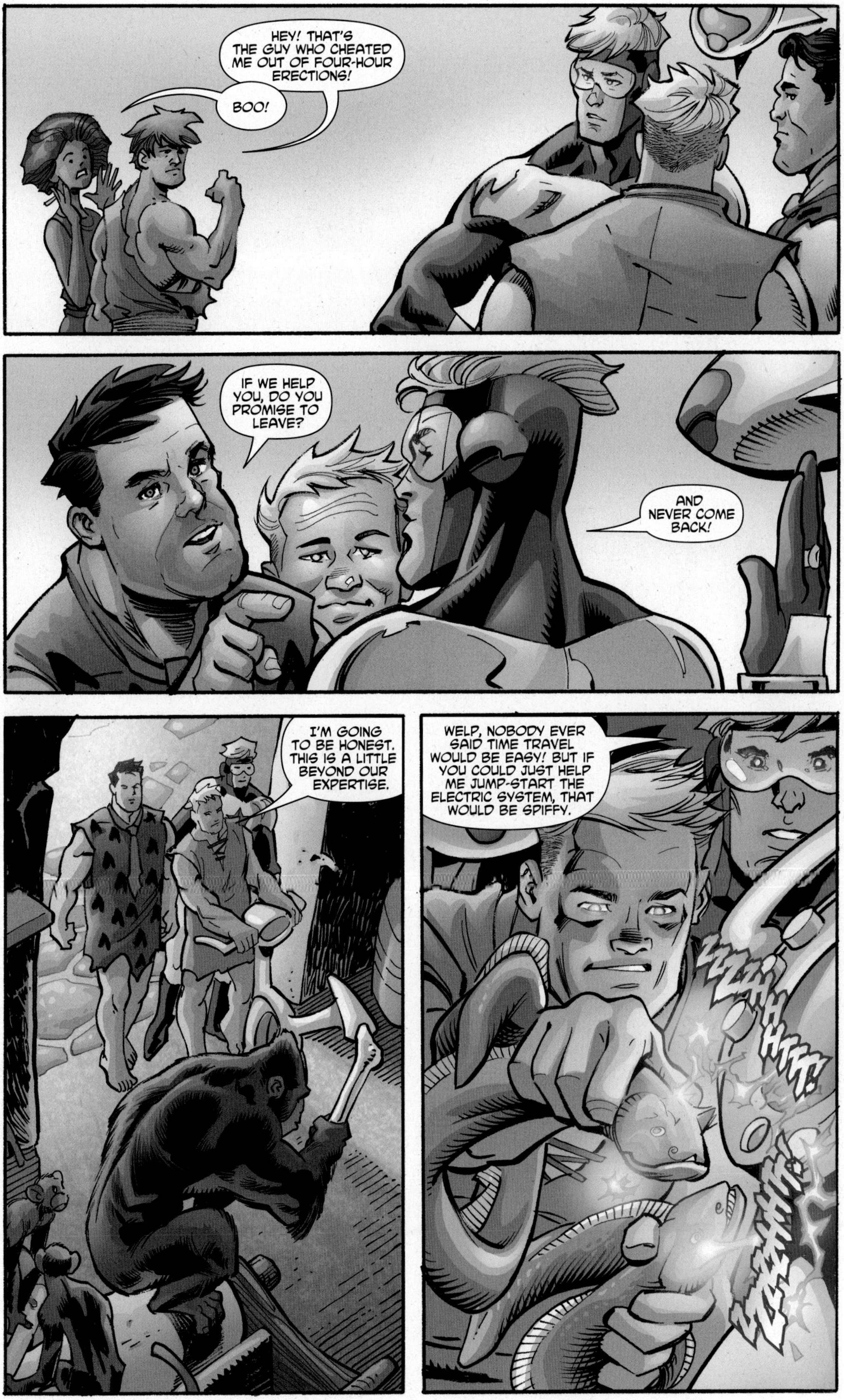
HEY! THAT'S THE GUY WHO CHEATED ME OUT OF FOUR-HOUR ERECTIONS!
BOO!
IF WE HELP YOU, DO YOU PROMISE TO LEAVE?
AND NEVER COME BACK!
I'M GOING TO BE HONEST. THIS IS A LITTLE BEYOND OUR EXPERTISE.
WELP, NOBODY EVER SAID TIME TRAVEL WOULD BE EASY! BUT IF YOU COULD JUST HELP ME JUMP-START THE ELECTRIC SYSTEM, THAT WOULD BE SPIFFY.

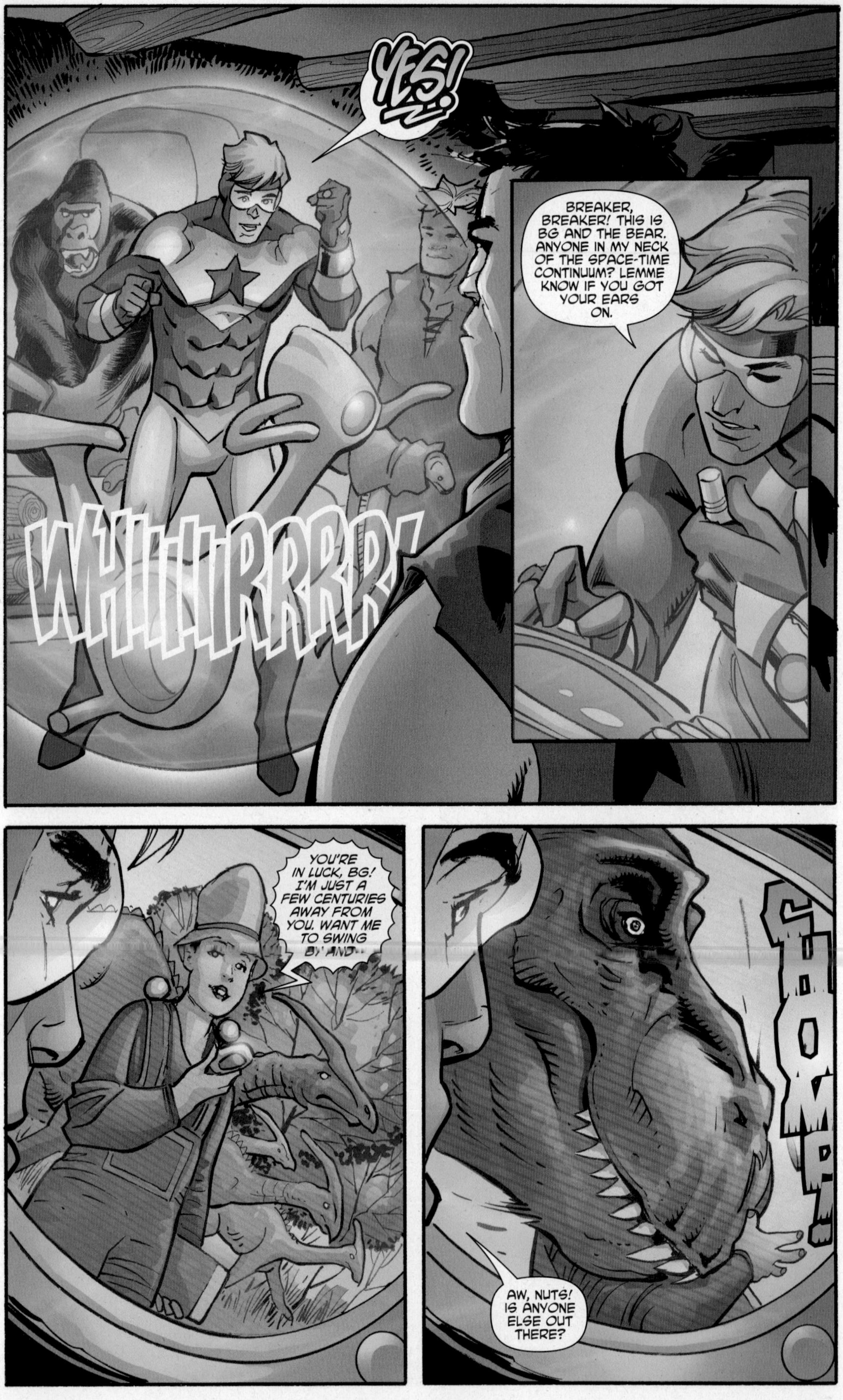
YES!
WHIIIIRRRR!
BREAKER, BREAKER! THIS IS BG AND THE BEAR. ANYONE IN MY NECK OF THE SPACE-TIME CONTINUUM? LEMME KNOW IF YOU GOT YOUR EARS ON.
YOU'RE IN LUCK, BG! I'M JUST A FEW CENTURIES AWAY FROM YOU. WANT ME TO SWING BY AND...
CHOMP!
AW, NUTS! IS ANYONE ELSE OUT THERE?

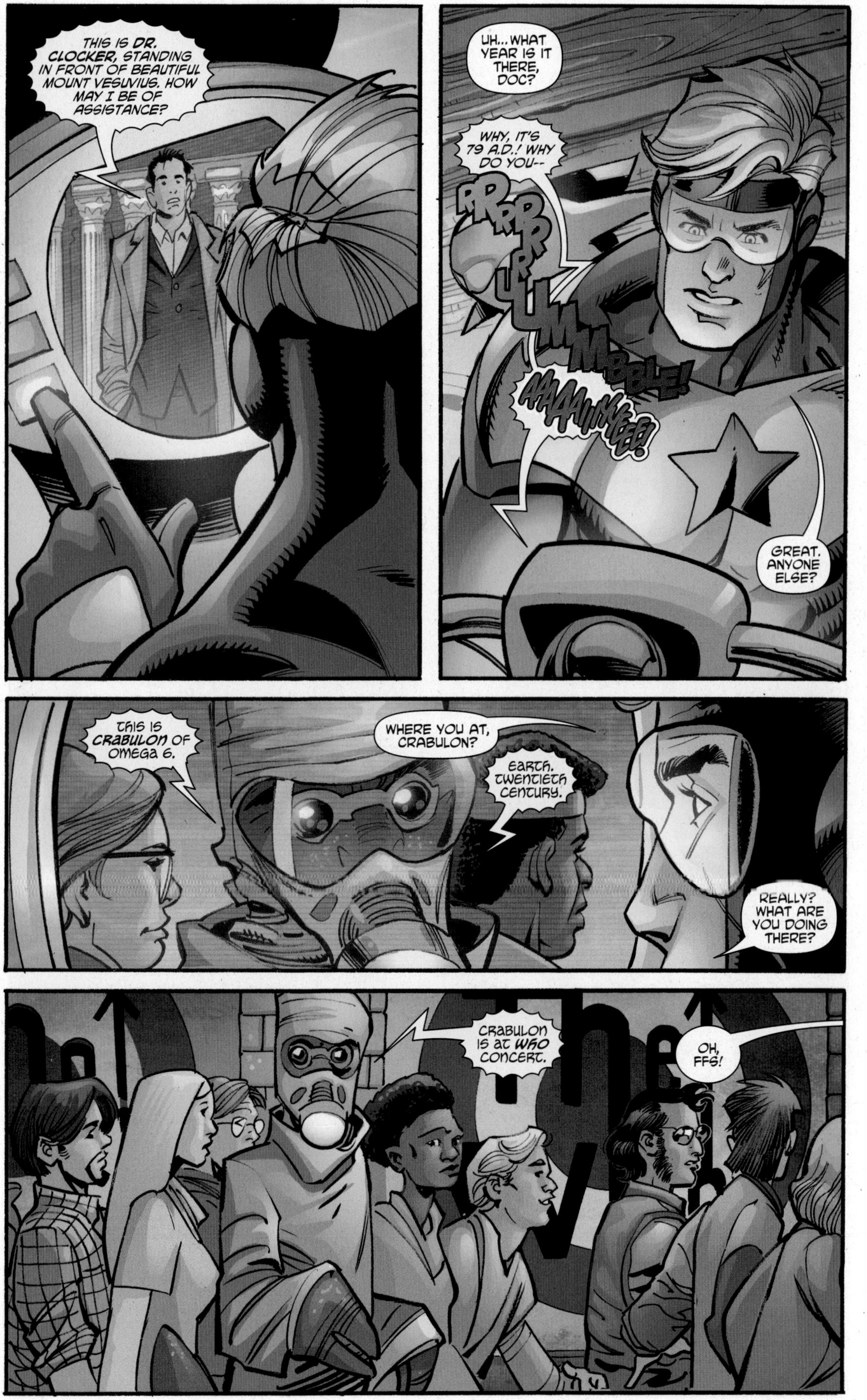
THIS IS DR. CLOCKER, STANDING IN FRONT OF BEAUTIFUL MOUNT VESUVIUS. HOW MAY I BE OF ASSISTANCE?
UH...WHAT YEAR IS IT THERE, DOC?
WHY, IT'S 79 A.D.! WHY DO YOU--
RRRRRRRUUMMMBBLE!
AAAAAIIIYEEE!
GREAT. ANYONE ELSE?
THIS IS CRABULON OF OMEGA 6.
WHERE YOU AT, CRABULON?
EARTH. TWENTIETH CENTURY.
REALLY? WHAT ARE YOU DOING THERE?
CRABULON IS AT WHO CONCERT.
OH, FFS!

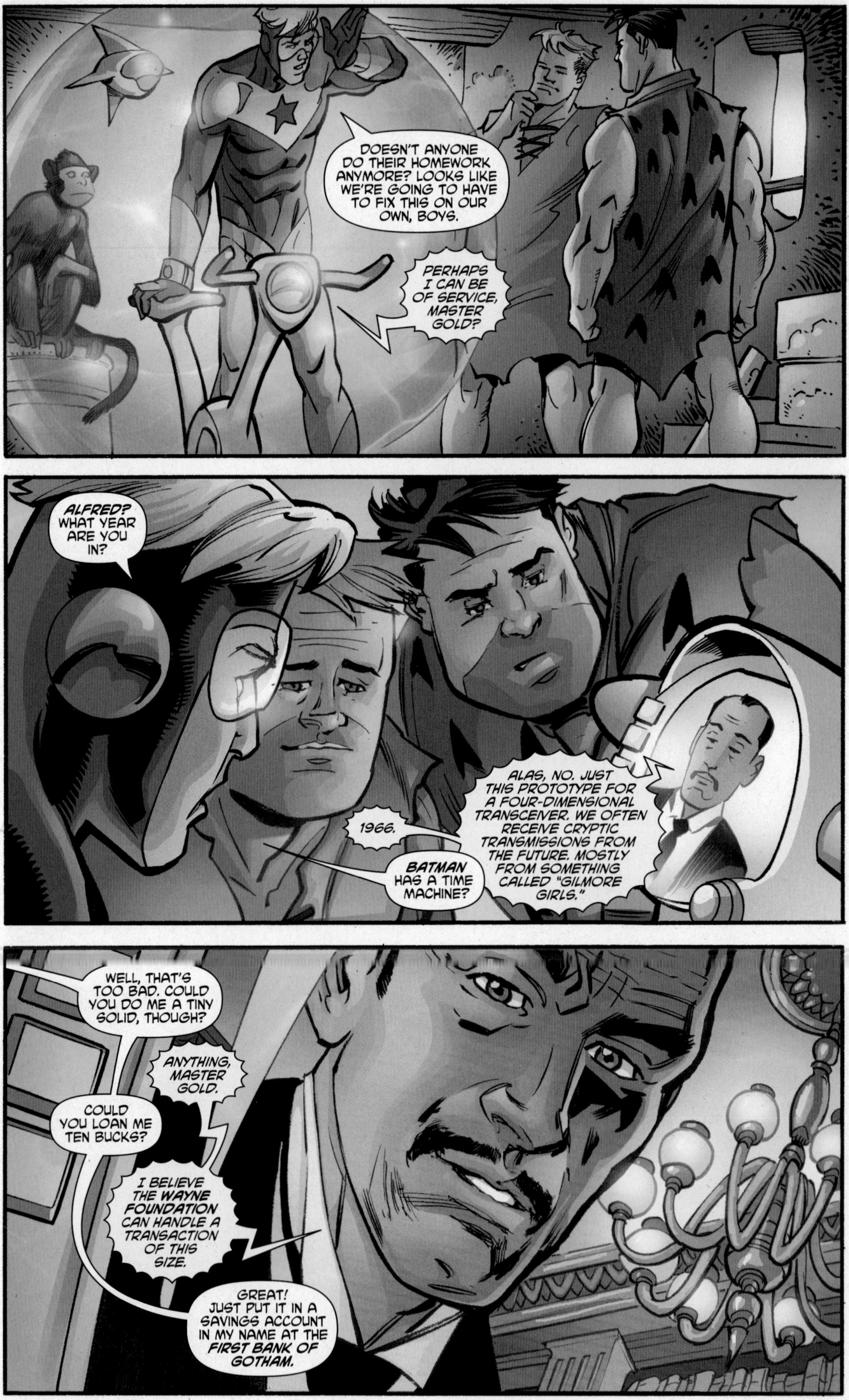
DOESN'T ANYONE DO THEIR HOMEWORK ANYMORE? LOOKS LIKE WE'RE GOING TO HAVE TO FIX THIS ON OUR OWN, BOYS.
PERHAPS I CAN BE OF SERVICE, MASTER GOLD?
ALFRED? WHAT YEAR ARE YOU IN?
1966.
ALAS, NO. JUST THIS PROTOTYPE FOR A FOUR-DIMENSIONAL TRANSCEIVER. WE OFTEN RECEIVE CRYPTIC TRANSMISSIONS FROM THE FUTURE. MOSTLY FROM SOMETHING CALLED "GILMORE GIRLS."
BATMAN HAS A TIME MACHINE?
WELL, THAT'S TOO BAD. COULD YOU DO ME A TINY SOLID, THOUGH?
ANYTHING, MASTER GOLD.
COULD YOU LOAN ME TEN BUCKS?
I BELIEVE THE WAYNE FOUNDATION CAN HANDLE A TRANSACTION OF THIS SIZE.
GREAT! JUST PUT IT IN A SAVINGS ACCOUNT IN MY NAME AT THE FIRST BANK OF GOTHAM.

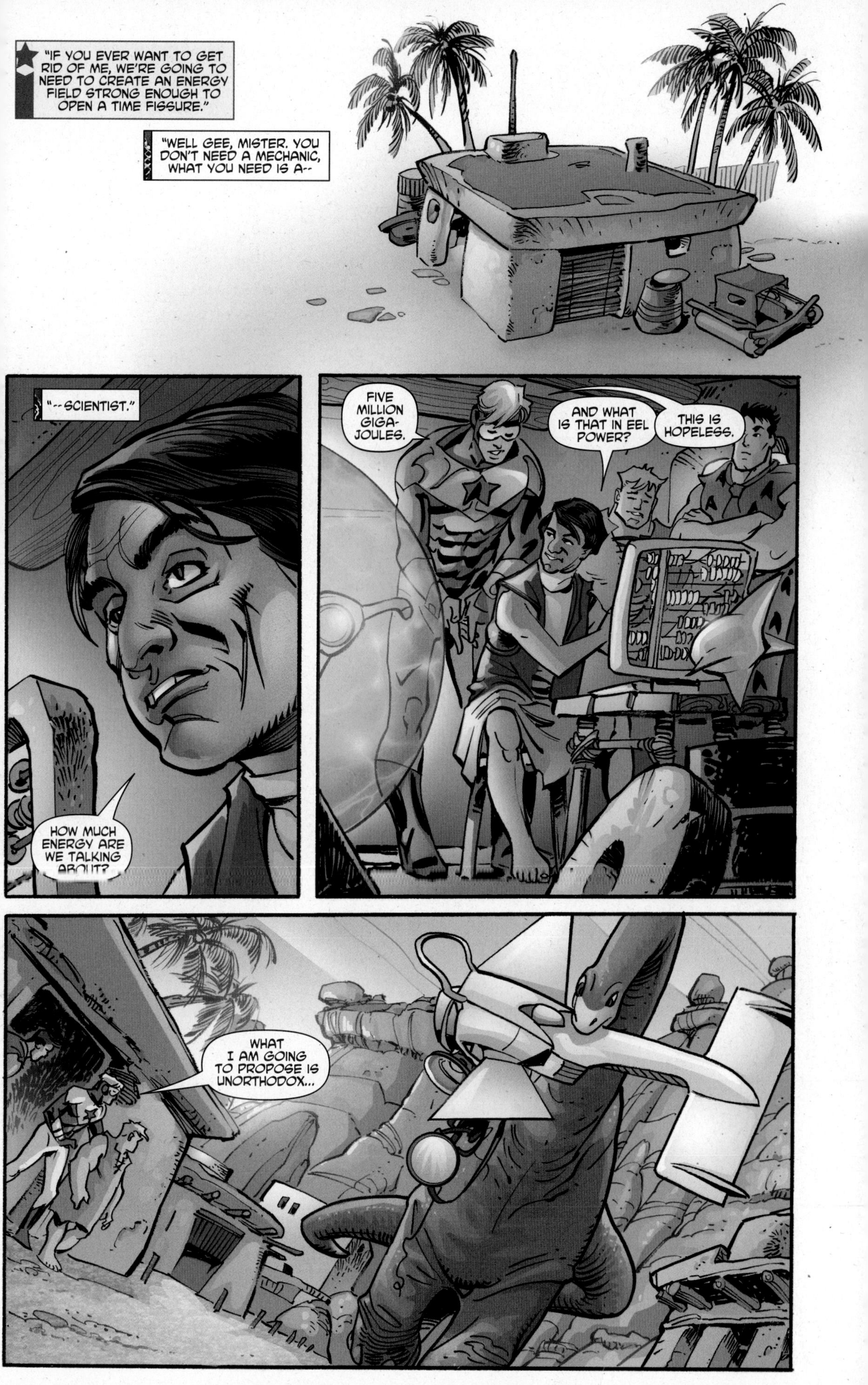
"IF YOU EVER WANT TO GET RID OF ME, WE'RE GOING TO NEED TO CREATE AN ENERGY FIELD STRONG ENOUGH TO OPEN A TIME FISSURE."
"WELL GEE, MISTER. YOU DON'T NEED A MECHANIC, WHAT YOU NEED IS A--
"--SCIENTIST."
HOW MUCH ENERGY ARE WE TALKING ABOUT?
FIVE MILLION GIGA-JOULES.
AND WHAT IS THAT IN EEL POWER?
THIS IS HOPELESS.
WHAT I AM GOING TO PROPOSE IS UNORTHODOX...

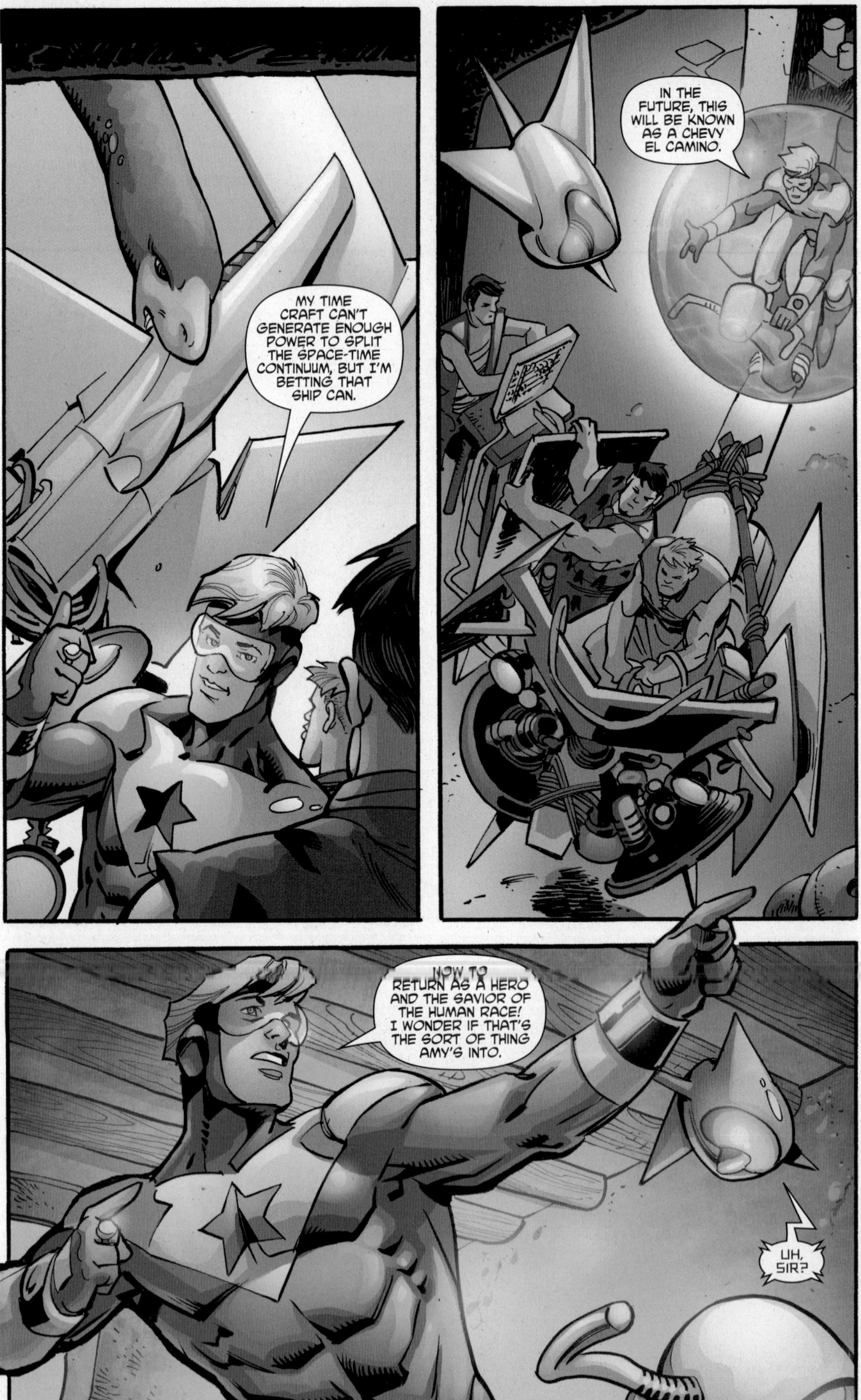
MY TIME CRAFT CAN'T GENERATE ENOUGH POWER TO SPLIT THE SPACE-TIME CONTINUUM, BUT I'M BETTING THAT SHIP CAN.
IN THE FUTURE, THIS WILL BE KNOWN AS A CHEVY EL CAMINO.
NOW TO RETURN AS A HERO AND THE SAVIOR OF THE HUMAN RACE! I WONDER IF THAT'S THE SORT OF THING AMY'S INTO.
UH, SIR?

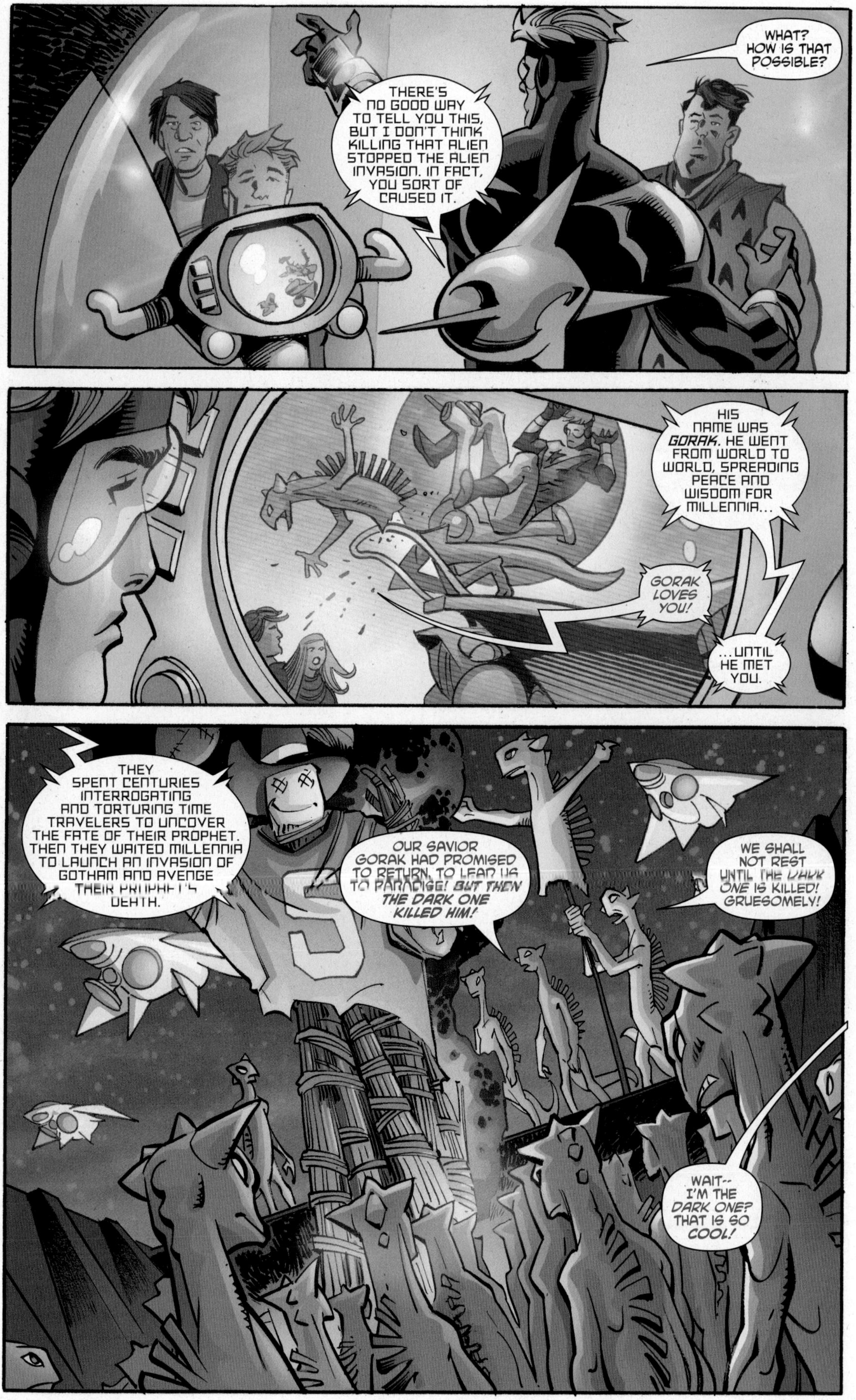
THERE'S NO GOOD WAY TO TELL YOU THIS, BUT I DON'T THINK KILLING THAT ALIEN STOPPED THE ALIEN INVASION. IN FACT, YOU SORT OF CAUSED IT.
WHAT? HOW IS THAT POSSIBLE?
HIS NAME WAS GORAK. HE WENT FROM WORLD TO WORLD, SPREADING PEACE AND WISDOM FOR MILLENNIA...
GORAK LOVES YOU!
...UNTIL HE MET YOU.
THEY SPENT CENTURIES INTERROGATING AND TORTURING TIME TRAVELERS TO UNCOVER THE FATE OF THEIR PROPHET. THEN THEY WAITED MILLENNIA TO LAUNCH AN INVASION OF GOTHAM AND AVENGE THEIR PROPHET'S DEATH.
OUR SAVIOR GORAK HAD PROMISED TO RETURN, TO LEAD US TO PARADISE! BUT THEN THE DARK ONE KILLED HIM!
WE SHALL NOT REST UNTIL THE DARK ONE IS KILLED! GRUESOMELY!
WAIT-- I'M THE DARK ONE? THAT IS SO COOL!

WE DON'T WANT THE TIME RIFT TO BE TOO BIG, SO LET ME KNOW BEFORE WE HIT FIVE MILLION GIGAJOULES.

UH...WHAT'S A MILLION?

WWWWRRRRRRRRRR!

OH NO!

NOW, SKEETS! NOW!

GOTHAM, 2472 A.D.

WE HAVE CAPTURED THE DARK ONE'S CITY! OUR TROOPS ARE SEARCHING THE STREETS FOR HIM NOW.

PRAISE GORAK!

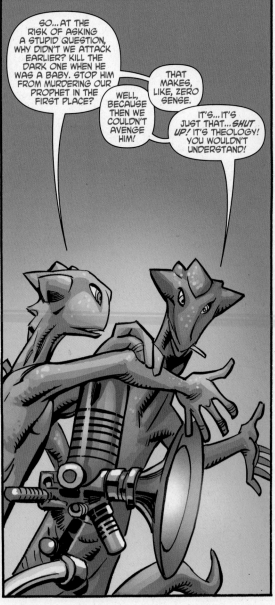

SO...AT THE RISK OF ASKING A STUPID QUESTION, WHY DIDN'T WE ATTACK EARLIER? KILL THE DARK ONE WHEN HE WAS A BABY. STOP HIM FROM MURDERING OUR PROPHET IN THE FIRST PLACE?

WELL, BECAUSE THEN WE COULDN'T AVENGE HIM!

THAT MAKES, LIKE, ZERO SENSE.

IT'S...IT'S JUST THAT...SHUT UP! IT'S THEOLOGY! YOU WOULDN'T UNDERSTAND!

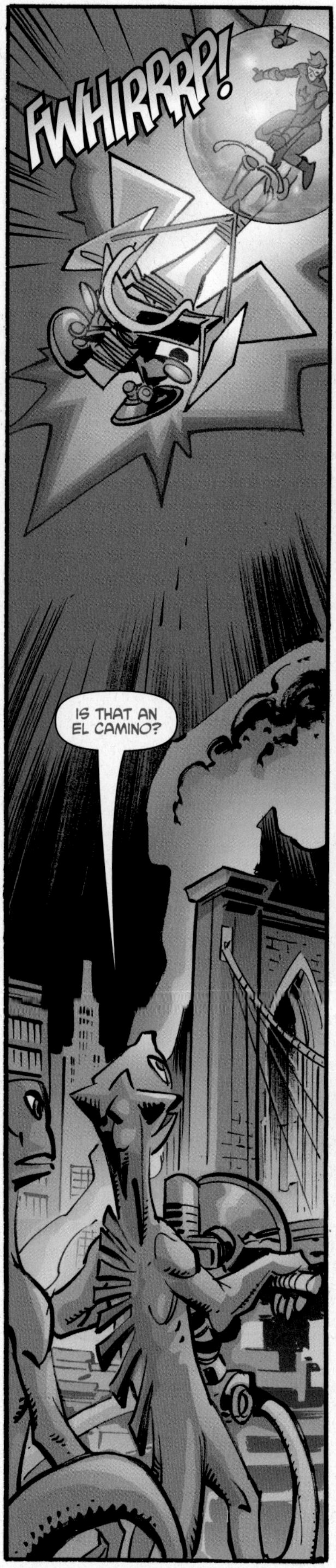
FWHIRRRP!
IS THAT AN EL CAMINO?

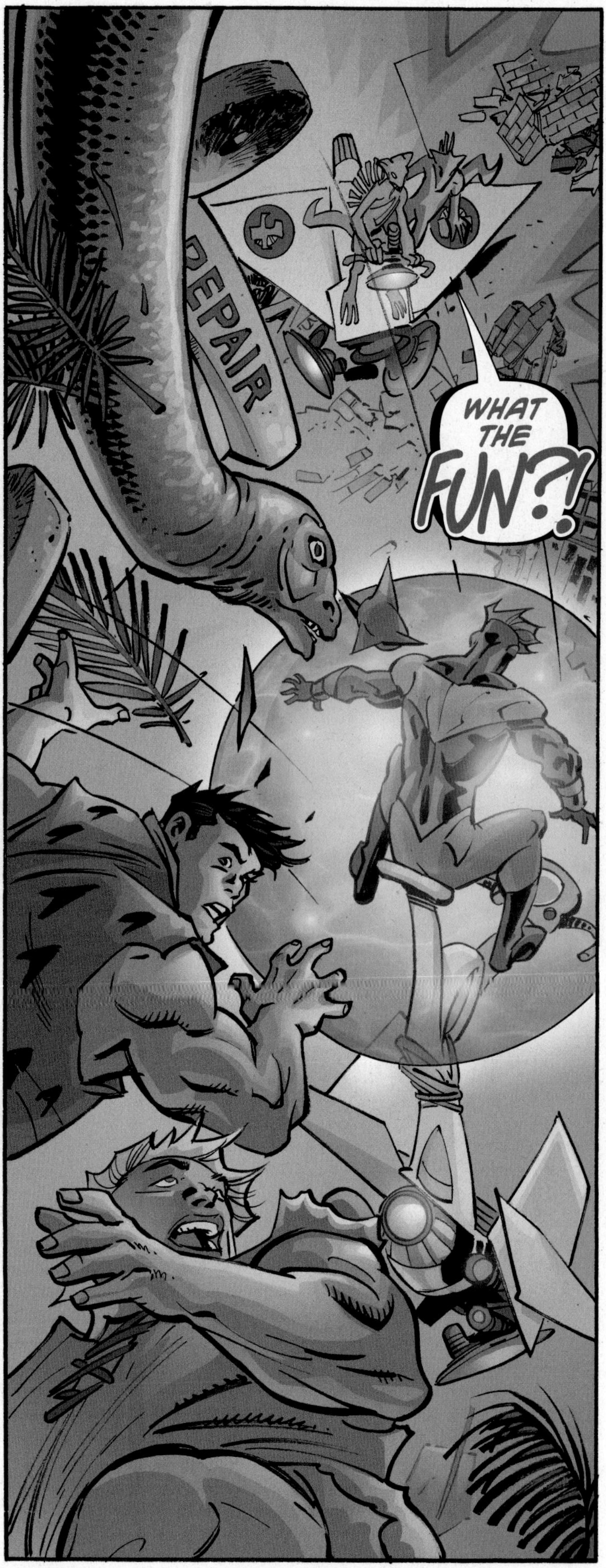
REPAIR
WHAT THE FUN?!

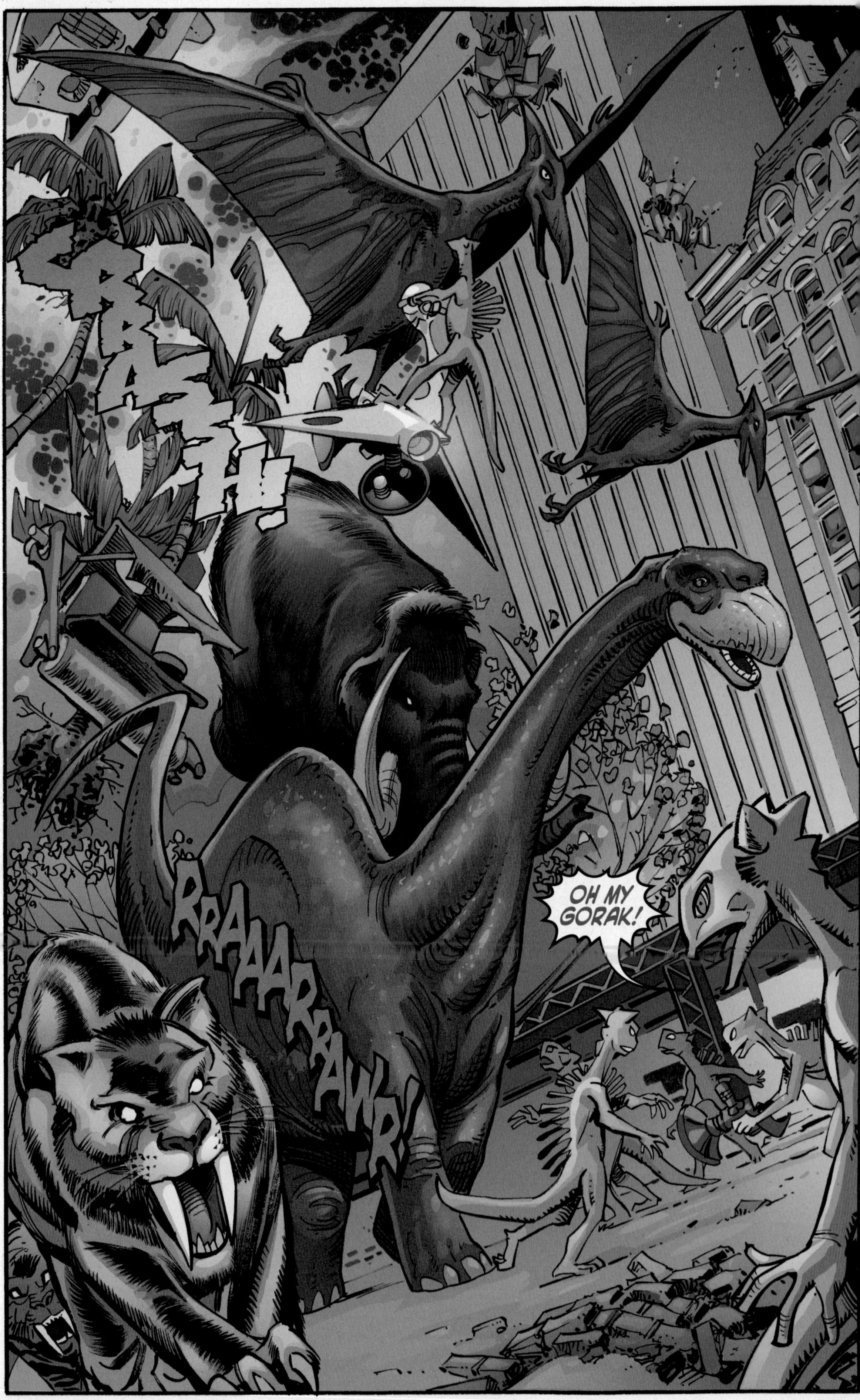
CRASH!
RRAAARRRAWR!
OH MY GORAK!

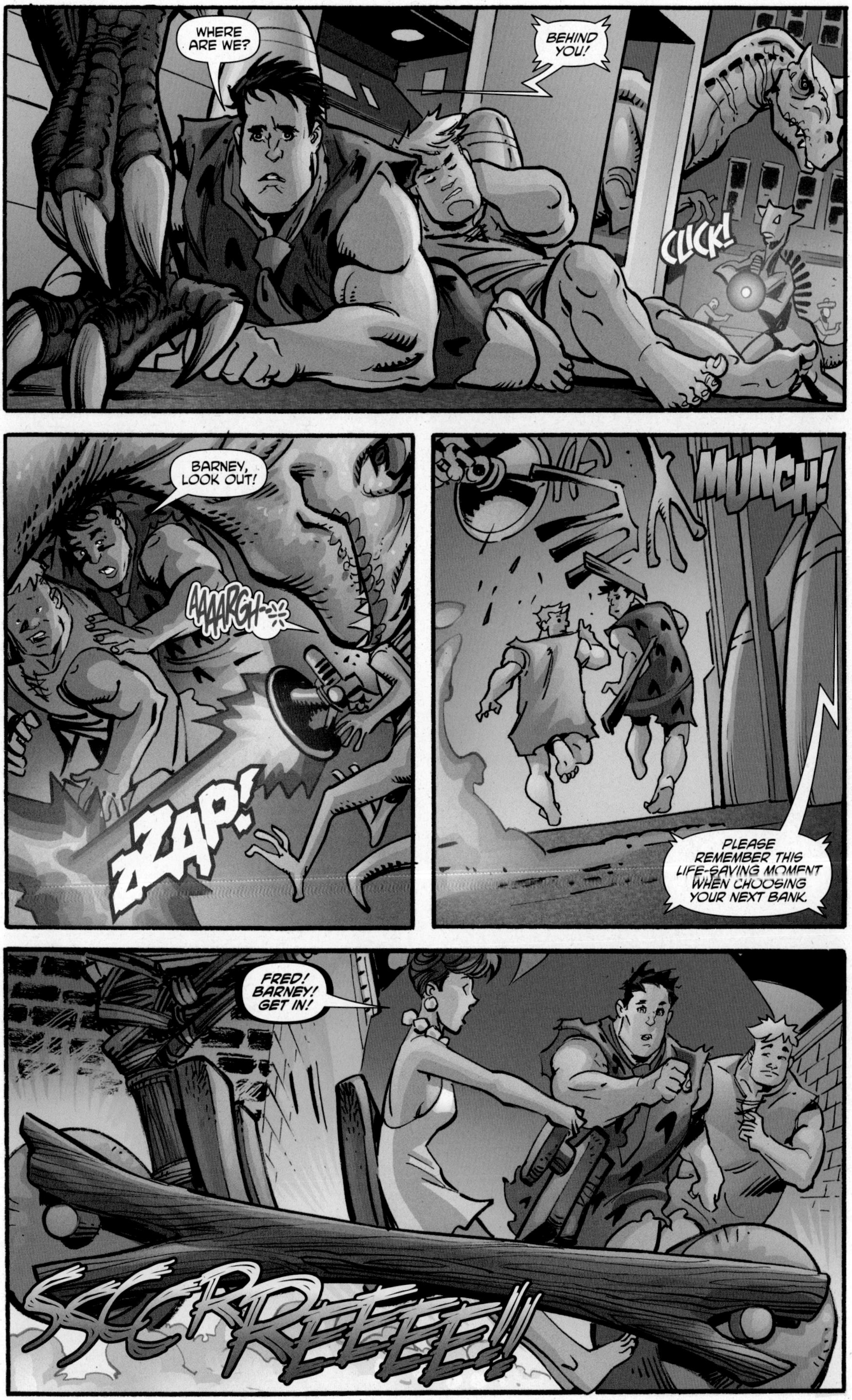
WHERE ARE WE?
BEHIND YOU!
CLICK!
BARNEY, LOOK OUT!
AAAARGH-
ZZAP!
MUNCH!
PLEASE REMEMBER THIS LIFE-SAVING MOMENT WHEN CHOOSING YOUR NEXT BANK.
FRED! BARNEY! GET IN!
SSCCRREEEEE!!

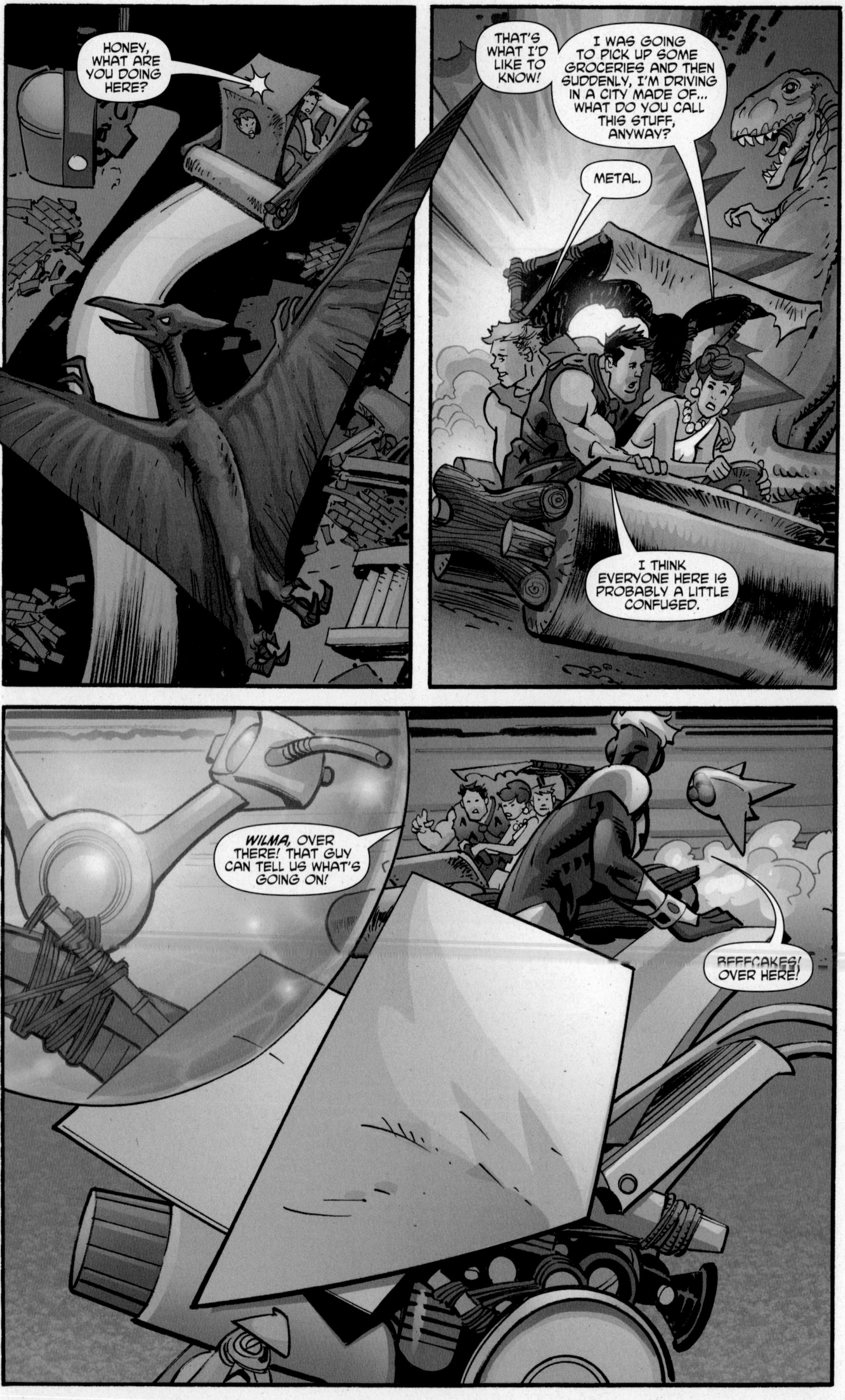
HONEY, WHAT ARE YOU DOING HERE?
THAT'S WHAT I'D LIKE TO KNOW!
I WAS GOING TO PICK UP SOME GROCERIES AND THEN SUDDENLY, I'M DRIVING IN A CITY MADE OF... WHAT DO YOU CALL THIS STUFF, ANYWAY?
METAL.
I THINK EVERYONE HERE IS PROBABLY A LITTLE CONFUSED.
WILMA, OVER THERE! THAT GUY CAN TELL US WHAT'S GOING ON!
BEEFCAKES! OVER HERE!

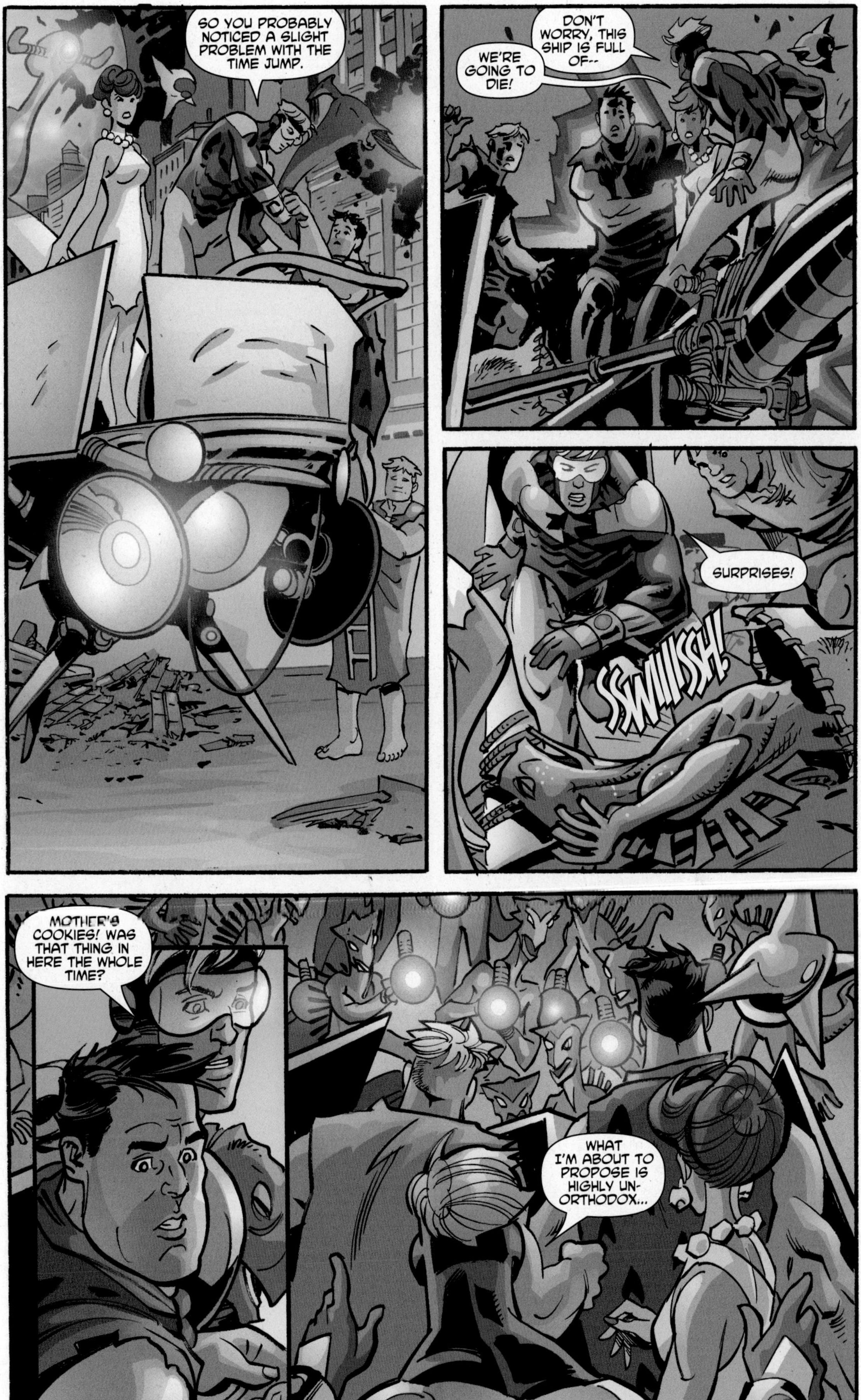
SO YOU PROBABLY NOTICED A SLIGHT PROBLEM WITH THE TIME JUMP.
DON'T WORRY, THIS SHIP IS FULL OF--
WE'RE GOING TO DIE!
SURPRISES!
SSWIIIISSH!
MOTHER'S COOKIES! WAS THAT THING IN HERE THE WHOLE TIME?
WHAT I'M ABOUT TO PROPOSE IS HIGHLY UN-ORTHODOX...

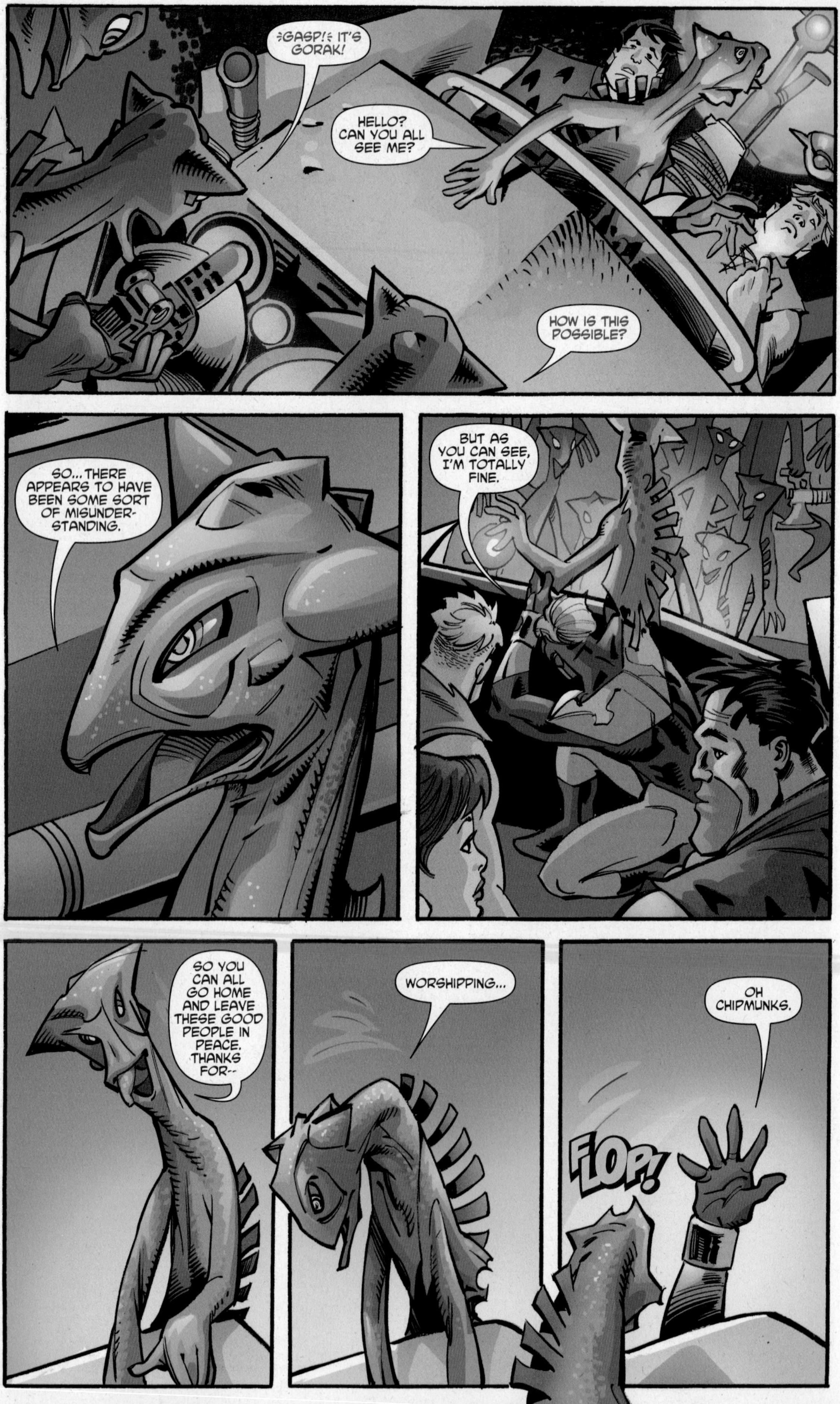

:GASP!: IT'S GORAK!
HELLO? CAN YOU ALL SEE ME?
HOW IS THIS POSSIBLE?
SO... THERE APPEARS TO HAVE BEEN SOME SORT OF MISUNDER-STANDING.
BUT AS YOU CAN SEE, I'M TOTALLY FINE.
SO YOU CAN ALL GO HOME AND LEAVE THESE GOOD PEOPLE IN PEACE. THANKS FOR--
WORSHIPPING...
OH CHIPMUNKS.
FLOP!

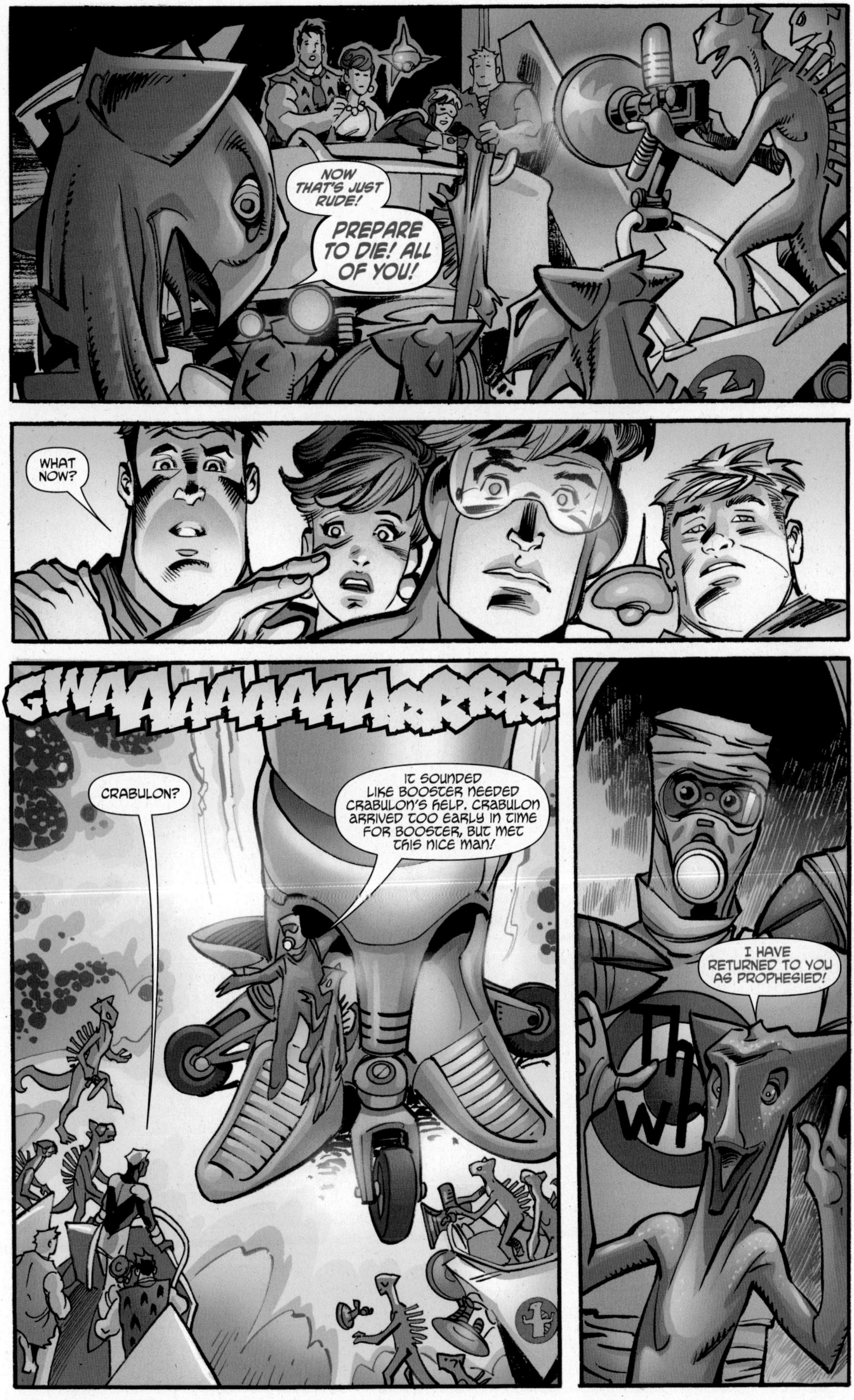
NOW THAT'S JUST RUDE!
PREPARE TO DIE! ALL OF YOU!
WHAT NOW?
GWAAAAAAAARRRR!
CRABULON?
IT SOUNDED LIKE BOOSTER NEEDED CRABULON'S HELP. CRABULON ARRIVED TOO EARLY IN TIME FOR BOOSTER, BUT MET THIS NICE MAN!
I HAVE RETURNED TO YOU AS PROPHESIED!

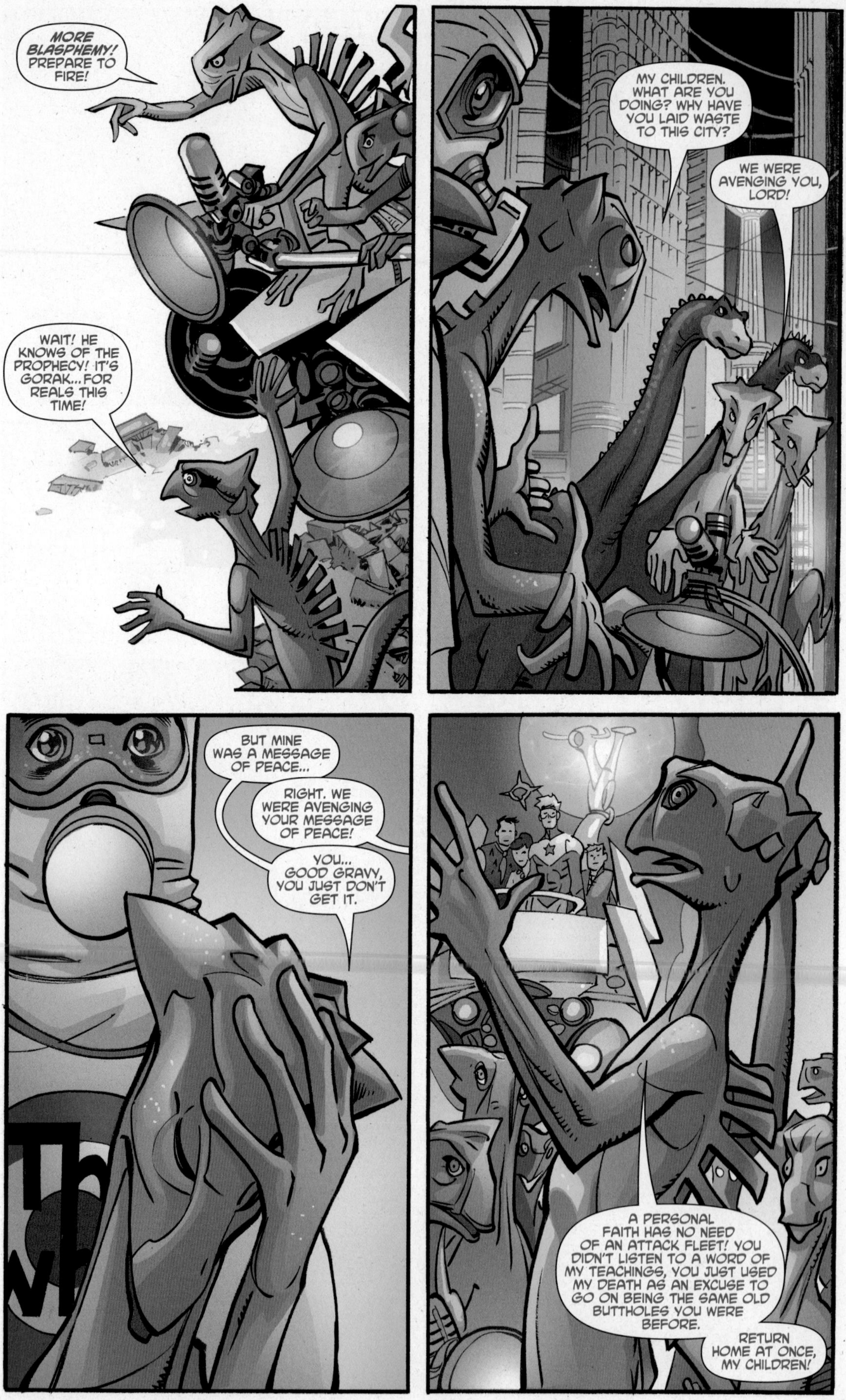
MORE BLASPHEMY! PREPARE TO FIRE!
WAIT! HE KNOWS OF THE PROPHECY! IT'S GORAK...FOR REALS THIS TIME!
MY CHILDREN. WHAT ARE YOU DOING? WHY HAVE YOU LAID WASTE TO THIS CITY?
WE WERE AVENGING YOU, LORD!
BUT MINE WAS A MESSAGE OF PEACE...
RIGHT. WE WERE AVENGING YOUR MESSAGE OF PEACE!
YOU... GOOD GRAVY, YOU JUST DON'T GET IT.
A PERSONAL FAITH HAS NO NEED OF AN ATTACK FLEET! YOU DIDN'T LISTEN TO A WORD OF MY TEACHINGS, YOU JUST USED MY DEATH AS AN EXCUSE TO GO ON BEING THE SAME OLD BUTTHOLES YOU WERE BEFORE.
RETURN HOME AT ONCE, MY CHILDREN!

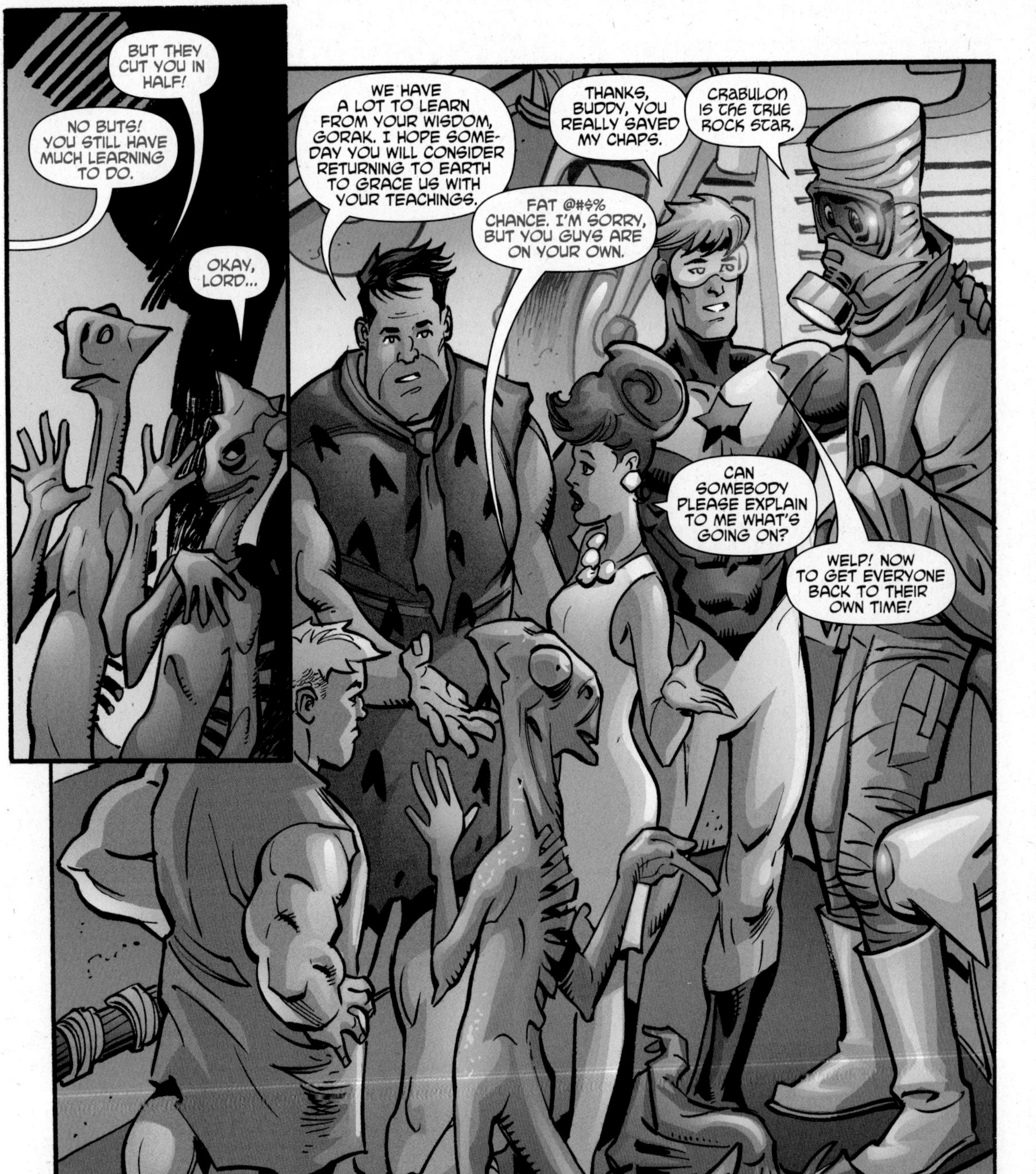
BUT THEY CUT YOU IN HALF!
NO BUTS! YOU STILL HAVE MUCH LEARNING TO DO.
OKAY, LORD...
WE HAVE A LOT TO LEARN FROM YOUR WISDOM, GORAK. I HOPE SOME-DAY YOU WILL CONSIDER RETURNING TO EARTH TO GRACE US WITH YOUR TEACHINGS.
THANKS, BUDDY, YOU REALLY SAVED MY CHAPS.
CRABULON IS THE TRUE ROCK STAR.
FAT @#$% CHANCE. I'M SORRY, BUT YOU GUYS ARE ON YOUR OWN.
CAN SOMEBODY PLEASE EXPLAIN TO ME WHAT'S GOING ON?
WELP! NOW TO GET EVERYONE BACK TO THEIR OWN TIME!

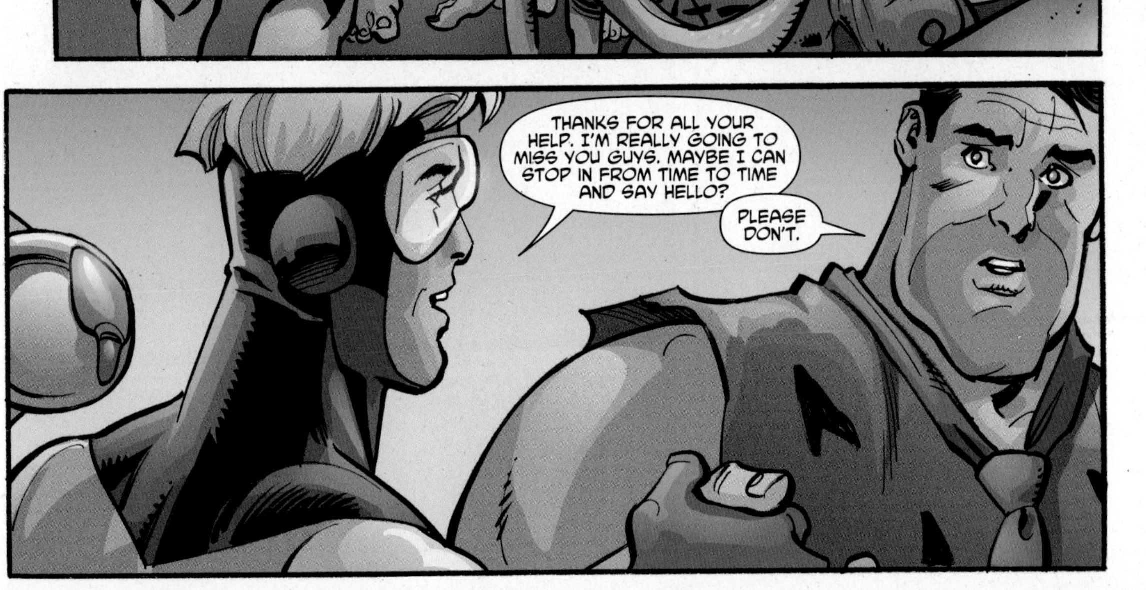
THANKS FOR ALL YOUR HELP. I'M REALLY GOING TO MISS YOU GUYS. MAYBE I CAN STOP IN FROM TIME TO TIME AND SAY HELLO?
PLEASE DON'T.

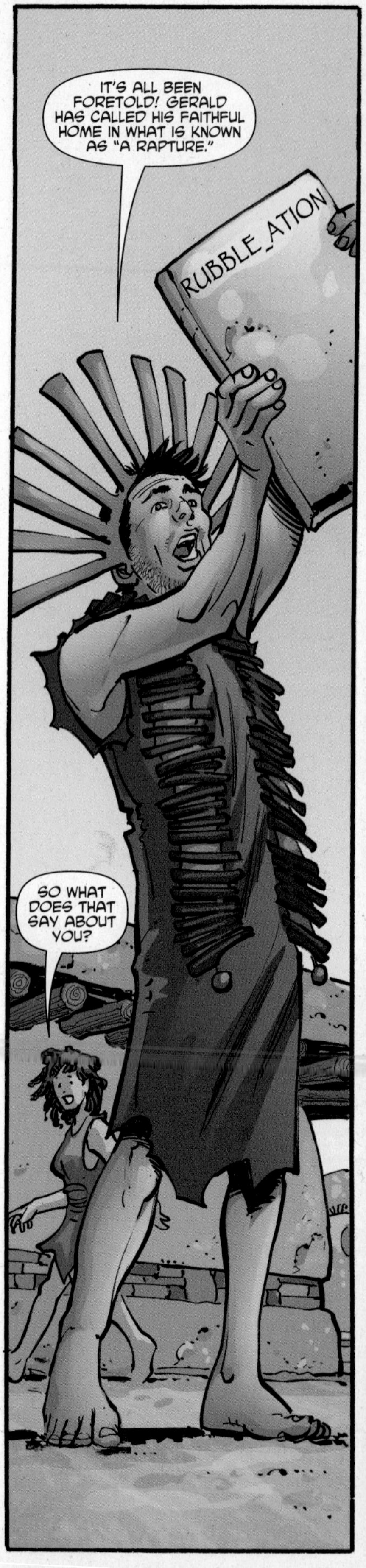
IT'S ALL BEEN FORETOLD! GERALD HAS CALLED HIS FAITHFUL HOME IN WHAT IS KNOWN AS "A RAPTURE."
RUBBLE_ATION
SO WHAT DOES THAT SAY ABOUT YOU?

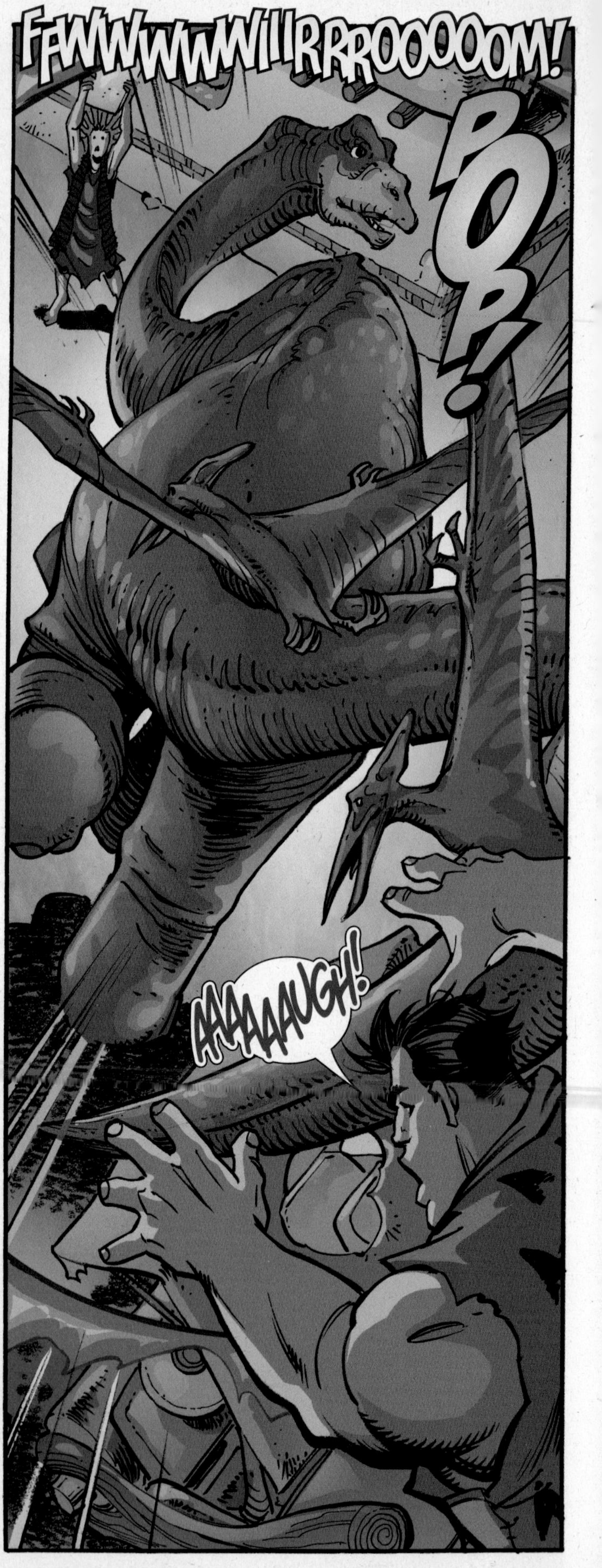
FFWWWWWWIIIRRROOOOOOM!
POP!
AAAAAAUGH!

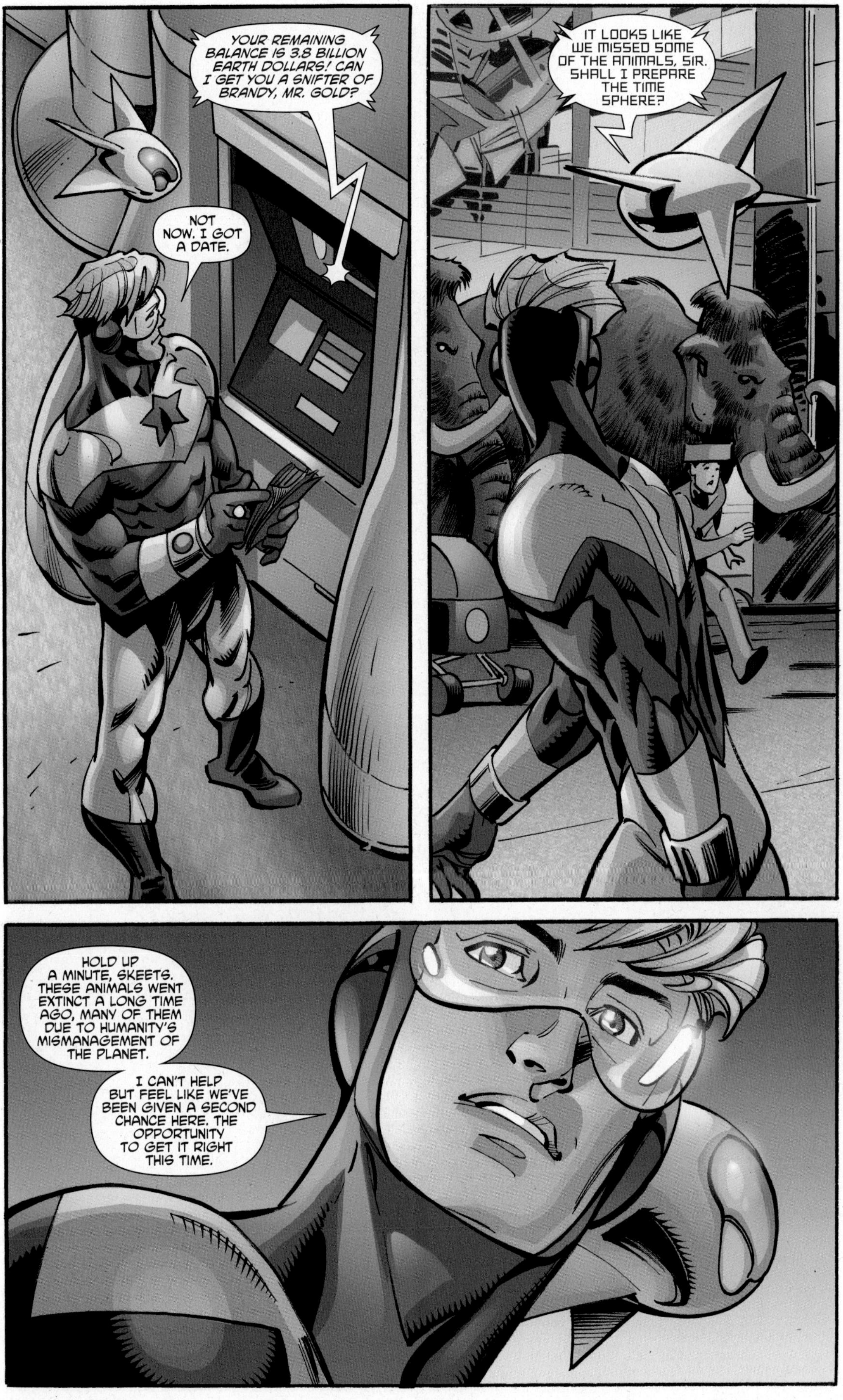
YOUR REMAINING BALANCE IS 3.8 BILLION EARTH DOLLARS! CAN I GET YOU A SNIFTER OF BRANDY, MR. GOLD?
NOT NOW. I GOT A DATE.
IT LOOKS LIKE WE MISSED SOME OF THE ANIMALS, SIR. SHALL I PREPARE THE TIME SPHERE?
HOLD UP A MINUTE, SKEETS. THESE ANIMALS WENT EXTINCT A LONG TIME AGO, MANY OF THEM DUE TO HUMANITY'S MISMANAGEMENT OF THE PLANET.
I CAN'T HELP BUT FEEL LIKE WE'VE BEEN GIVEN A SECOND CHANCE HERE. THE OPPORTUNITY TO GET IT RIGHT THIS TIME.

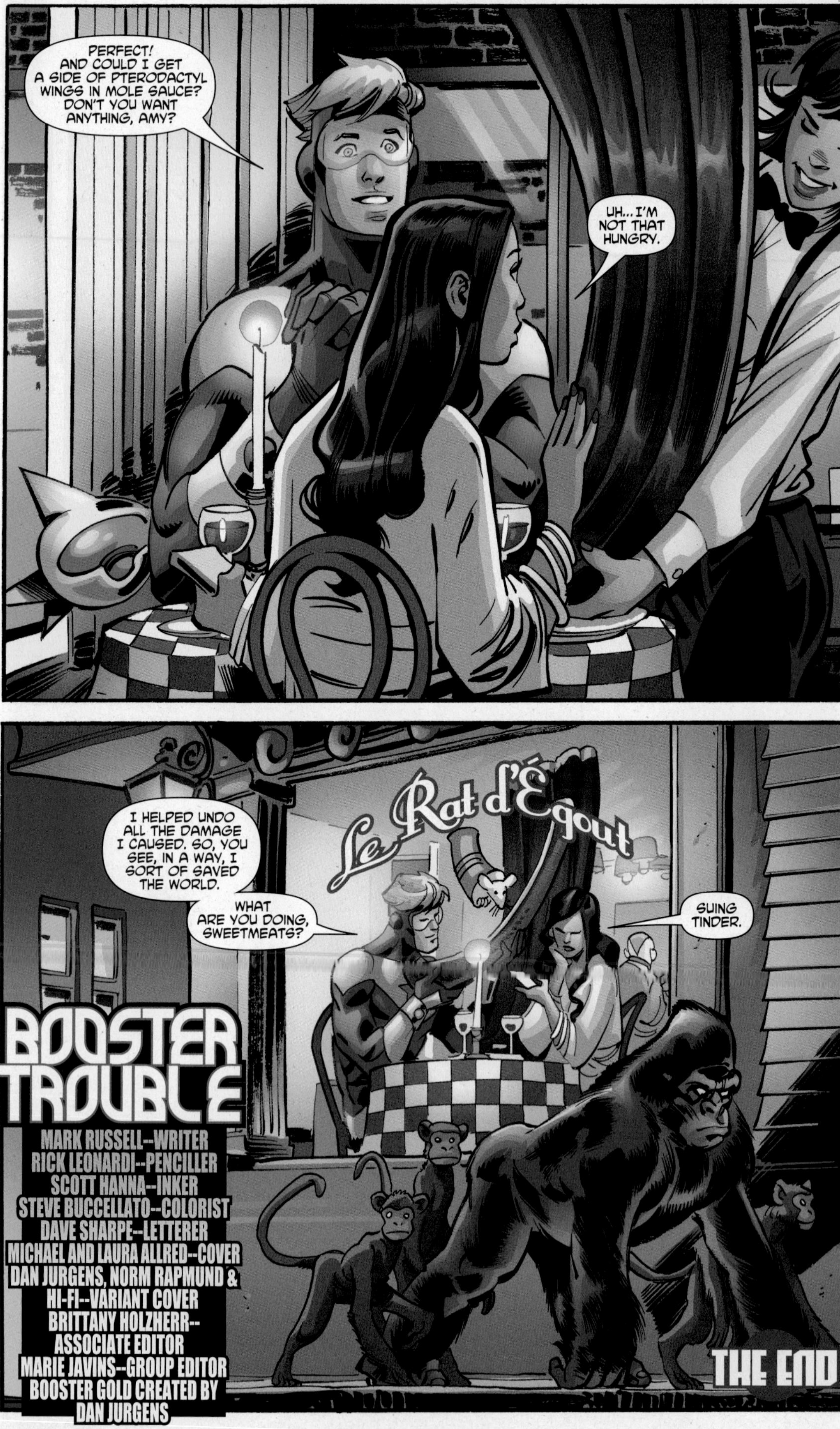
PERFECT! AND COULD I GET A SIDE OF PTERODACTYL WINGS IN MOLE SAUCE? DON'T YOU WANT ANYTHING, AMY?
UH... I'M NOT THAT HUNGRY.
Le Rat d'Égout
I HELPED UNDO ALL THE DAMAGE I CAUSED. SO, YOU SEE, IN A WAY, I SORT OF SAVED THE WORLD.
WHAT ARE YOU DOING, SWEETMEATS?
SUING TINDER.
BOOSTER TROUBLE
MARK RUSSELL--WRITER
RICK LEONARDI--PENCILLER
SCOTT HANNA--INKER
STEVE BUCCELLATO--COLORIST
DAVE SHARPE--LETTERER
MICHAEL AND LAURA ALLRED--COVER
DAN JURGENS, NORM RAPMUND & HI-FI--VARIANT COVER
BRITTANY HOLZHERR--ASSOCIATE EDITOR
MARIE JAVINS--GROUP EDITOR
BOOSTER GOLD CREATED BY DAN JURGENS
THE END

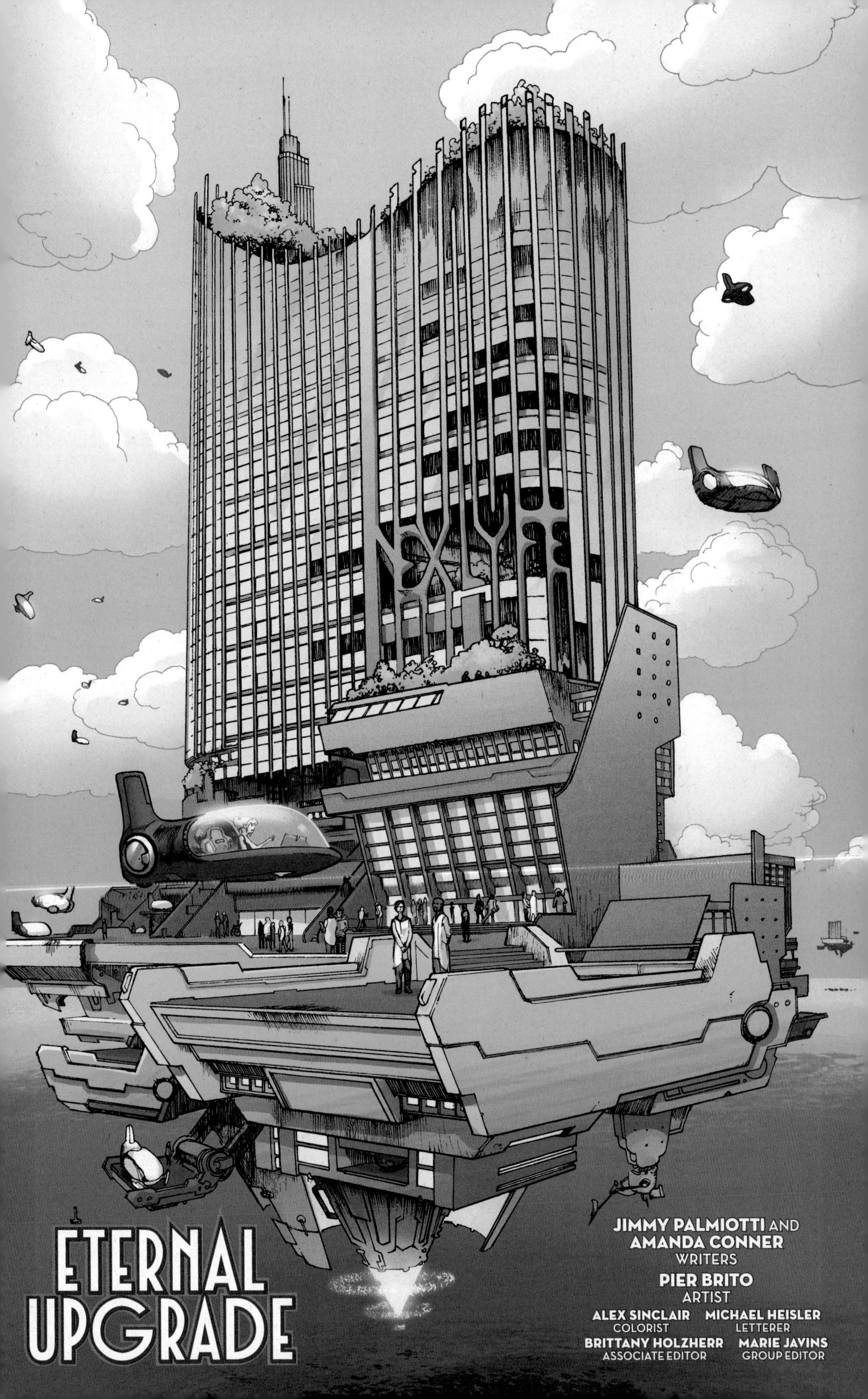
ETERNAL
UPGRADE
JIMMY PALMIOTTI AND
AMANDA CONNER
WRITERS
PIER BRITO
ARTIST
ALEX SINCLAIR
COLORIST
MICHAEL HEISLER
LETTERER
BRITTANY HOLZHERR
ASSOCIATE EDITOR
MARIE JAVINS
GROUP EDITOR

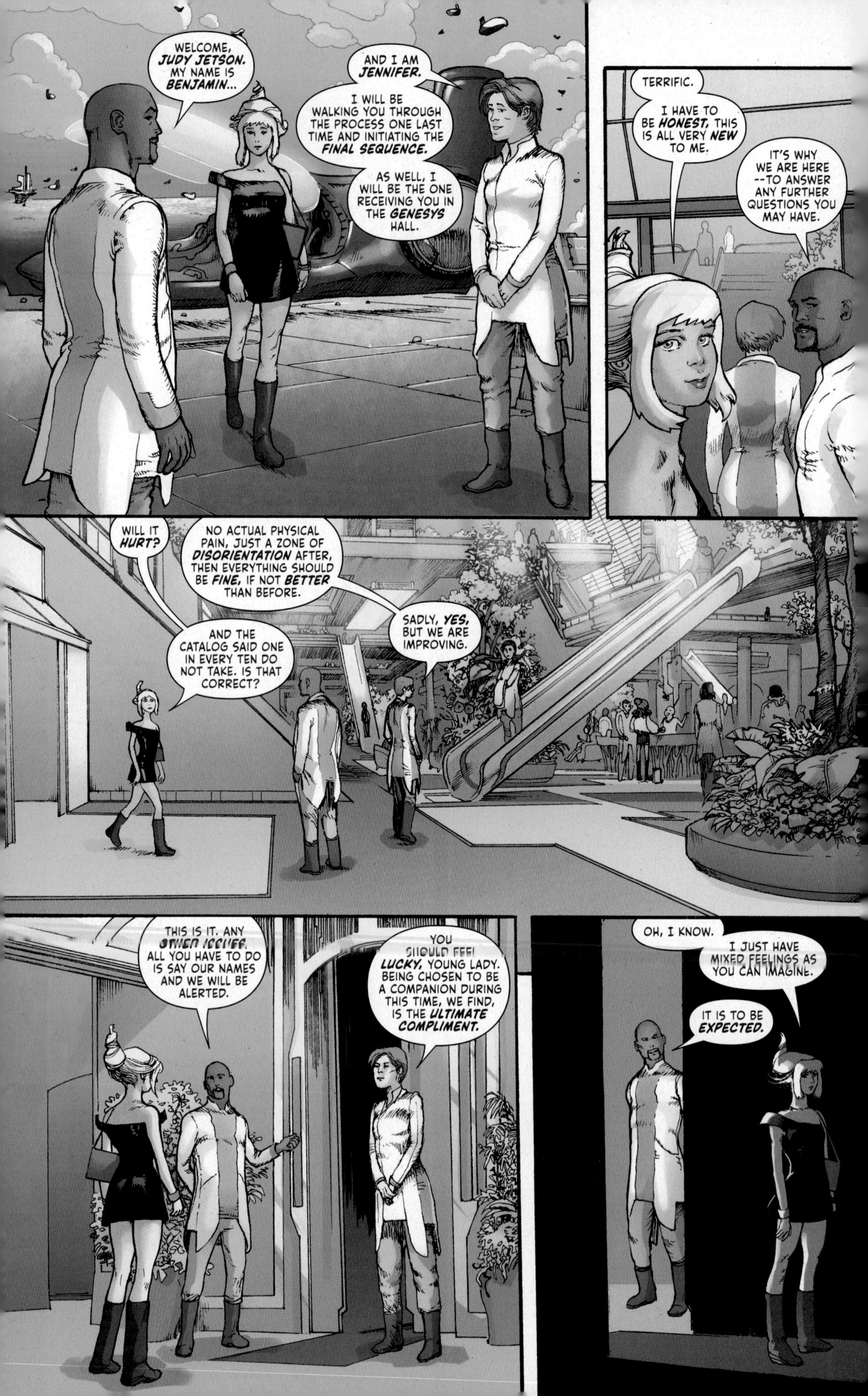
WELCOME, JUDY JETSON. MY NAME IS BENJAMIN...
AND I AM JENNIFER.
I WILL BE WALKING YOU THROUGH THE PROCESS ONE LAST TIME AND INITIATING THE FINAL SEQUENCE.
AS WELL, I WILL BE THE ONE RECEIVING YOU IN THE GENESYS HALL.
TERRIFIC.
I HAVE TO BE HONEST, THIS IS ALL VERY NEW TO ME.
IT'S WHY WE ARE HERE --TO ANSWER ANY FURTHER QUESTIONS YOU MAY HAVE.
WILL IT HURT?
NO ACTUAL PHYSICAL PAIN, JUST A ZONE OF DISORIENTATION AFTER, THEN EVERYTHING SHOULD BE FINE, IF NOT BETTER THAN BEFORE.
AND THE CATALOG SAID ONE IN EVERY TEN DO NOT TAKE. IS THAT CORRECT?
SADLY, YES, BUT WE ARE IMPROVING.
THIS IS IT. ANY OTHER ISSUES, ALL YOU HAVE TO DO IS SAY OUR NAMES AND WE WILL BE ALERTED.
YOU SHOULD FEEL LUCKY, YOUNG LADY. BEING CHOSEN TO BE A COMPANION DURING THIS TIME, WE FIND, IS THE ULTIMATE COMPLIMENT.
OH, I KNOW.
I JUST HAVE MIXED FEELINGS AS YOU CAN IMAGINE.
IT IS TO BE EXPECTED.

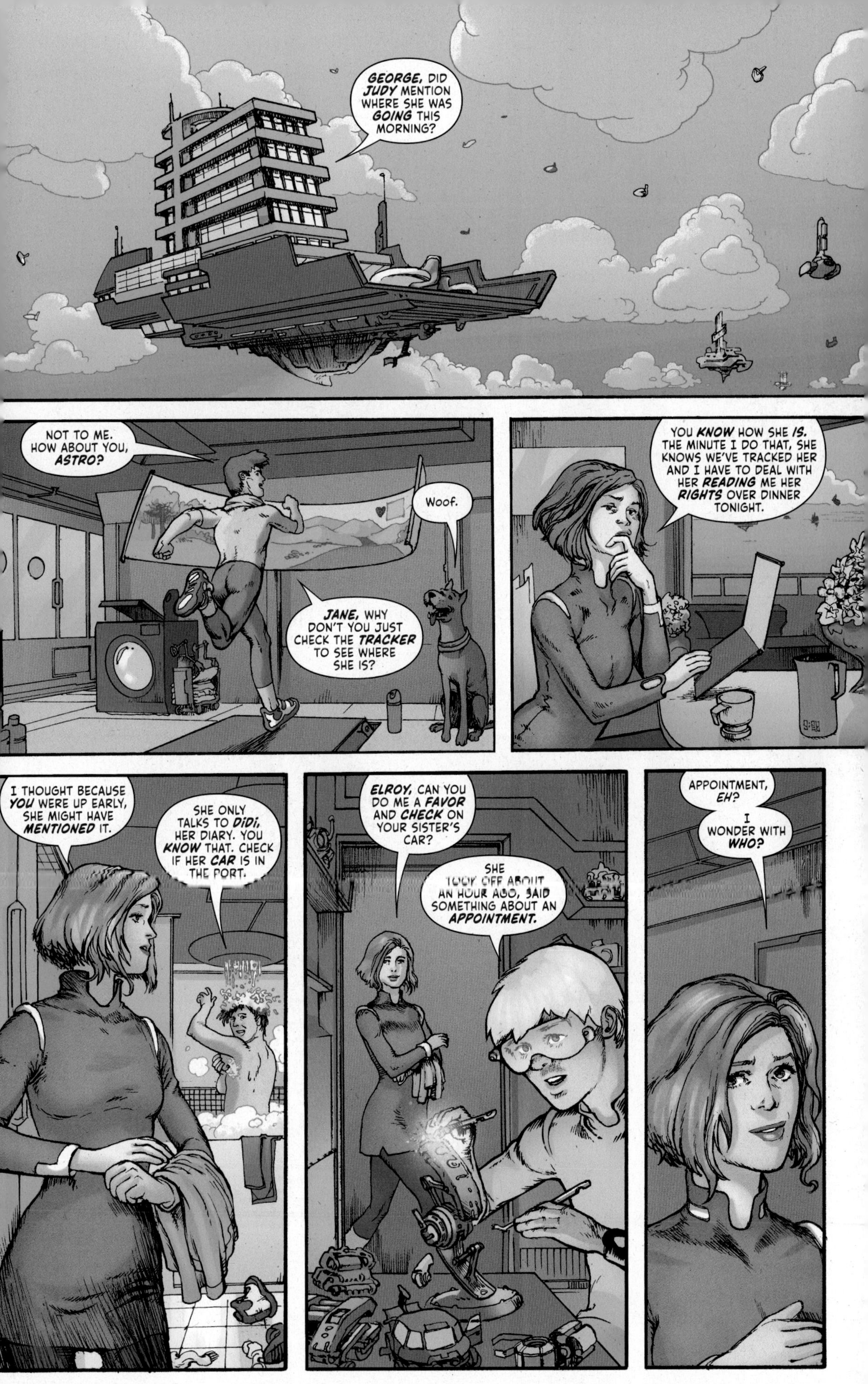
GEORGE, DID JUDY MENTION WHERE SHE WAS GOING THIS MORNING?
NOT TO ME. HOW ABOUT YOU, ASTRO?
Woof.
JANE, WHY DON'T YOU JUST CHECK THE TRACKER TO SEE WHERE SHE IS?
YOU KNOW HOW SHE IS. THE MINUTE I DO THAT, SHE KNOWS WE'VE TRACKED HER AND I HAVE TO DEAL WITH HER READING ME HER RIGHTS OVER DINNER TONIGHT.
I THOUGHT BECAUSE YOU WERE UP EARLY, SHE MIGHT HAVE MENTIONED IT.
SHE ONLY TALKS TO DiDi, HER DIARY. YOU KNOW THAT. CHECK IF HER CAR IS IN THE PORT.
ELROY, CAN YOU DO ME A FAVOR AND CHECK ON YOUR SISTER'S CAR?
SHE TOOK OFF ABOUT AN HOUR AGO, SAID SOMETHING ABOUT AN APPOINTMENT.
APPOINTMENT, EH?
I WONDER WITH WHO?

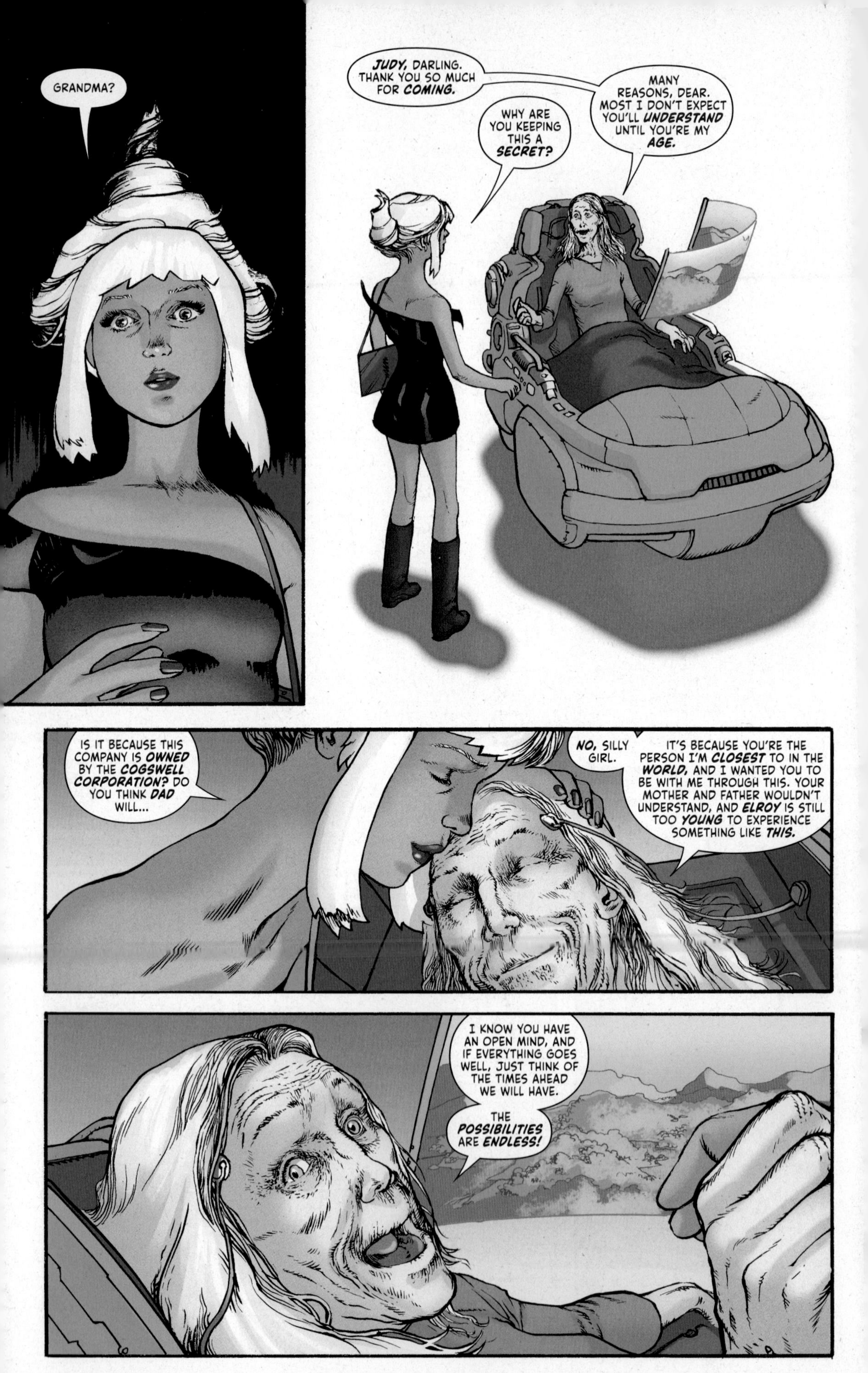
GRANDMA?
JUDY, DARLING. THANK YOU SO MUCH FOR COMING.
WHY ARE YOU KEEPING THIS A SECRET?
MANY REASONS, DEAR. MOST I DON'T EXPECT YOU'LL UNDERSTAND UNTIL YOU'RE MY AGE.
IS IT BECAUSE THIS COMPANY IS OWNED BY THE COGSWELL CORPORATION? DO YOU THINK DAD WILL...
NO, SILLY GIRL.
IT'S BECAUSE YOU'RE THE PERSON I'M CLOSEST TO IN THE WORLD, AND I WANTED YOU TO BE WITH ME THROUGH THIS. YOUR MOTHER AND FATHER WOULDN'T UNDERSTAND, AND ELROY IS STILL TOO YOUNG TO EXPERIENCE SOMETHING LIKE THIS.
I KNOW YOU HAVE AN OPEN MIND, AND IF EVERYTHING GOES WELL, JUST THINK OF THE TIMES AHEAD WE WILL HAVE.
THE POSSIBILITIES ARE ENDLESS!

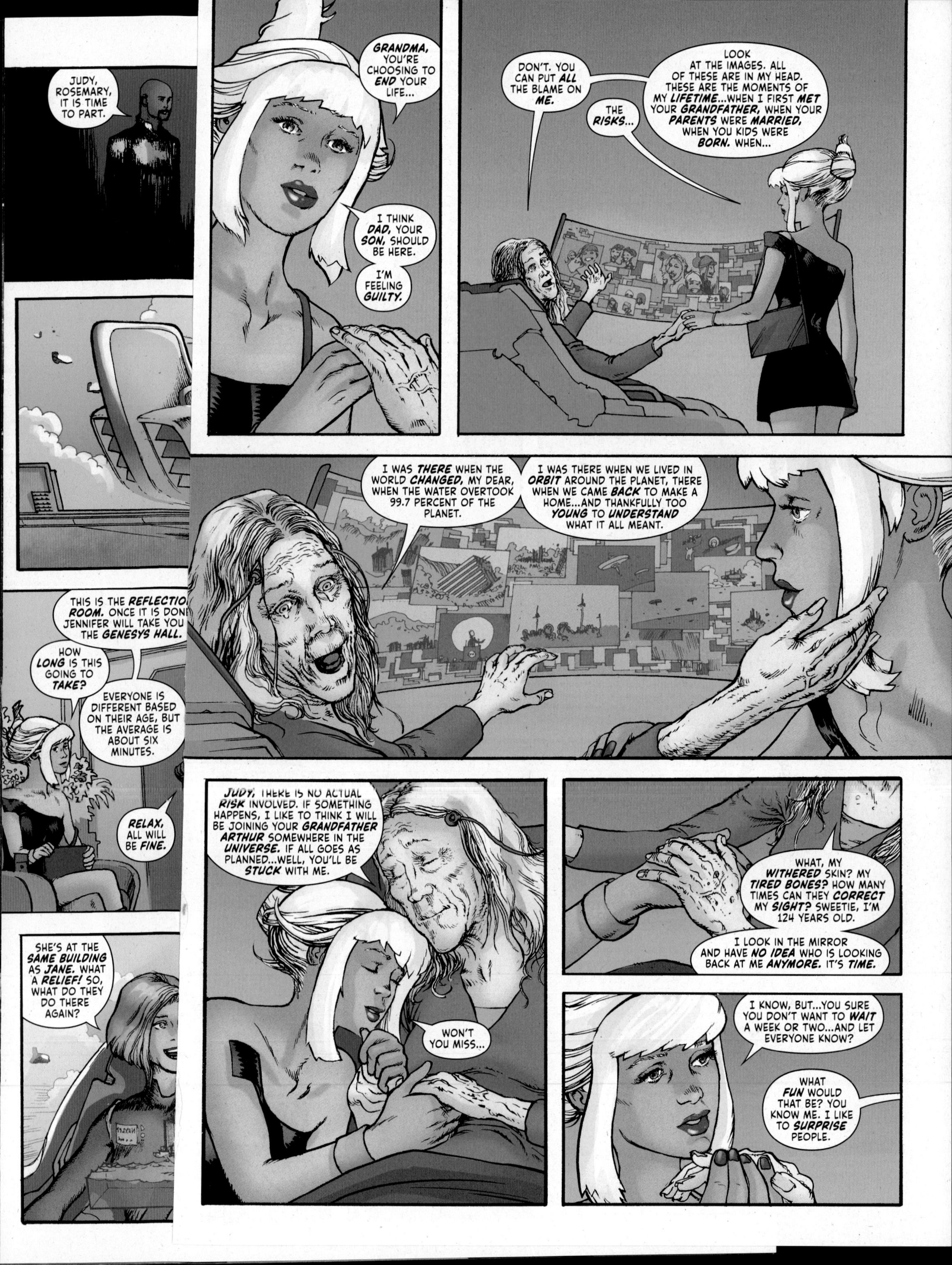

JUDY, ROSEMARY, IT IS TIME TO PART.
THIS IS THE REFLECTIO ROOM. ONCE IT IS DON JENNIFER WILL TAKE YOU THE GENESYS HALL.
HOW LONG IS THIS GOING TO TAKE?
EVERYONE IS DIFFERENT BASED ON THEIR AGE, BUT THE AVERAGE IS ABOUT SIX MINUTES.
RELAX, ALL WILL BE FINE.
SHE'S AT THE SAME BUILDING AS JANE. WHAT A RELIEF! SO, WHAT DO THEY DO THERE AGAIN?
GRANDMA, YOU'RE CHOOSING TO END YOUR LIFE...
I THINK DAD, YOUR SON, SHOULD BE HERE.
I'M FEELING GUILTY.
DON'T. YOU CAN PUT ALL THE BLAME ON ME.
THE RISKS...
LOOK AT THE IMAGES. ALL OF THESE ARE IN MY HEAD. THESE ARE THE MOMENTS OF MY LIFETIME...WHEN I FIRST MET YOUR GRANDFATHER, WHEN YOUR PARENTS WERE MARRIED, WHEN YOU KIDS WERE BORN. WHEN...
I WAS THERE WHEN THE WORLD CHANGED, MY DEAR, WHEN THE WATER OVERTOOK 99.7 PERCENT OF THE PLANET.
I WAS THERE WHEN WE LIVED IN ORBIT AROUND THE PLANET, THERE WHEN WE CAME BACK TO MAKE A HOME...AND THANKFULLY TOO YOUNG TO UNDERSTAND WHAT IT ALL MEANT.
JUDY, THERE IS NO ACTUAL RISK INVOLVED. IF SOMETHING HAPPENS, I LIKE TO THINK I WILL BE JOINING YOUR GRANDFATHER ARTHUR SOMEWHERE IN THE UNIVERSE. IF ALL GOES AS PLANNED...WELL, YOU'LL BE STUCK WITH ME.
WON'T YOU MISS...
WHAT, MY WITHERED SKIN? MY TIRED BONES? HOW MANY TIMES CAN THEY CORRECT MY SIGHT? SWEETIE, I'M 124 YEARS OLD.
I LOOK IN THE MIRROR AND HAVE NO IDEA WHO IS LOOKING BACK AT ME ANYMORE. IT'S TIME.
I KNOW, BUT...YOU SURE YOU DON'T WANT TO WAIT A WEEK OR TWO...AND LET EVERYONE KNOW?
WHAT FUN WOULD THAT BE? YOU KNOW ME. I LIKE TO SURPRISE PEOPLE.

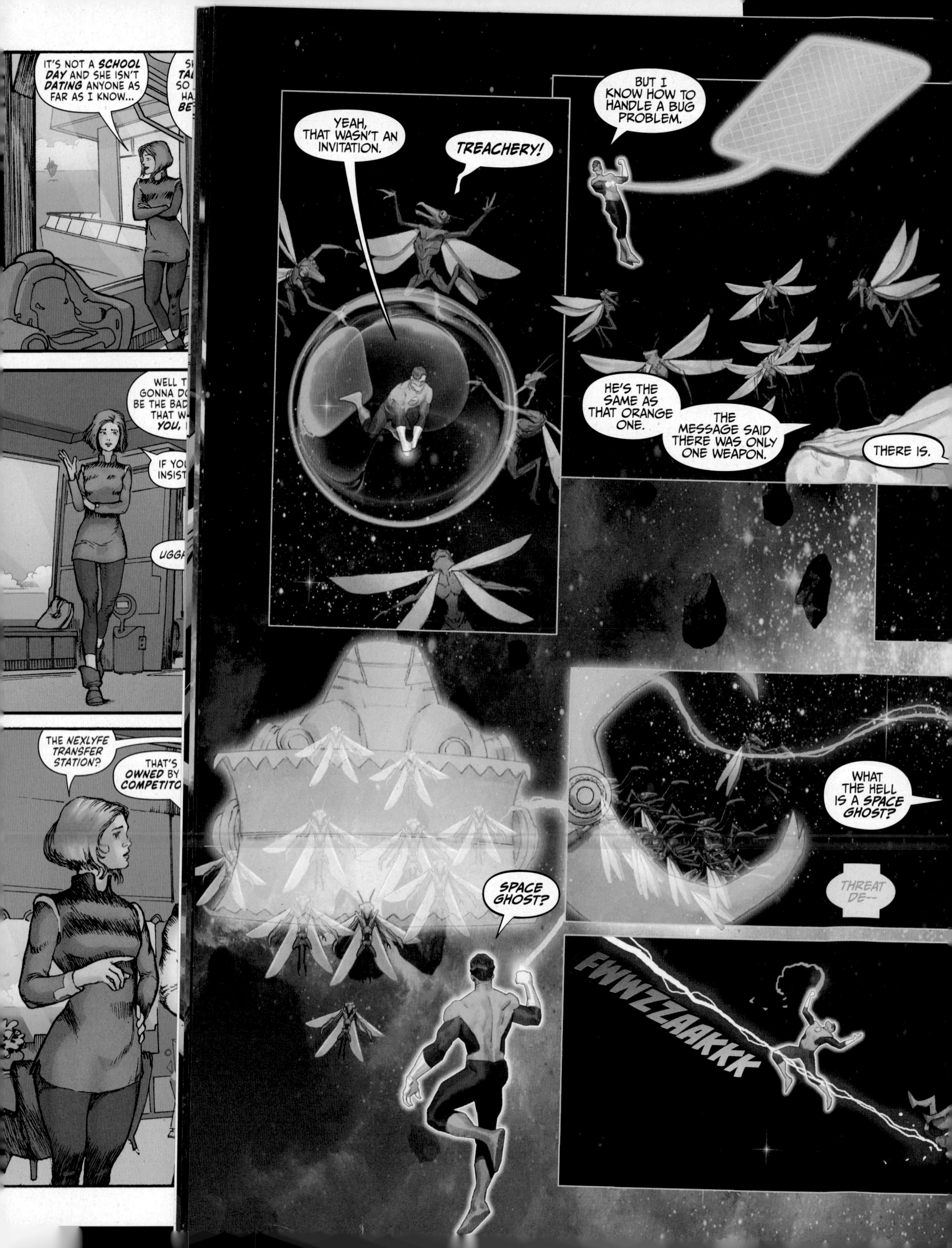
IT'S NOT A SCHOOL DAY AND SHE ISN'T DATING ANYONE AS FAR AS I KNOW...
THE NEXLYFE TRANSFER STATION?
YEAH, THAT WASN'T AN INVITATION.
TREACHERY!
BUT I KNOW HOW TO HANDLE A BUG PROBLEM.
HE'S THE SAME AS THAT ORANGE ONE.
THE MESSAGE SAID THERE WAS ONLY ONE WEAPON.
THERE IS.
SPACE GHOST?
WHAT THE HELL IS A SPACE GHOST?
THREAT DE--
FWWZZAAKKK

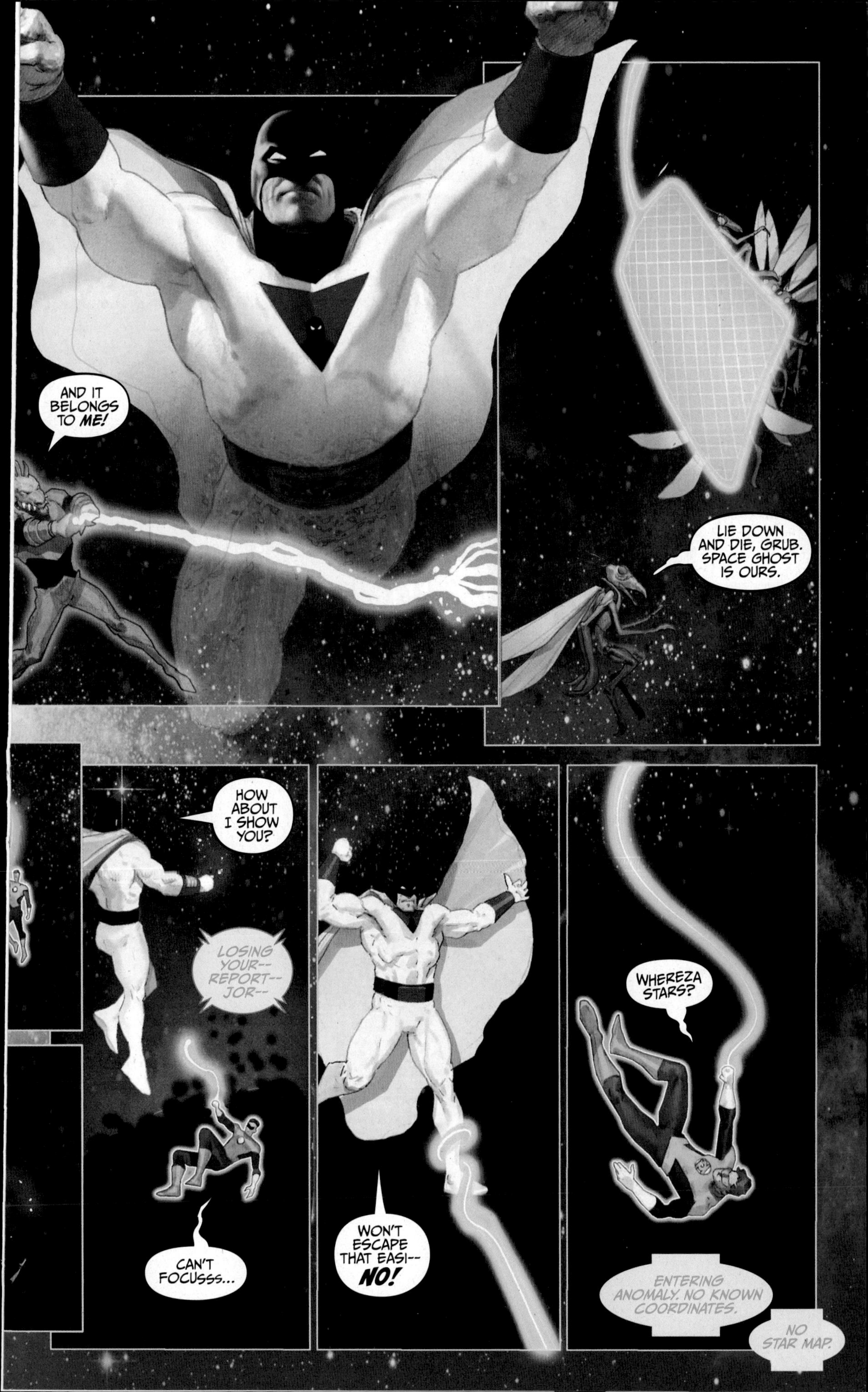
AND IT BELONGS TO ME!
LIE DOWN AND DIE, GRUB. SPACE GHOST IS OURS.
HOW ABOUT I SHOW YOU?
LOSING YOUR-- REPORT-- JOR--
CAN'T FOCUSSS...
WON'T ESCAPE THAT EASI-- NO!
WHEREZA STARS?
ENTERING ANOMALY. NO KNOWN COORDINATES.
NO STAR MAP.

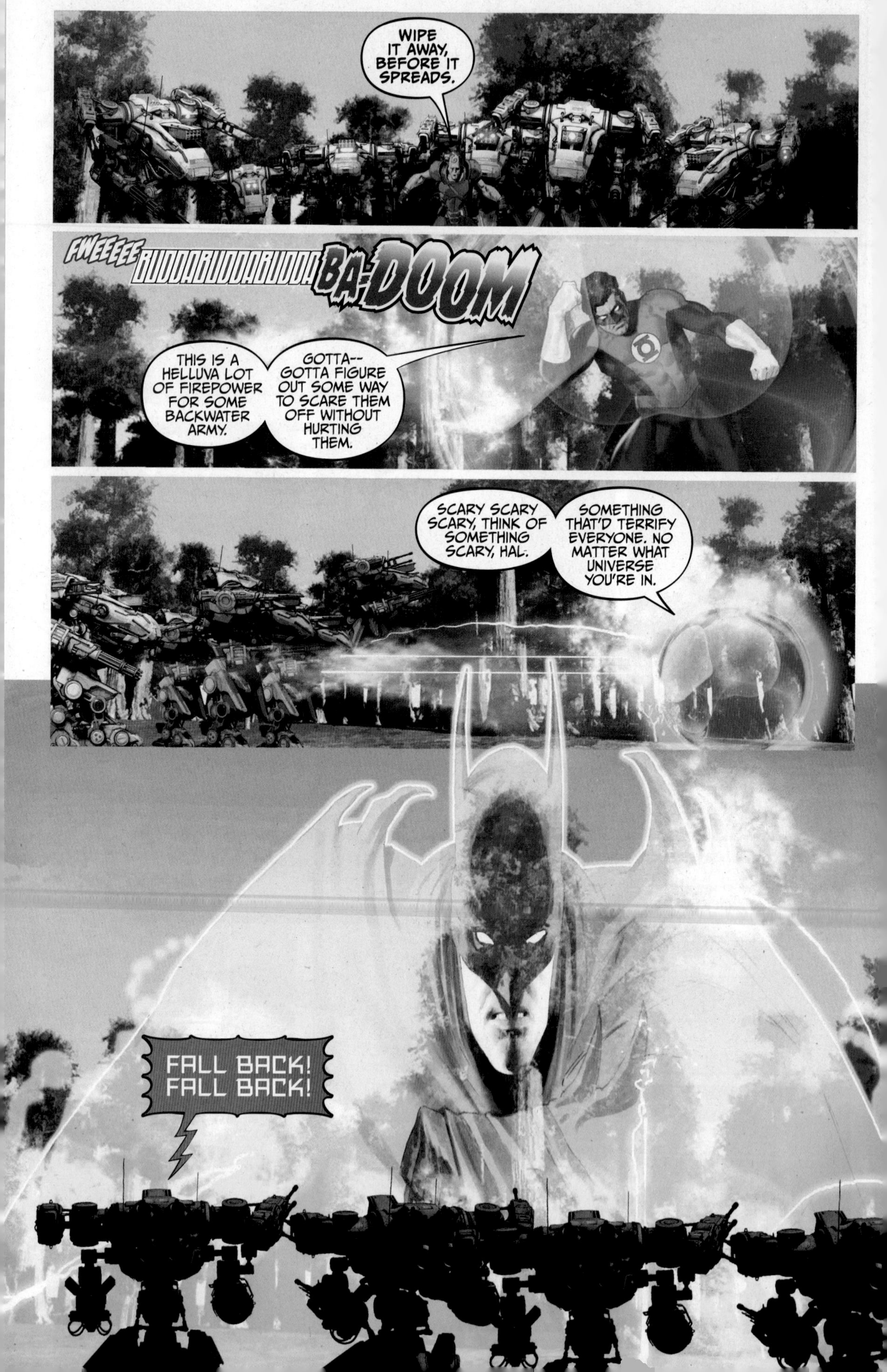
WIPE IT AWAY, BEFORE IT SPREADS.
FWEEEEE BUDDABUDDABUDDA BA-DOOM
THIS IS A HELLUVA LOT OF FIREPOWER FOR SOME BACKWATER ARMY.
GOTTA-- GOTTA FIGURE OUT SOME WAY TO SCARE THEM OFF WITHOUT HURTING THEM.
SCARY SCARY SCARY, THINK OF SOMETHING SCARY, HAL.
SOMETHING THAT'D TERRIFY EVERYONE. NO MATTER WHAT UNIVERSE YOU'RE IN.
FALL BACK! FALL BACK!

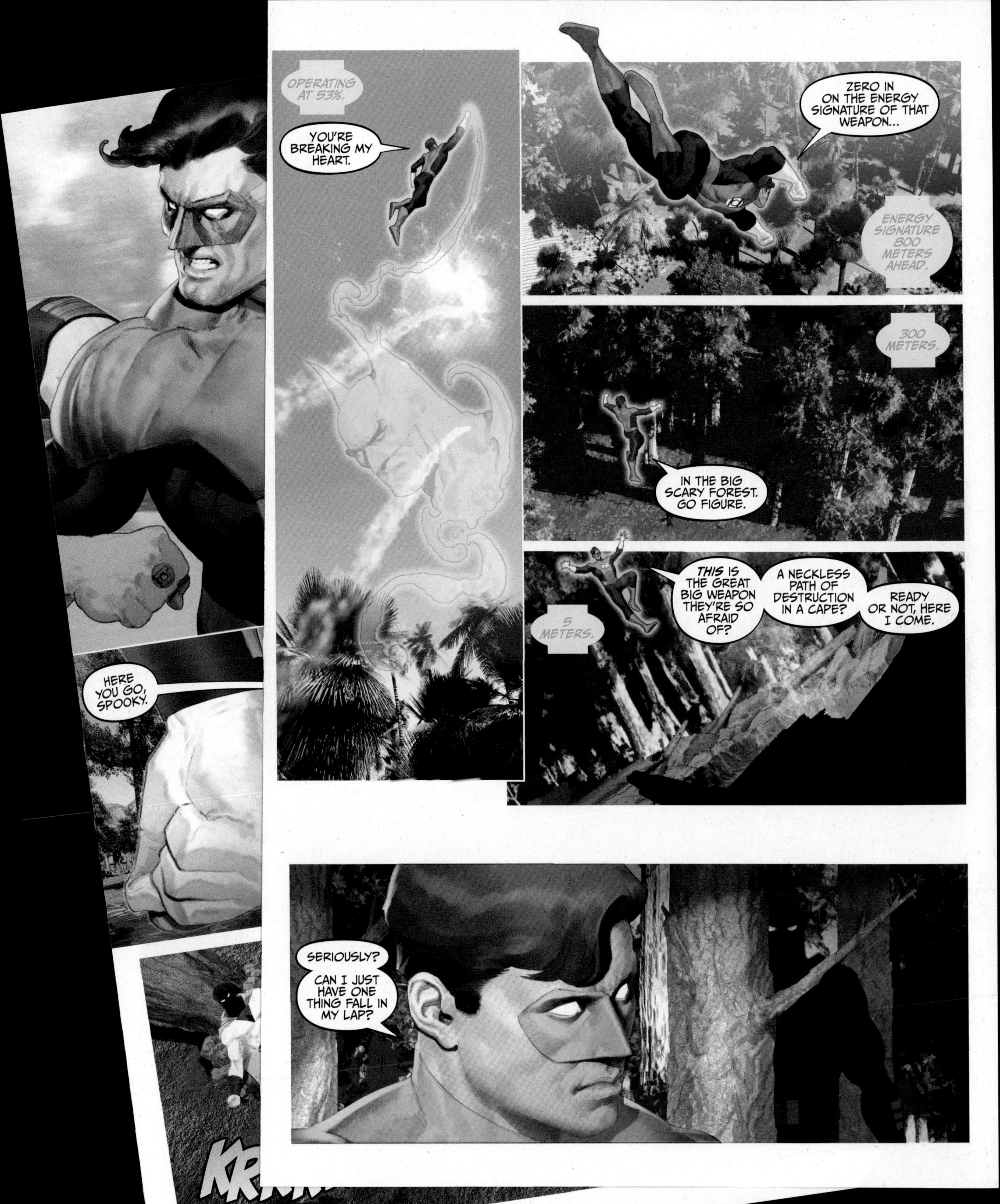
HERE YOU GO, SPOOKY.
OPERATING AT 53%.
YOU'RE BREAKING MY HEART.
ZERO IN ON THE ENERGY SIGNATURE OF THAT WEAPON...
ENERGY SIGNATURE 800 METERS AHEAD.
300 METERS.
IN THE BIG SCARY FOREST. GO FIGURE.
5 METERS.
THIS IS THE GREAT BIG WEAPON THEY'RE SO AFRAID OF?
A NECKLESS PATH OF DESTRUCTION IN A CAPE?
READY OR NOT, HERE I COME.
SERIOUSLY?
CAN I JUST HAVE ONE THING FALL IN MY LAP?

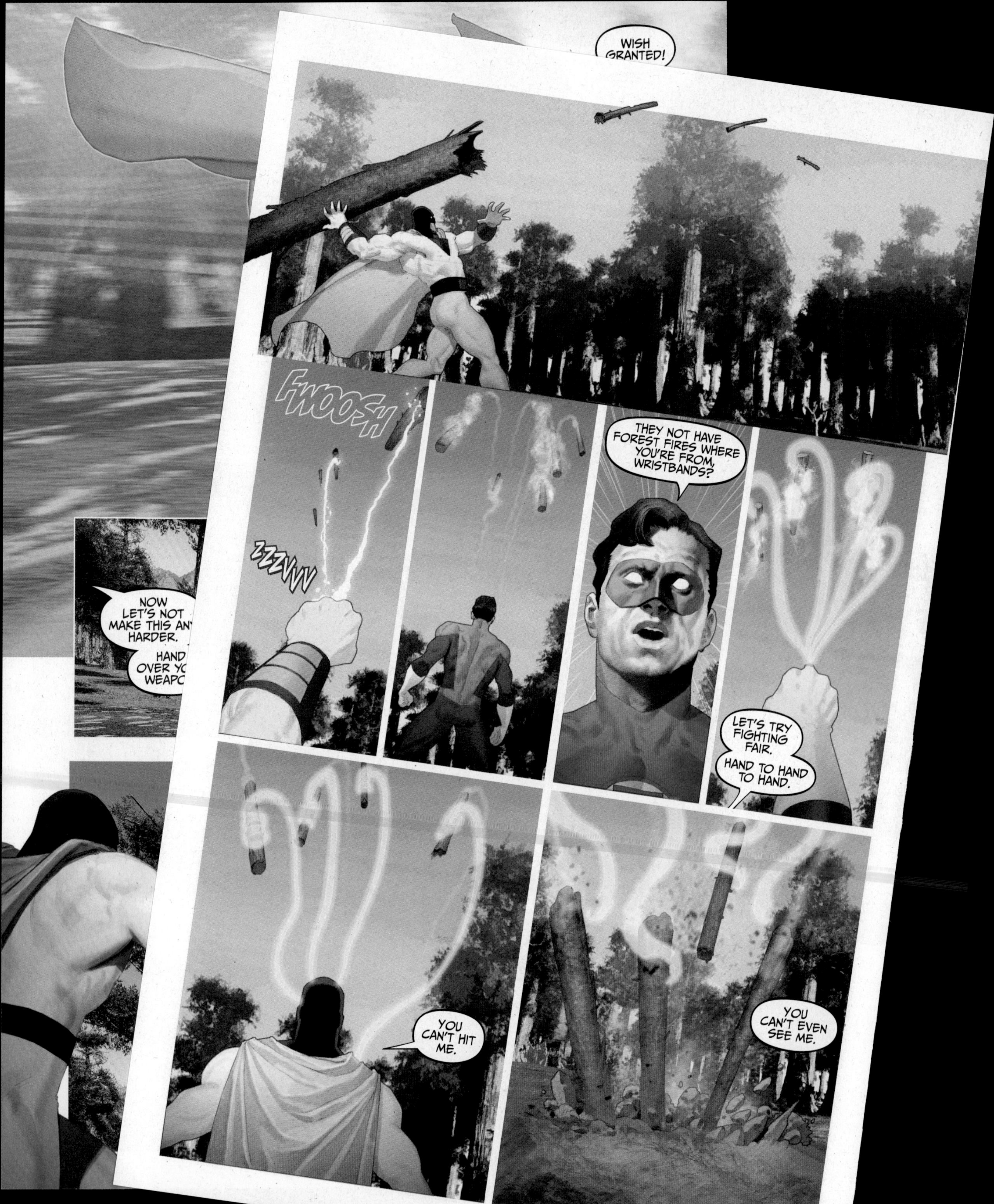
WISH GRANTED!
NOW LET'S NOT MAKE THIS AN HARDER.
HAND OVER YO WEAPO
FWOOSH
ZZZVVV
THEY NOT HAVE FOREST FIRES WHERE YOU'RE FROM, WRISTBANDS?
LET'S TRY FIGHTING FAIR.
HAND TO HAND TO HAND.
YOU CAN'T HIT ME.
YOU CAN'T EVEN SEE ME.

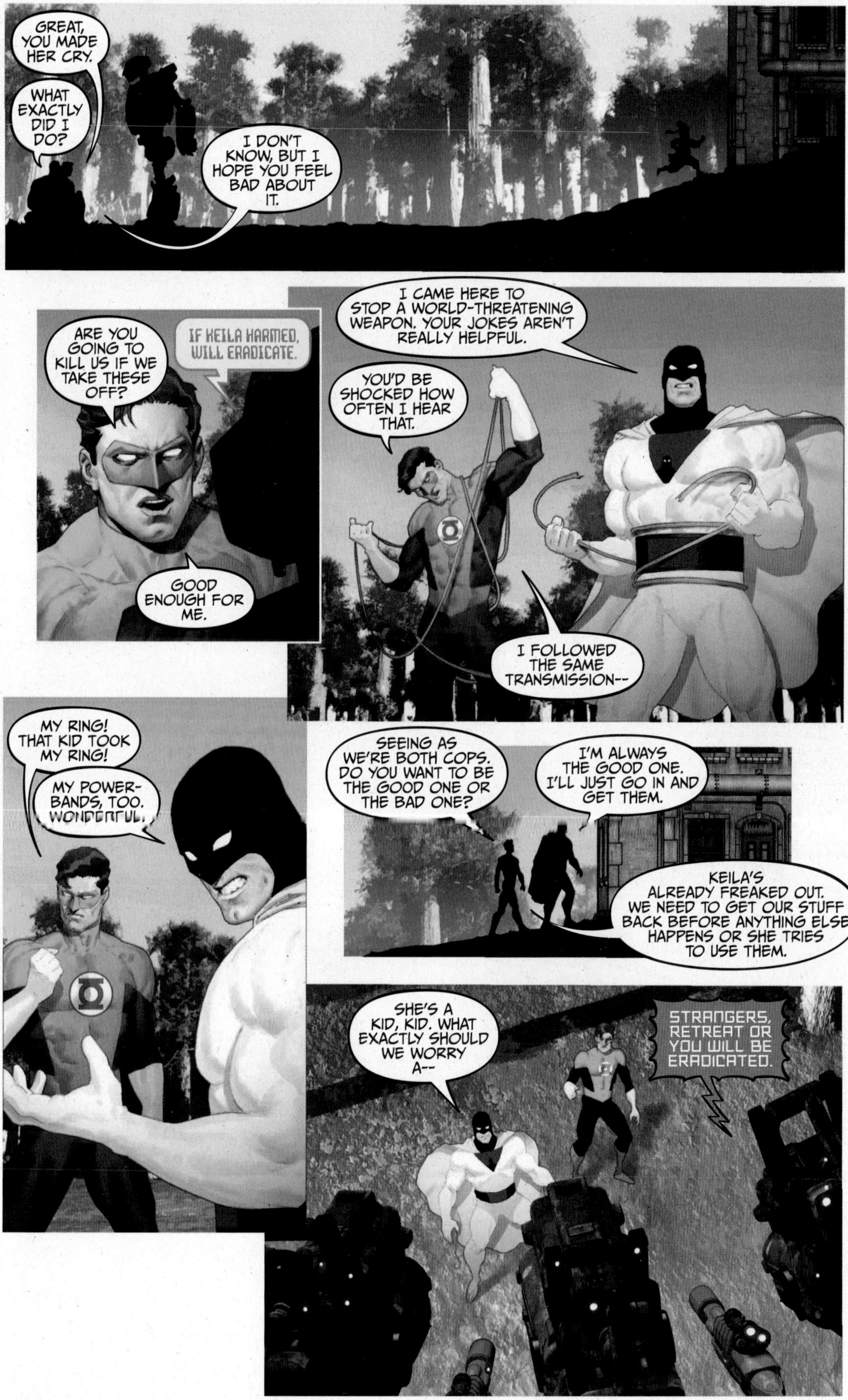
GREAT, YOU MADE HER CRY.
WHAT EXACTLY DID I DO?
I DON'T KNOW, BUT I HOPE YOU FEEL BAD ABOUT IT.
ARE YOU GOING TO KILL US IF WE TAKE THESE OFF?
IF KEILA HARMED, WILL ERADICATE.
GOOD ENOUGH FOR ME.
I CAME HERE TO STOP A WORLD-THREATENING WEAPON. YOUR JOKES AREN'T REALLY HELPFUL.
YOU'D BE SHOCKED HOW OFTEN I HEAR THAT.
I FOLLOWED THE SAME TRANSMISSION--
MY RING! THAT KID TOOK MY RING!
MY POWER-BANDS, TOO. WONDERFUL.
SEEING AS WE'RE BOTH COPS. DO YOU WANT TO BE THE GOOD ONE OR THE BAD ONE?
I'M ALWAYS THE GOOD ONE. I'LL JUST GO IN AND GET THEM.
KEILA'S ALREADY FREAKED OUT. WE NEED TO GET OUR STUFF BACK BEFORE ANYTHING ELSE HAPPENS OR SHE TRIES TO USE THEM.
SHE'S A KID, KID. WHAT EXACTLY SHOULD WE WORRY A--
STRANGERS, RETREAT OR YOU WILL BE ERADICATED.

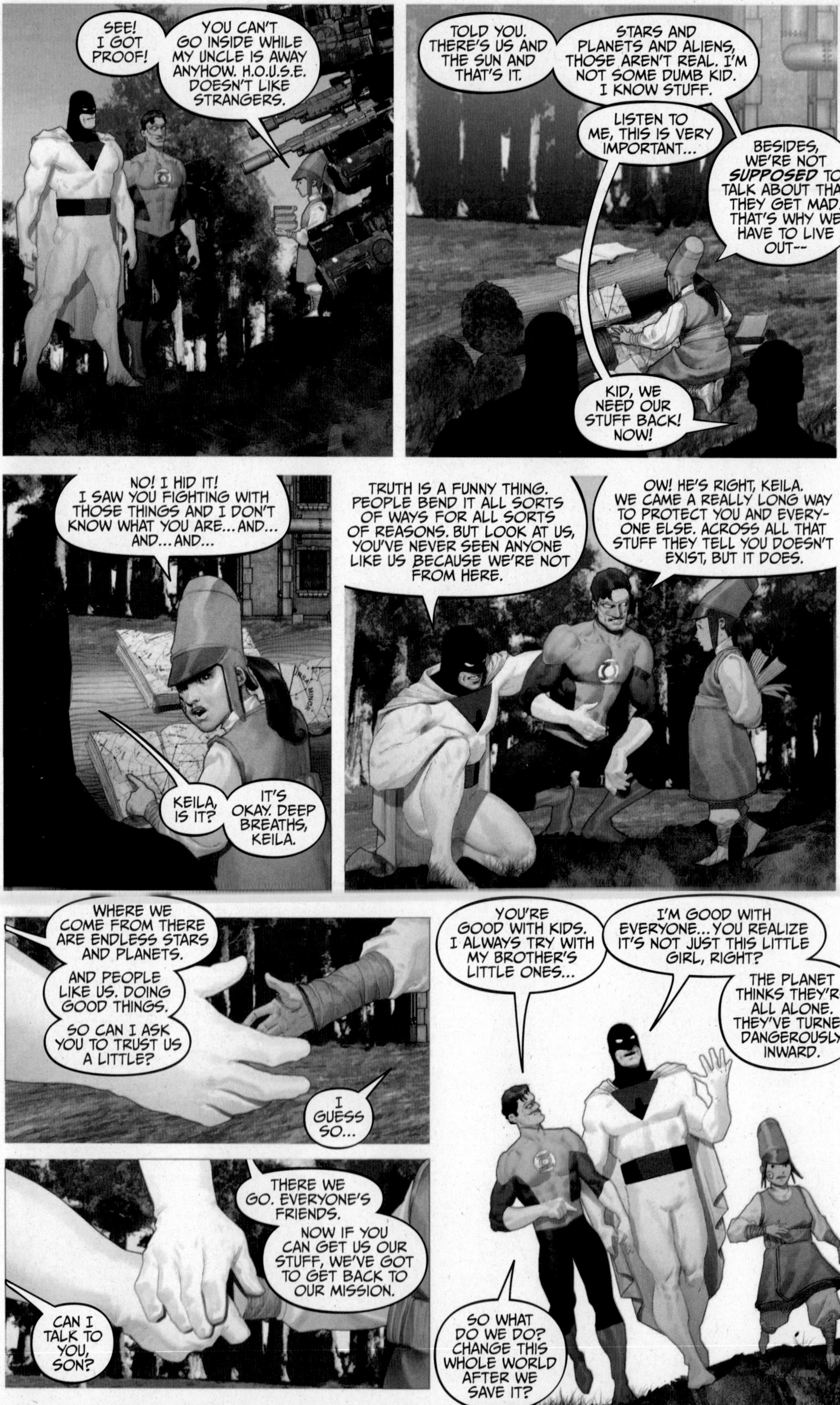
SEE! I GOT PROOF!
YOU CAN'T GO INSIDE WHILE MY UNCLE IS AWAY ANYHOW. H.O.U.S.E. DOESN'T LIKE STRANGERS.
TOLD YOU. THERE'S US AND THE SUN AND THAT'S IT.
STARS AND PLANETS AND ALIENS, THOSE AREN'T REAL. I'M NOT SOME DUMB KID. I KNOW STUFF.
LISTEN TO ME, THIS IS VERY IMPORTANT...
BESIDES, WE'RE NOT SUPPOSED TO TALK ABOUT THAT THEY GET MAD. THAT'S WHY WE HAVE TO LIVE OUT--
KID, WE NEED OUR STUFF BACK! NOW!
NO! I HID IT! I SAW YOU FIGHTING WITH THOSE THINGS AND I DON'T KNOW WHAT YOU ARE... AND... AND... AND... AND...
KEILA, IS IT?
IT'S OKAY. DEEP BREATHS, KEILA.
TRUTH IS A FUNNY THING. PEOPLE BEND IT ALL SORTS OF WAYS FOR ALL SORTS OF REASONS. BUT LOOK AT US, YOU'VE NEVER SEEN ANYONE LIKE US BECAUSE WE'RE NOT FROM HERE.
OW! HE'S RIGHT, KEILA. WE CAME A REALLY LONG WAY TO PROTECT YOU AND EVERYONE ELSE. ACROSS ALL THAT STUFF THEY TELL YOU DOESN'T EXIST, BUT IT DOES.
WHERE WE COME FROM THERE ARE ENDLESS STARS AND PLANETS.
AND PEOPLE LIKE US. DOING GOOD THINGS.
SO CAN I ASK YOU TO TRUST US A LITTLE?
I GUESS SO...
THERE WE GO. EVERYONE'S FRIENDS.
NOW IF YOU CAN GET US OUR STUFF, WE'VE GOT TO GET BACK TO OUR MISSION.
CAN I TALK TO YOU, SON?
YOU'RE GOOD WITH KIDS. I ALWAYS TRY WITH MY BROTHER'S LITTLE ONES...
I'M GOOD WITH EVERYONE... YOU REALIZE IT'S NOT JUST THIS LITTLE GIRL, RIGHT?
THE PLANET THINKS THEY'RE ALL ALONE. THEY'VE TURNED DANGEROUSLY INWARD.
SO WHAT DO WE DO? CHANGE THIS WHOLE WORLD AFTER WE SAVE IT?

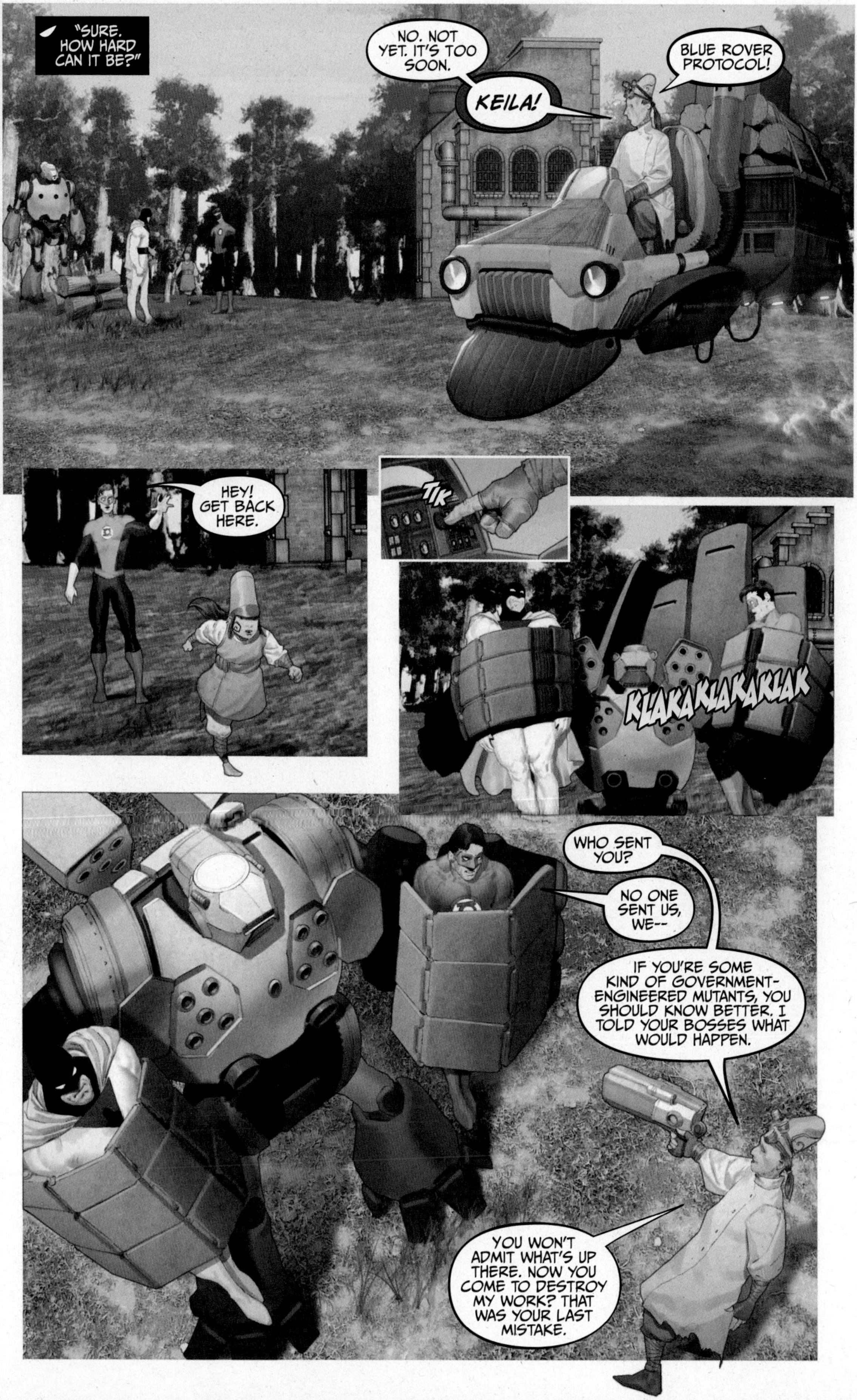
"SURE. HOW HARD CAN IT BE?"
NO. NOT YET. IT'S TOO SOON.
KEILA!
BLUE ROVER PROTOCOL!
HEY! GET BACK HERE.
TIK
KLAKAKLAKAKLAK
WHO SENT YOU?
NO ONE SENT US, WE--
IF YOU'RE SOME KIND OF GOVERNMENT-ENGINEERED MUTANTS, YOU SHOULD KNOW BETTER. I TOLD YOUR BOSSES WHAT WOULD HAPPEN.
YOU WON'T ADMIT WHAT'S UP THERE. NOW YOU COME TO DESTROY MY WORK? THAT WAS YOUR LAST MISTAKE.

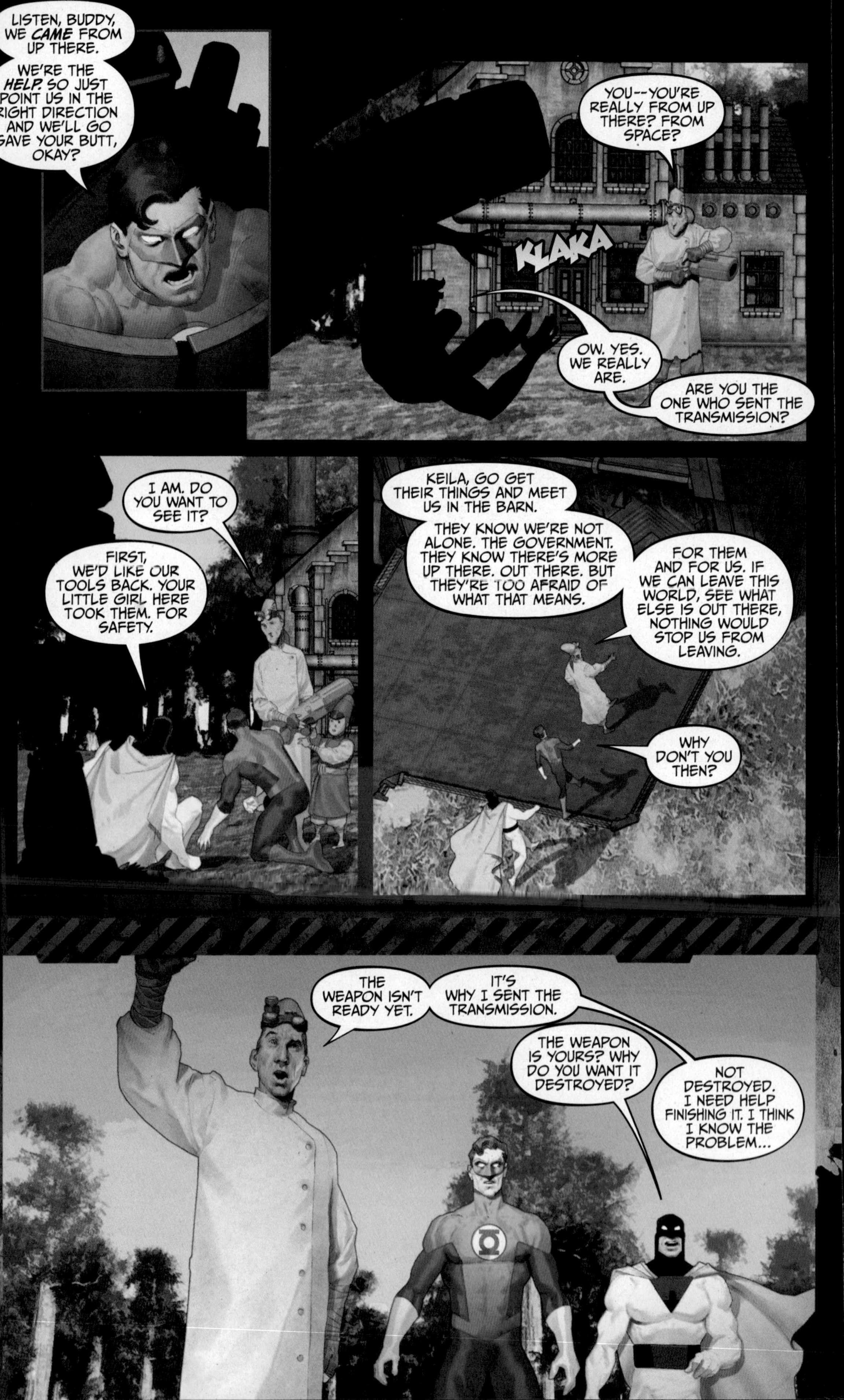
LISTEN, BUDDY, WE CAME FROM UP THERE.
WE'RE THE HELP. SO JUST POINT US IN THE RIGHT DIRECTION AND WE'LL GO SAVE YOUR BUTT, OKAY?
YOU--YOU'RE REALLY FROM UP THERE? FROM SPACE?
KLAKA
OW. YES. WE REALLY ARE.
ARE YOU THE ONE WHO SENT THE TRANSMISSION?
I AM. DO YOU WANT TO SEE IT?
FIRST, WE'D LIKE OUR TOOLS BACK. YOUR LITTLE GIRL HERE TOOK THEM. FOR SAFETY.
KEILA, GO GET THEIR THINGS AND MEET US IN THE BARN.
THEY KNOW WE'RE NOT ALONE. THE GOVERNMENT. THEY KNOW THERE'S MORE UP THERE. OUT THERE. BUT THEY'RE TOO AFRAID OF WHAT THAT MEANS.
FOR THEM AND FOR US. IF WE CAN LEAVE THIS WORLD, SEE WHAT ELSE IS OUT THERE, NOTHING WOULD STOP US FROM LEAVING.
WHY DON'T YOU THEN?
THE WEAPON ISN'T READY YET.
IT'S WHY I SENT THE TRANSMISSION.
THE WEAPON IS YOURS? WHY DO YOU WANT IT DESTROYED?
NOT DESTROYED. I NEED HELP FINISHING IT. I THINK I KNOW THE PROBLEM...

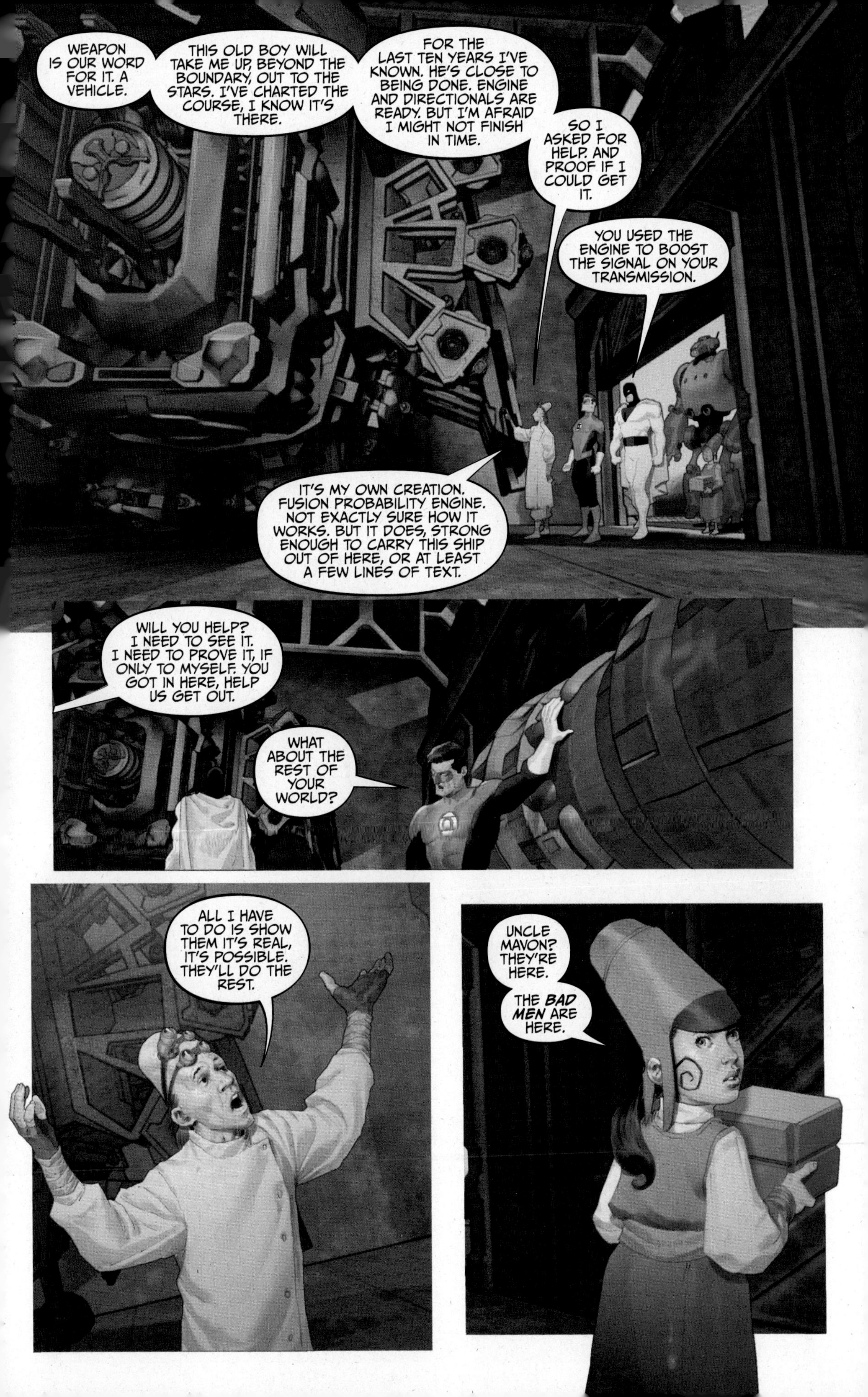
WEAPON IS OUR WORD FOR IT. A VEHICLE.
THIS OLD BOY WILL TAKE ME UP, BEYOND THE BOUNDARY, OUT TO THE STARS. I'VE CHARTED THE COURSE, I KNOW IT'S THERE.
FOR THE LAST TEN YEARS I'VE KNOWN. HE'S CLOSE TO BEING DONE. ENGINE AND DIRECTIONALS ARE READY. BUT I'M AFRAID I MIGHT NOT FINISH IN TIME.
SO I ASKED FOR HELP. AND PROOF IF I COULD GET IT.
YOU USED THE ENGINE TO BOOST THE SIGNAL ON YOUR TRANSMISSION.
IT'S MY OWN CREATION. FUSION PROBABILITY ENGINE. NOT EXACTLY SURE HOW IT WORKS. BUT IT DOES, STRONG ENOUGH TO CARRY THIS SHIP OUT OF HERE, OR AT LEAST A FEW LINES OF TEXT.
WILL YOU HELP? I NEED TO SEE IT. I NEED TO PROVE IT, IF ONLY TO MYSELF. YOU GOT IN HERE, HELP US GET OUT.
WHAT ABOUT THE REST OF YOUR WORLD?
ALL I HAVE TO DO IS SHOW THEM IT'S REAL, IT'S POSSIBLE. THEY'LL DO THE REST.
UNCLE MAVON? THEY'RE HERE.
THE *BAD MEN* ARE HERE.

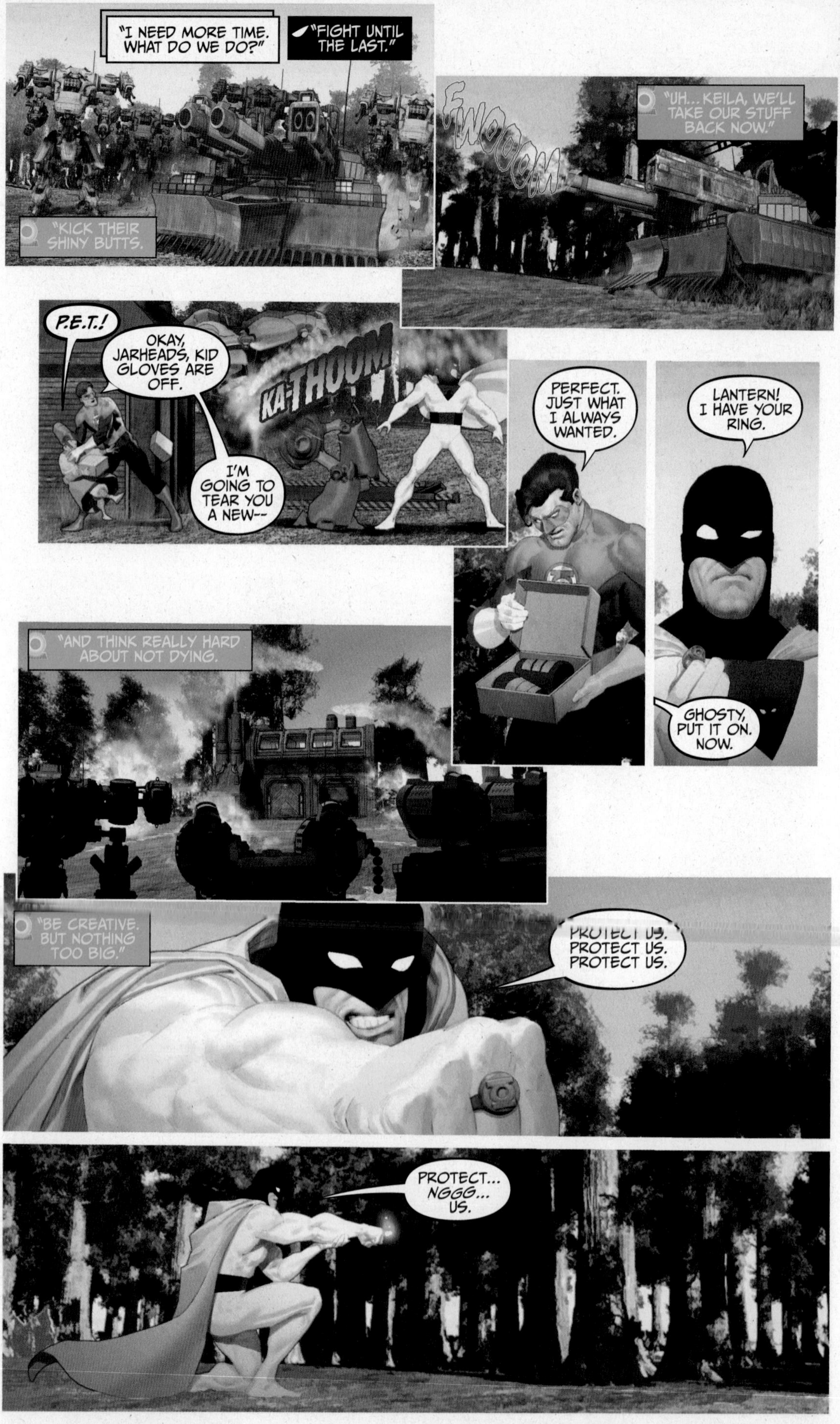
"I NEED MORE TIME. WHAT DO WE DO?"
"FIGHT UNTIL THE LAST."
"KICK THEIR SHINY BUTTS.
FWOOOM
"UH... KEILA, WE'LL TAKE OUR STUFF BACK NOW."
P.E.T.!
OKAY, JARHEADS, KID GLOVES ARE OFF.
KA-THOOM
I'M GOING TO TEAR YOU A NEW--
PERFECT. JUST WHAT I ALWAYS WANTED.
LANTERN! I HAVE YOUR RING.
GHOSTY, PUT IT ON. NOW.
"AND THINK REALLY HARD ABOUT NOT DYING.
"BE CREATIVE. BUT NOTHING TOO BIG."
PROTECT US. PROTECT US. PROTECT US.
PROTECT... NGGG... US.

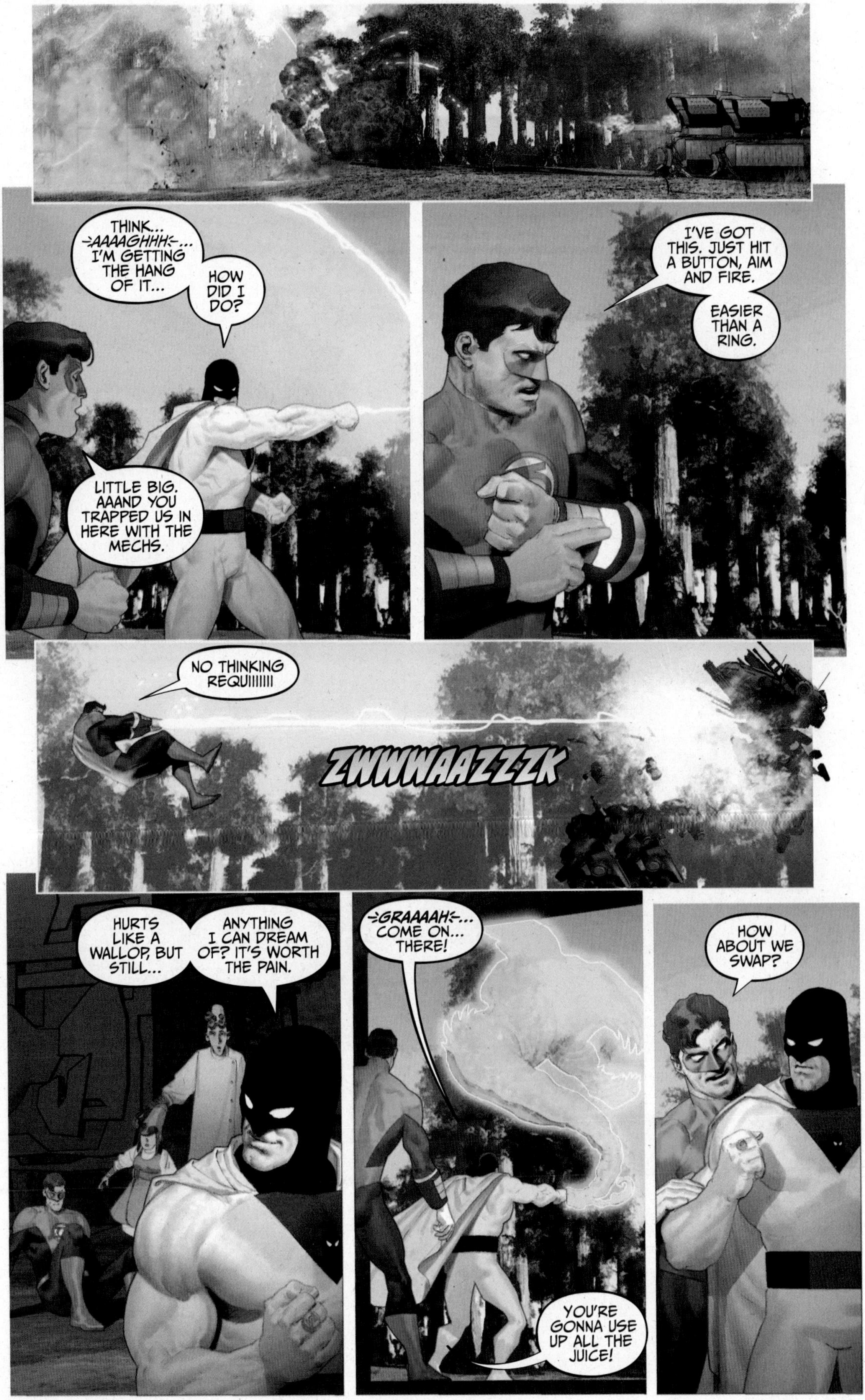
THINK... -AAAAGHHH-... I'M GETTING THE HANG OF IT...
HOW DID I DO?
LITTLE BIG. AAAND YOU TRAPPED US IN HERE WITH THE MECHS.
I'VE GOT THIS. JUST HIT A BUTTON, AIM AND FIRE.
EASIER THAN A RING.
NO THINKING REQUIIIIIII
ZWWWAAZZZK
HURTS LIKE A WALLOP, BUT STILL...
ANYTHING I CAN DREAM OF? IT'S WORTH THE PAIN.
-GRAAAAH-... COME ON... THERE!
YOU'RE GONNA USE UP ALL THE JUICE!
HOW ABOUT WE SWAP?

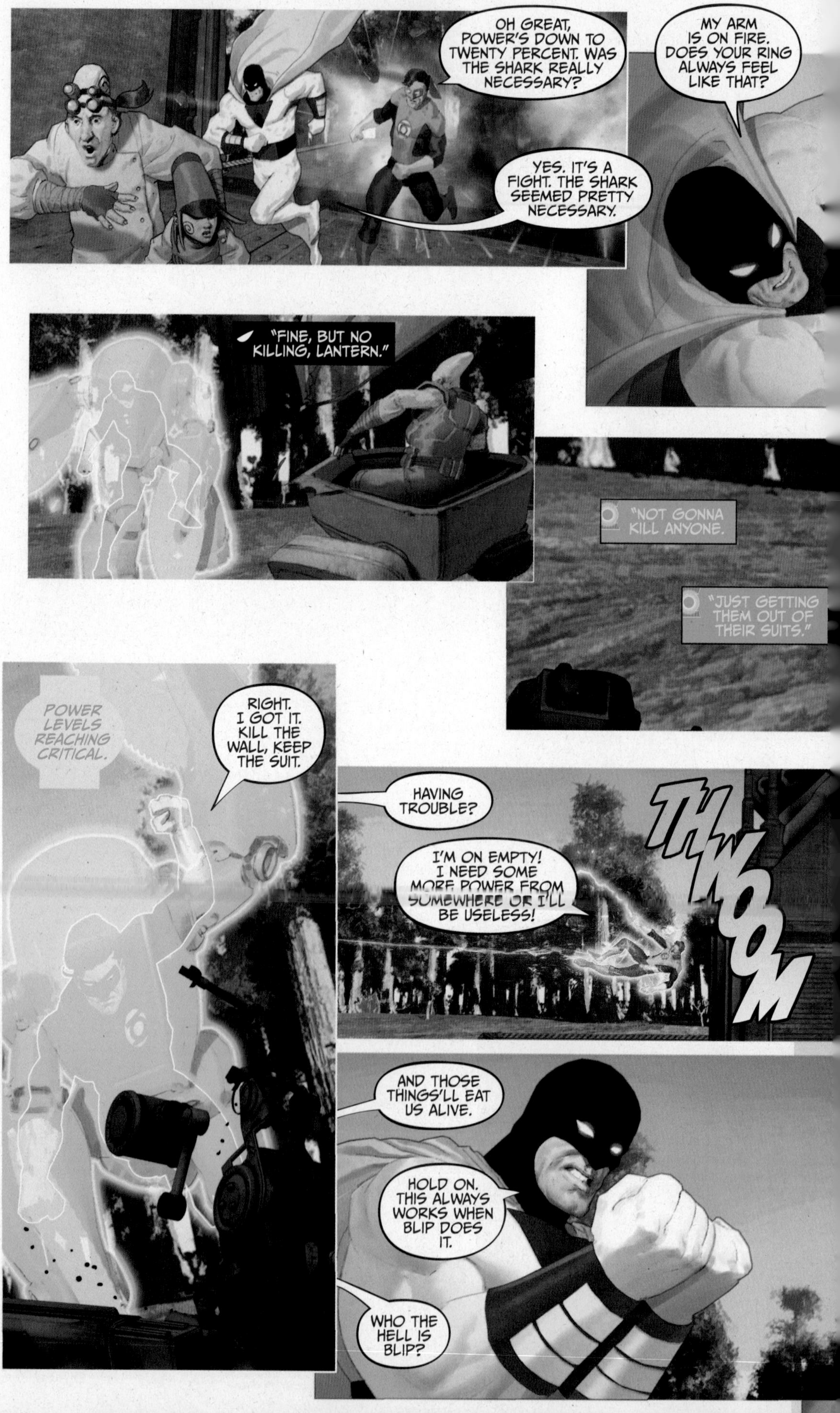
OH GREAT, POWER'S DOWN TO TWENTY PERCENT. WAS THE SHARK REALLY NECESSARY?
YES. IT'S A FIGHT. THE SHARK SEEMED PRETTY NECESSARY.
MY ARM IS ON FIRE. DOES YOUR RING ALWAYS FEEL LIKE THAT?
"FINE, BUT NO KILLING, LANTERN."
"NOT GONNA KILL ANYONE.
"JUST GETTING THEM OUT OF THEIR SUITS."
POWER LEVELS REACHING CRITICAL.
RIGHT. I GOT IT. KILL THE WALL, KEEP THE SUIT.
HAVING TROUBLE?
I'M ON EMPTY! I NEED SOME MORE POWER FROM SOMEWHERE OR I'LL BE USELESS!
THWOOM
AND THOSE THINGS'LL EAT US ALIVE.
HOLD ON. THIS ALWAYS WORKS WHEN BLIP DOES IT.
WHO THE HELL IS BLIP?

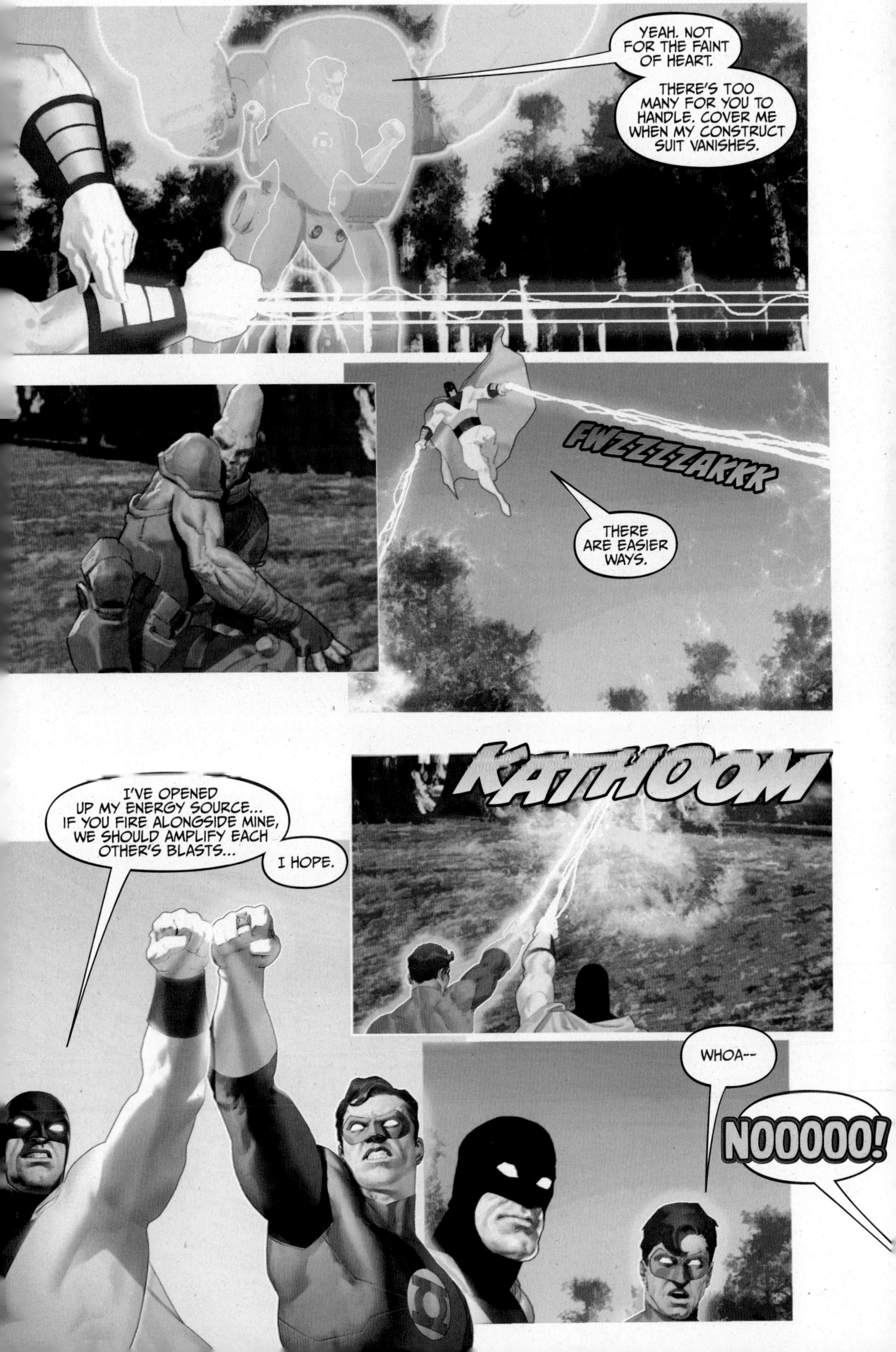
YEAH. NOT FOR THE FAINT OF HEART.
THERE'S TOO MANY FOR YOU TO HANDLE. COVER ME WHEN MY CONSTRUCT SUIT VANISHES.
FWZZZZZAKKK
THERE ARE EASIER WAYS.
I'VE OPENED UP MY ENERGY SOURCE... IF YOU FIRE ALONGSIDE MINE, WE SHOULD AMPLIFY EACH OTHER'S BLASTS...
I HOPE.
KATHOOM
WHOA--
NOOOOO!

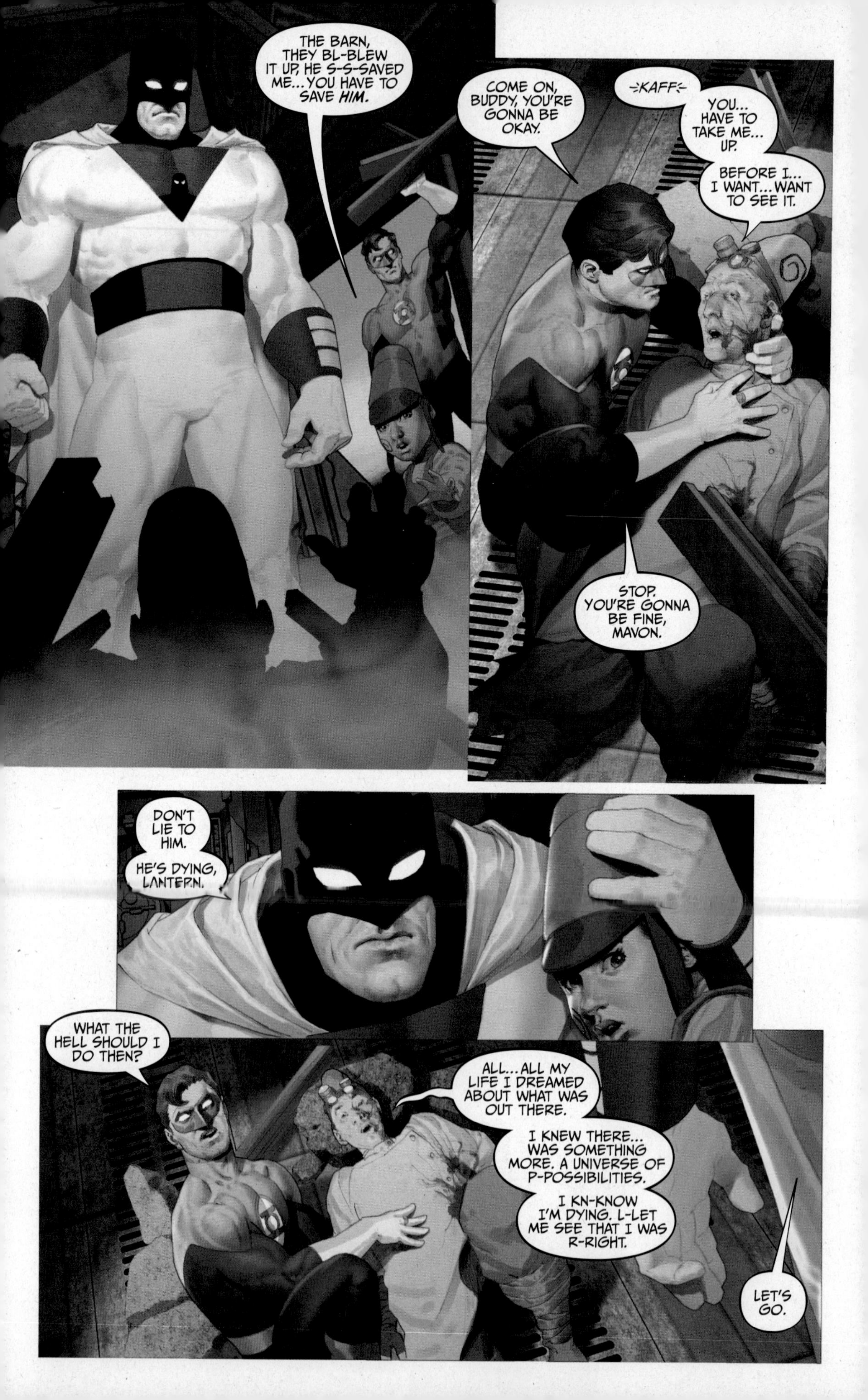
THE BARN, THEY BL-BLEW IT UP, HE S-S-SAVED ME...YOU HAVE TO SAVE *HIM*.
COME ON, BUDDY, YOU'RE GONNA BE OKAY.
-KAFF-
YOU... HAVE TO TAKE ME... UP.
BEFORE I... I WANT...WANT TO SEE IT.
STOP. YOU'RE GONNA BE FINE, MAVON.
DON'T LIE TO HIM.
HE'S DYING, LANTERN.
WHAT THE HELL SHOULD I DO THEN?
ALL...ALL MY LIFE I DREAMED ABOUT WHAT WAS OUT THERE.
I KNEW THERE... WAS SOMETHING MORE. A UNIVERSE OF P-POSSIBILITIES.
I KN-KNOW I'M DYING. L-LET ME SEE THAT I WAS R-RIGHT.
LET'S GO.

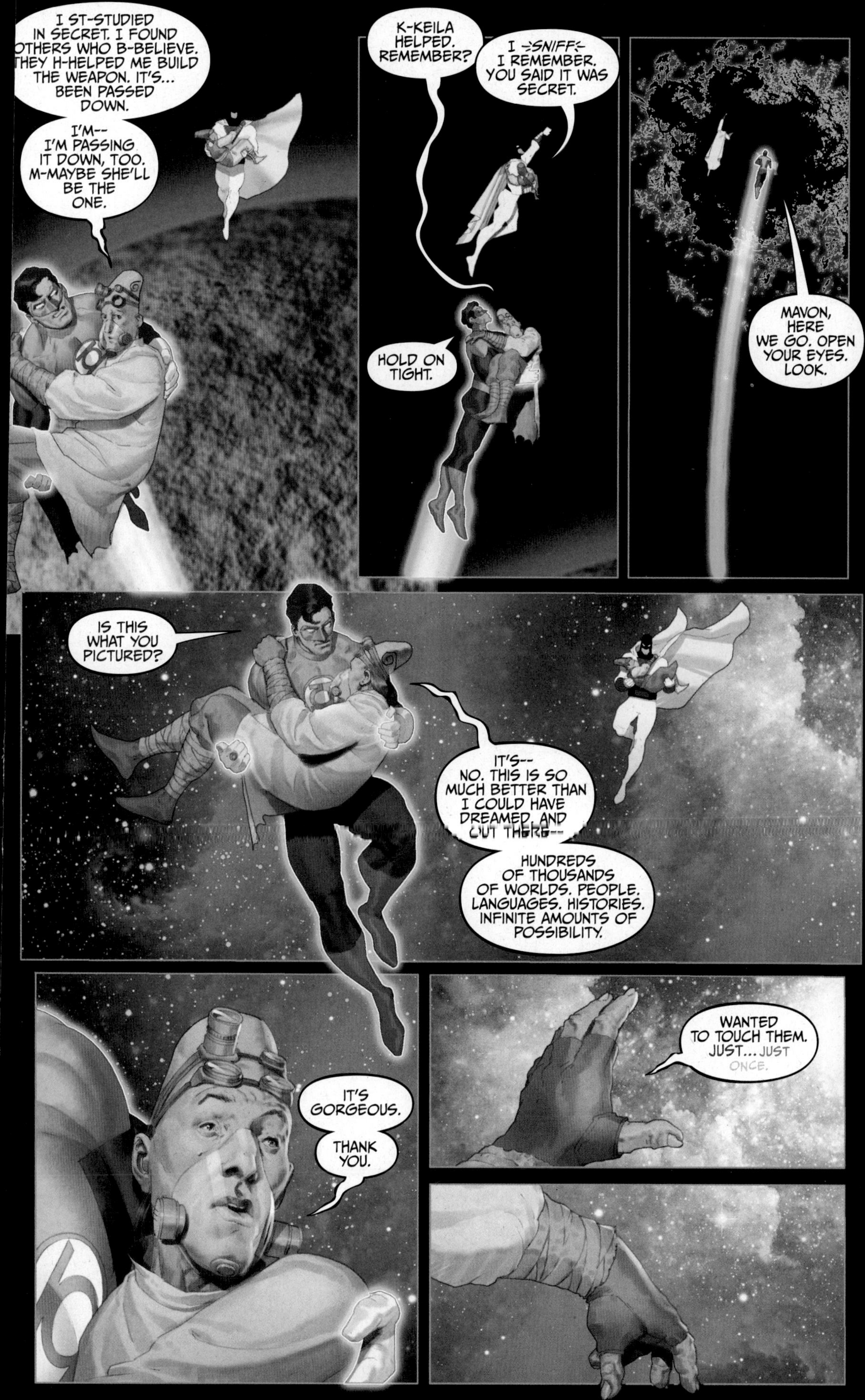
I ST-STUDIED IN SECRET. I FOUND OTHERS WHO B-BELIEVE. THEY H-HELPED ME BUILD THE WEAPON. IT'S... BEEN PASSED DOWN.
I'M-- I'M PASSING IT DOWN, TOO. M-MAYBE SHE'LL BE THE ONE.
K-KEILA HELPED. REMEMBER?
I -SNIFF- I REMEMBER. YOU SAID IT WAS SECRET.
HOLD ON TIGHT.
MAVON, HERE WE GO. OPEN YOUR EYES. LOOK.
IS THIS WHAT YOU PICTURED?
IT'S-- NO. THIS IS SO MUCH BETTER THAN I COULD HAVE DREAMED. AND OUT THERE--
HUNDREDS OF THOUSANDS OF WORLDS. PEOPLE. LANGUAGES. HISTORIES. INFINITE AMOUNTS OF POSSIBILITY.
IT'S GORGEOUS.
THANK YOU.
WANTED TO TOUCH THEM. JUST... JUST ONCE.

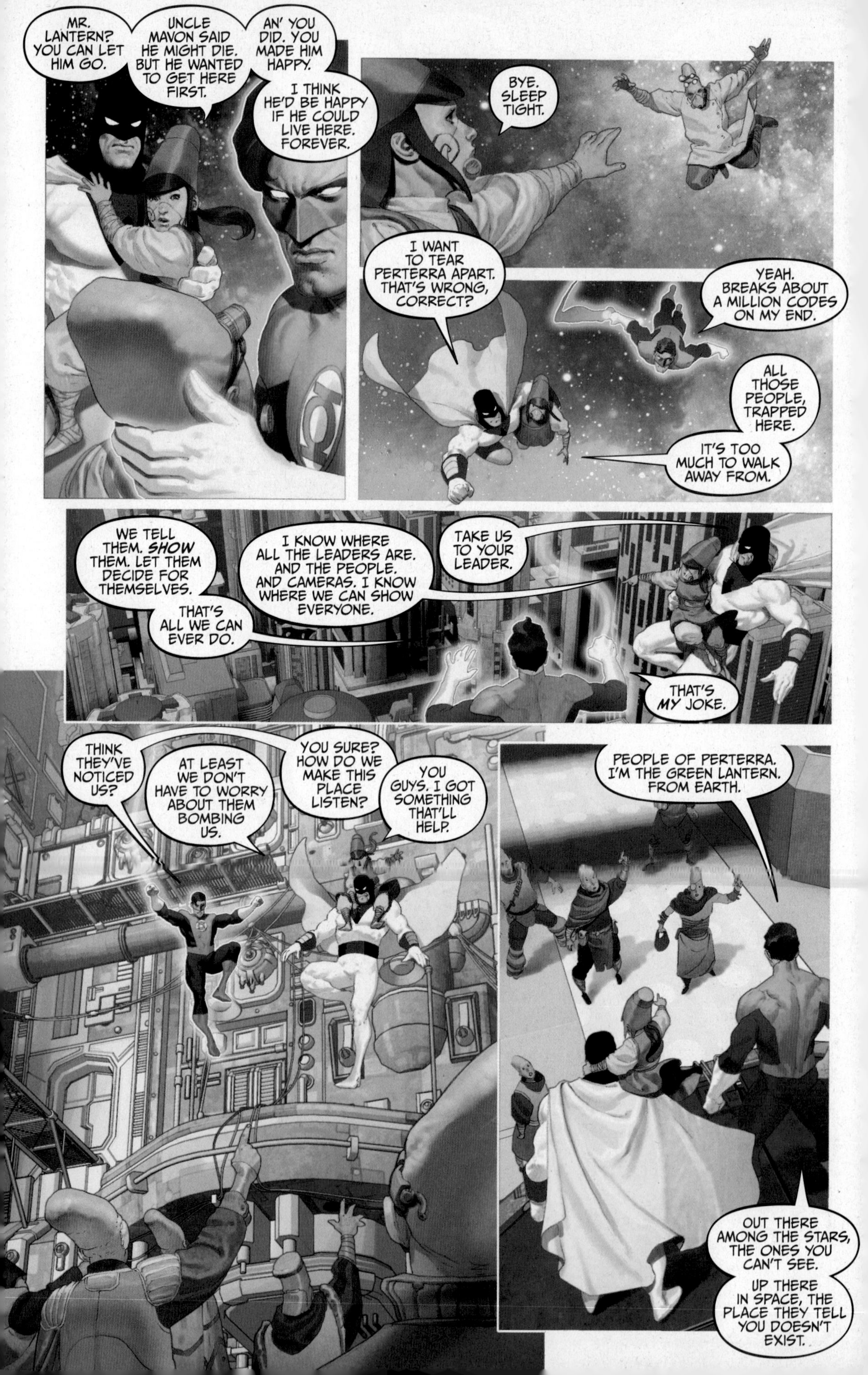

MR. LANTERN? YOU CAN LET HIM GO.
UNCLE MAVON SAID HE MIGHT DIE. BUT HE WANTED TO GET HERE FIRST.
AN' YOU DID. YOU MADE HIM HAPPY.
I THINK HE'D BE HAPPY IF HE COULD LIVE HERE. FOREVER.
BYE. SLEEP TIGHT.
I WANT TO TEAR PERTERRA APART. THAT'S WRONG, CORRECT?
YEAH. BREAKS ABOUT A MILLION CODES ON MY END.
ALL THOSE PEOPLE, TRAPPED HERE.
IT'S TOO MUCH TO WALK AWAY FROM.
WE TELL THEM. *SHOW* THEM. LET THEM DECIDE FOR THEMSELVES.
THAT'S ALL WE CAN EVER DO.
I KNOW WHERE ALL THE LEADERS ARE. AND THE PEOPLE. AND CAMERAS. I KNOW WHERE WE CAN SHOW EVERYONE.
TAKE US TO YOUR LEADER.
THAT'S *MY* JOKE.
THINK THEY'VE NOTICED US?
AT LEAST WE DON'T HAVE TO WORRY ABOUT THEM BOMBING US.
YOU SURE? HOW DO WE MAKE THIS PLACE LISTEN?
YOU GUYS. I GOT SOMETHING THAT'LL HELP.
PEOPLE OF PERTERRA. I'M THE GREEN LANTERN. FROM EARTH.
OUT THERE AMONG THE STARS, THE ONES YOU CAN'T SEE.
UP THERE IN SPACE, THE PLACE THEY TELL YOU DOESN'T EXIST.

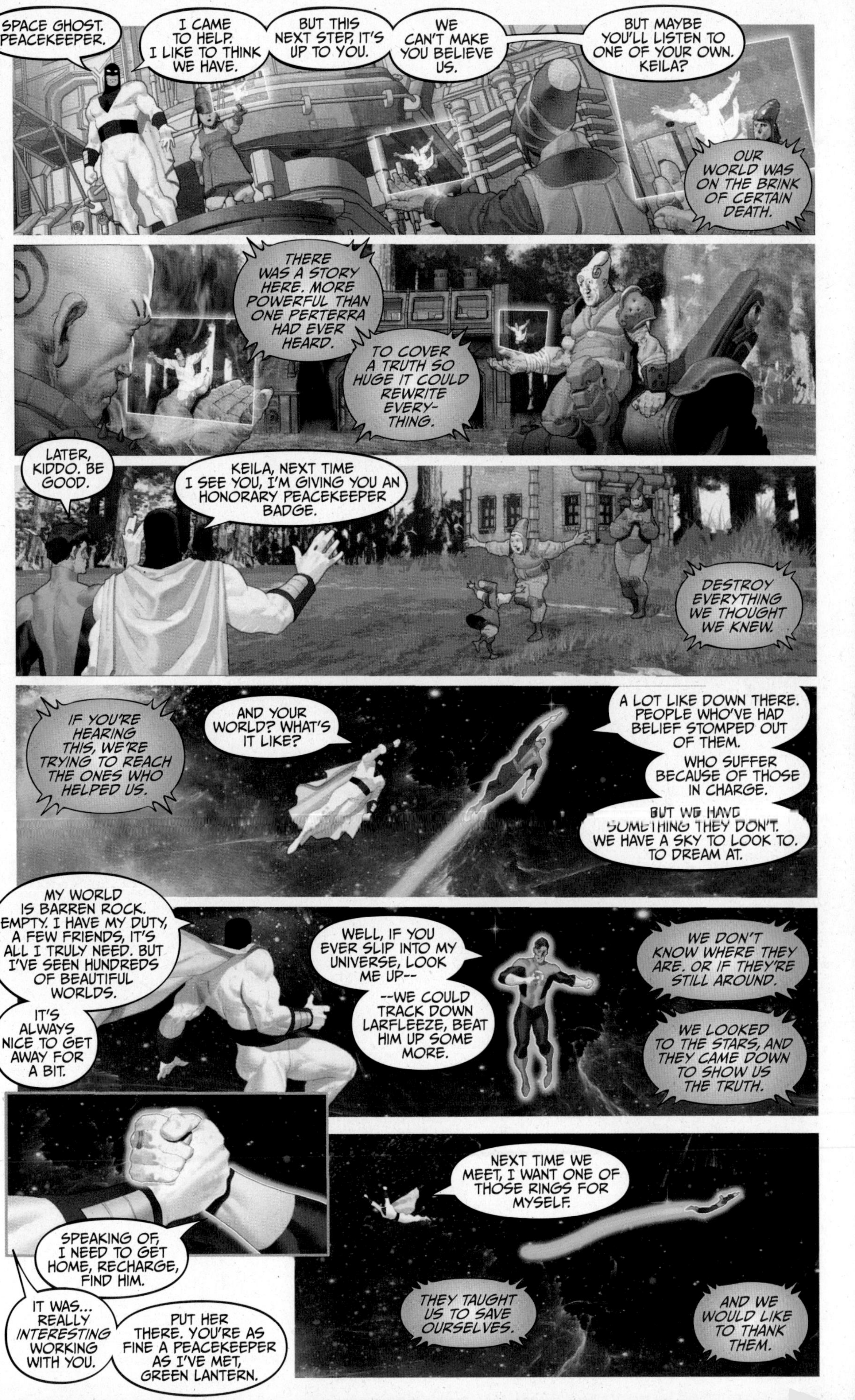
SPACE GHOST. PEACEKEEPER.
I CAME TO HELP. I LIKE TO THINK WE HAVE.
BUT THIS NEXT STEP, IT'S UP TO YOU.
WE CAN'T MAKE YOU BELIEVE US.
BUT MAYBE YOU'LL LISTEN TO ONE OF YOUR OWN. KEILA?
OUR WORLD WAS ON THE BRINK OF CERTAIN DEATH.
THERE WAS A STORY HERE. MORE POWERFUL THAN ONE PERTERRA HAD EVER HEARD.
TO COVER A TRUTH SO HUGE IT COULD REWRITE EVERY-THING.
LATER, KIDDO. BE GOOD.
KEILA, NEXT TIME I SEE YOU, I'M GIVING YOU AN HONORARY PEACEKEEPER BADGE.
DESTROY EVERYTHING WE THOUGHT WE KNEW.
IF YOU'RE HEARING THIS, WE'RE TRYING TO REACH THE ONES WHO HELPED US.
AND YOUR WORLD? WHAT'S IT LIKE?
A LOT LIKE DOWN THERE. PEOPLE WHO'VE HAD BELIEF STOMPED OUT OF THEM.
WHO SUFFER BECAUSE OF THOSE IN CHARGE.
BUT WE HAVE SOMETHING THEY DON'T. WE HAVE A SKY TO LOOK TO. TO DREAM AT.
MY WORLD IS BARREN ROCK. EMPTY. I HAVE MY DUTY, A FEW FRIENDS, IT'S ALL I TRULY NEED. BUT I'VE SEEN HUNDREDS OF BEAUTIFUL WORLDS.
IT'S ALWAYS NICE TO GET AWAY FOR A BIT.
WELL, IF YOU EVER SLIP INTO MY UNIVERSE, LOOK ME UP--
--WE COULD TRACK DOWN LARFLEEZE, BEAT HIM UP SOME MORE.
WE DON'T KNOW WHERE THEY ARE. OR IF THEY'RE STILL AROUND.
WE LOOKED TO THE STARS, AND THEY CAME DOWN TO SHOW US THE TRUTH.
SPEAKING OF, I NEED TO GET HOME, RECHARGE, FIND HIM.
IT WAS... REALLY INTERESTING WORKING WITH YOU.
PUT HER THERE. YOU'RE AS FINE A PEACEKEEPER AS I'VE MET, GREEN LANTERN.
NEXT TIME WE MEET, I WANT ONE OF THOSE RINGS FOR MYSELF.
THEY TAUGHT US TO SAVE OURSELVES.
AND WE WOULD LIKE TO THANK THEM.

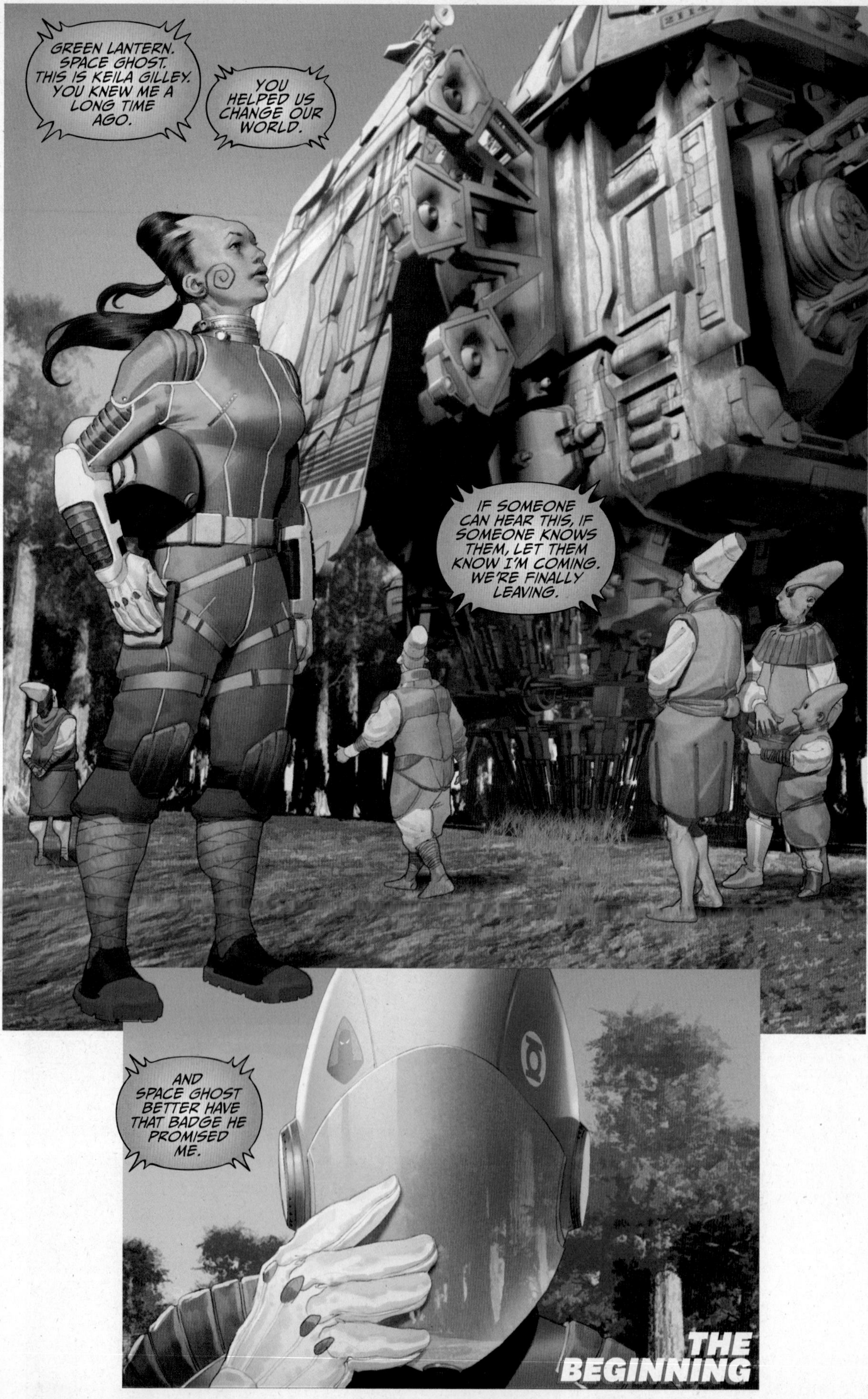
GREEN LANTERN. SPACE GHOST. THIS IS KEILA GILLEY. YOU KNEW ME A LONG TIME AGO.
YOU HELPED US CHANGE OUR WORLD.
IF SOMEONE CAN HEAR THIS, IF SOMEONE KNOWS THEM, LET THEM KNOW I'M COMING. WE'RE FINALLY LEAVING.
AND SPACE GHOST BETTER HAVE THAT BADGE HE PROMISED ME.
THE BEGINNING

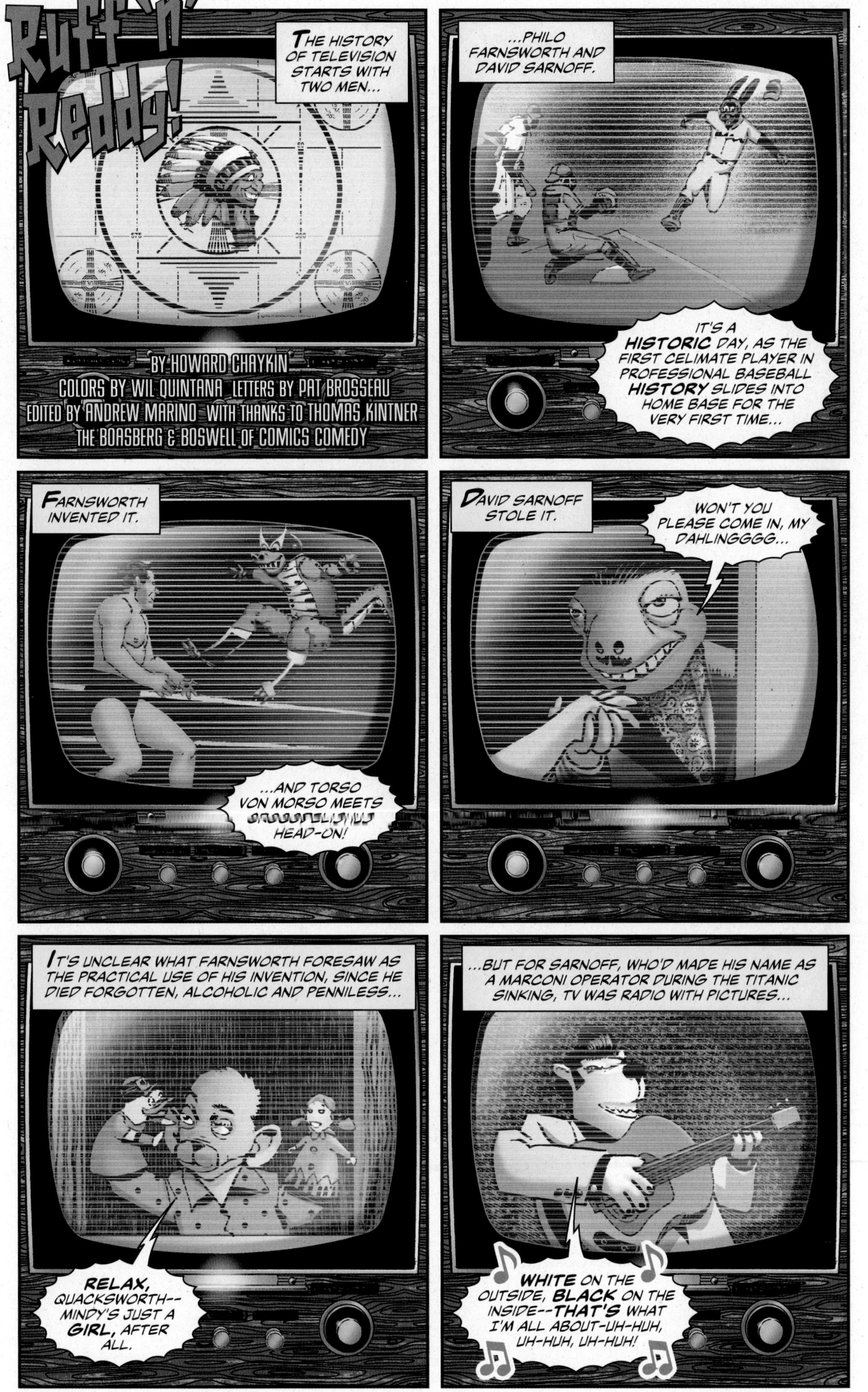

Ruff 'n' Reddy!
THE HISTORY OF TELEVISION STARTS WITH TWO MEN...
BY HOWARD CHAYKIN
COLORS BY WIL QUINTANA LETTERS BY PAT BROSSEAU
EDITED BY ANDREW MARINO WITH THANKS TO THOMAS KINTNER
THE BOASBERG & BOSWELL OF COMICS COMEDY
...PHILO FARNSWORTH AND DAVID SARNOFF.
IT'S A HISTORIC DAY, AS THE FIRST CELIMATE PLAYER IN PROFESSIONAL BASEBALL HISTORY SLIDES INTO HOME BASE FOR THE VERY FIRST TIME...
FARNSWORTH INVENTED IT.
...AND TORSO VON MORSO MEETS
HEAD-ON!
DAVID SARNOFF STOLE IT.
WON'T YOU PLEASE COME IN, MY DAHLINGGGG...
IT'S UNCLEAR WHAT FARNSWORTH FORESAW AS THE PRACTICAL USE OF HIS INVENTION, SINCE HE DIED FORGOTTEN, ALCOHOLIC AND PENNILESS...
RELAX, QUACKSWORTH-- MINDY'S JUST A GIRL, AFTER ALL.
...BUT FOR SARNOFF, WHO'D MADE HIS NAME AS A MARCONI OPERATOR DURING THE TITANIC SINKING, TV WAS RADIO WITH PICTURES...
WHITE ON THE OUTSIDE, BLACK ON THE INSIDE--THAT'S WHAT I'M ALL ABOUT-UH-HUH, UH-HUH, UH-HUH!

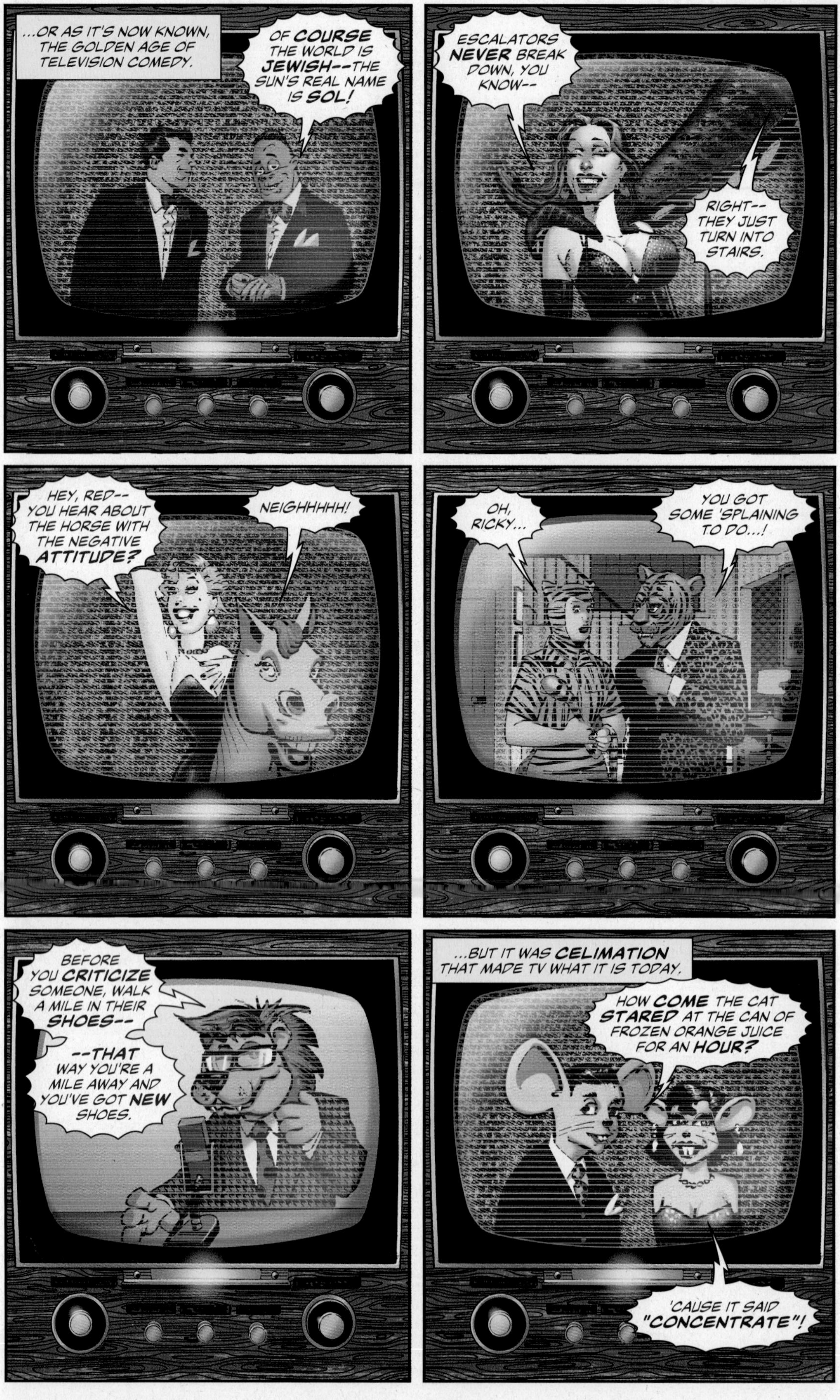
...OR AS IT'S NOW KNOWN, THE GOLDEN AGE OF TELEVISION COMEDY.
OF COURSE THE WORLD IS JEWISH--THE SUN'S REAL NAME IS SOL!
ESCALATORS NEVER BREAK DOWN, YOU KNOW--
RIGHT--THEY JUST TURN INTO STAIRS.
HEY, RED--YOU HEAR ABOUT THE HORSE WITH THE NEGATIVE ATTITUDE?
NEIGHHHHH!
OH, RICKY...
YOU GOT SOME 'SPLAINING TO DO...!
BEFORE YOU CRITICIZE SOMEONE, WALK A MILE IN THEIR SHOES--
--THAT WAY YOU'RE A MILE AWAY AND YOU'VE GOT NEW SHOES.
...BUT IT WAS CELIMATION THAT MADE TV WHAT IT IS TODAY.
HOW COME THE CAT STARED AT THE CAN OF FROZEN ORANGE JUICE FOR AN HOUR?
'CAUSE IT SAID "CONCENTRATE"!

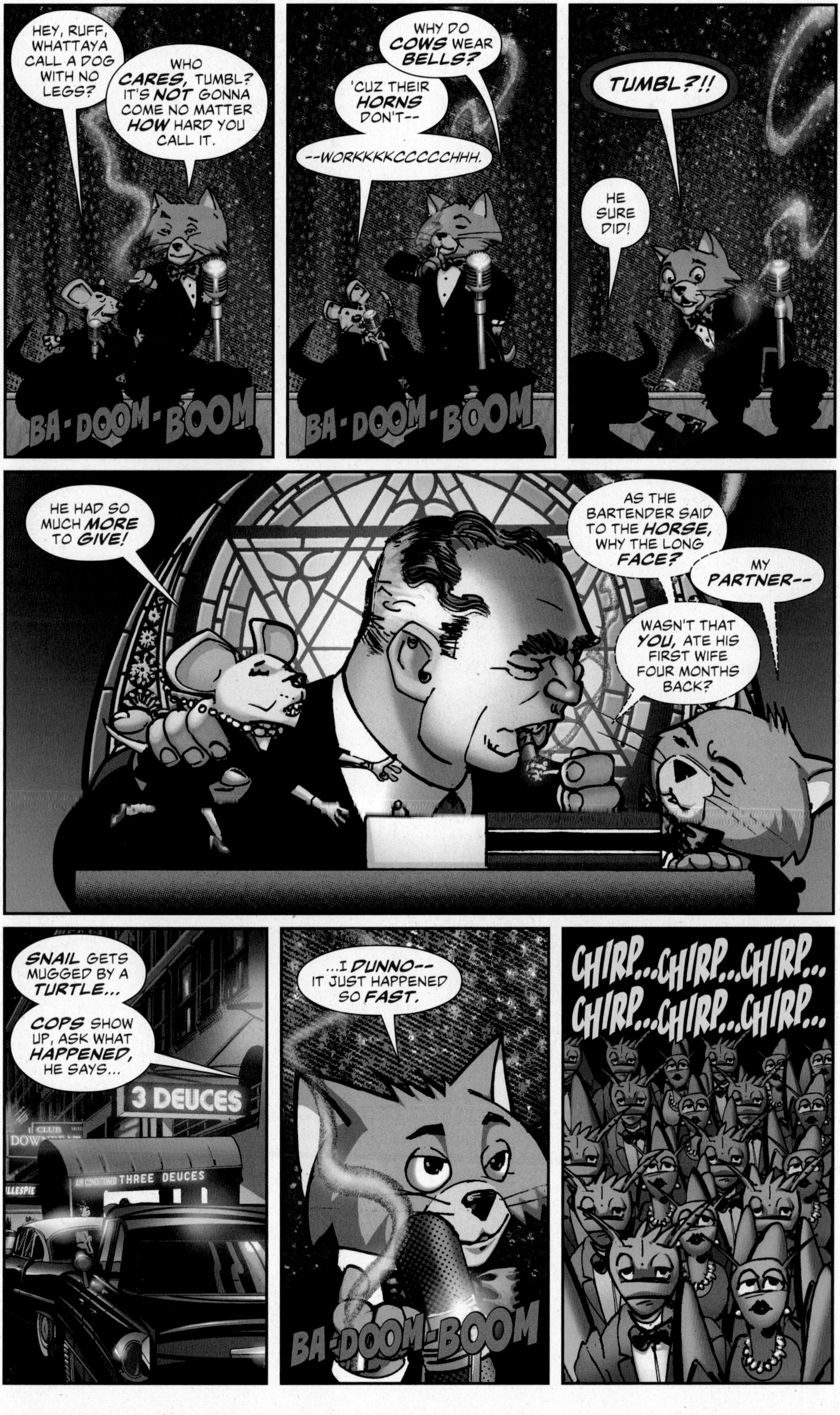
HEY, RUFF, WHATTAYA CALL A DOG WITH NO LEGS?
WHO CARES, TUMBL? IT'S NOT GONNA COME NO MATTER HOW HARD YOU CALL IT.
BA-DOOM-BOOM
WHY DO COWS WEAR BELLS?
'CUZ THEIR HORNS DON'T--
--WORKKKKCCCCCHHH.
BA-DOOM-BOOM
TUMBL?!!
HE SURE DID!
HE HAD SO MUCH MORE TO GIVE!
AS THE BARTENDER SAID TO THE HORSE, WHY THE LONG FACE?
MY PARTNER--
WASN'T THAT YOU, ATE HIS FIRST WIFE FOUR MONTHS BACK?
SNAIL GETS MUGGED BY A TURTLE...
COPS SHOW UP, ASK WHAT HAPPENED, HE SAYS...
3 DEUCES
CLUB
AIR CONDITIONED THREE DEUCES
...I DUNNO-- IT JUST HAPPENED SO FAST.
BA-DOOM-BOOM
CHIRP...CHIRP...CHIRP...
CHIRP...CHIRP...CHIRP...

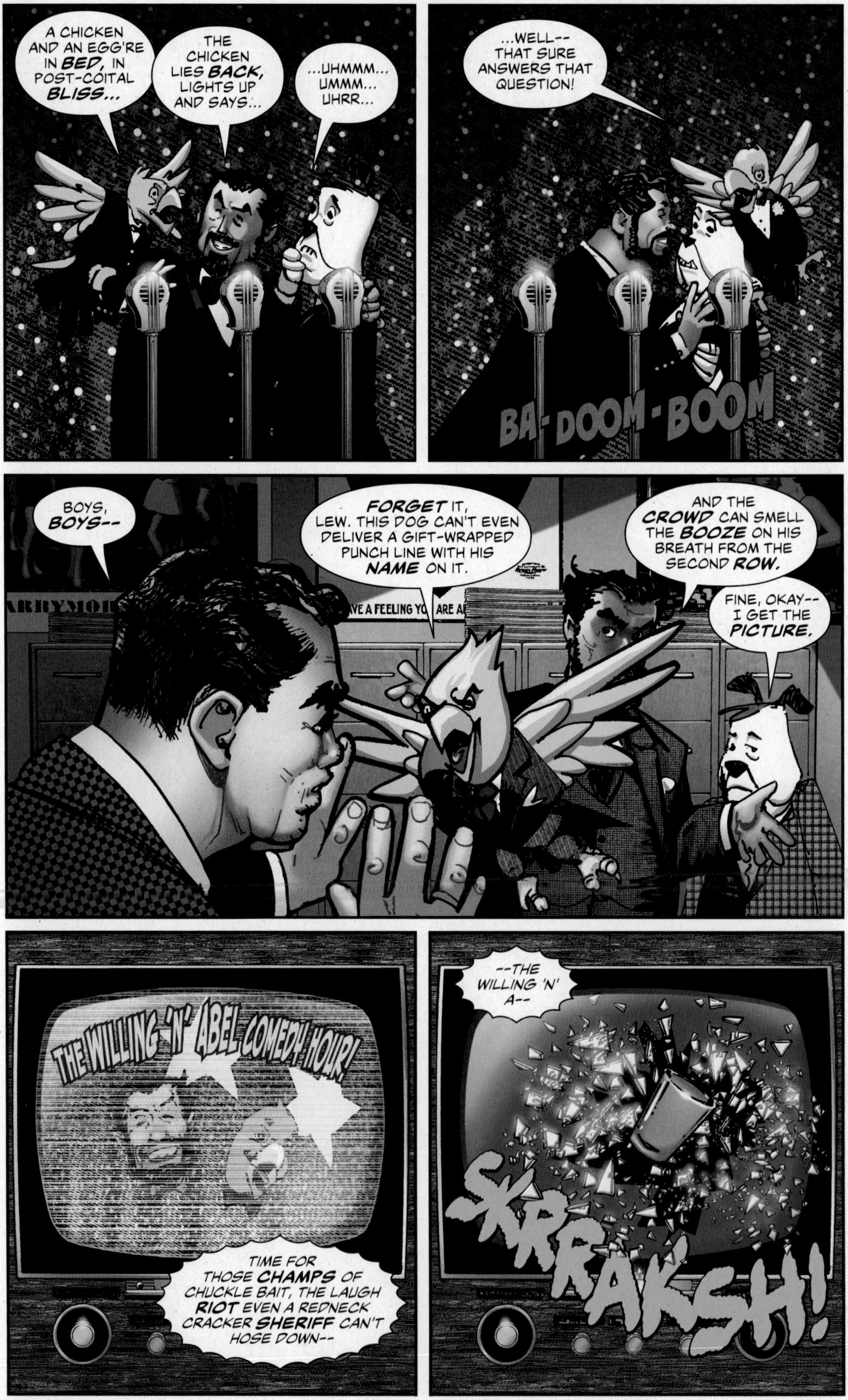
A CHICKEN AND AN EGG'RE IN BED, IN POST-COITAL BLISS...
THE CHICKEN LIES BACK, LIGHTS UP AND SAYS...
...UHMMM... UMMM... UHRR...
...WELL-- THAT SURE ANSWERS THAT QUESTION!
BA-DOOM-BOOM
BOYS, BOYS--
FORGET IT, LEW. THIS DOG CAN'T EVEN DELIVER A GIFT-WRAPPED PUNCH LINE WITH HIS NAME ON IT.
AND THE CROWD CAN SMELL THE BOOZE ON HIS BREATH FROM THE SECOND ROW.
FINE, OKAY-- I GET THE PICTURE.
THE WILLING 'N' ABEL COMEDY HOUR!
TIME FOR THOSE CHAMPS OF CHUCKLE BAIT, THE LAUGH RIOT EVEN A REDNECK CRACKER SHERIFF CAN'T HOSE DOWN--
--THE WILLING 'N' A--
SKRRAKSH!

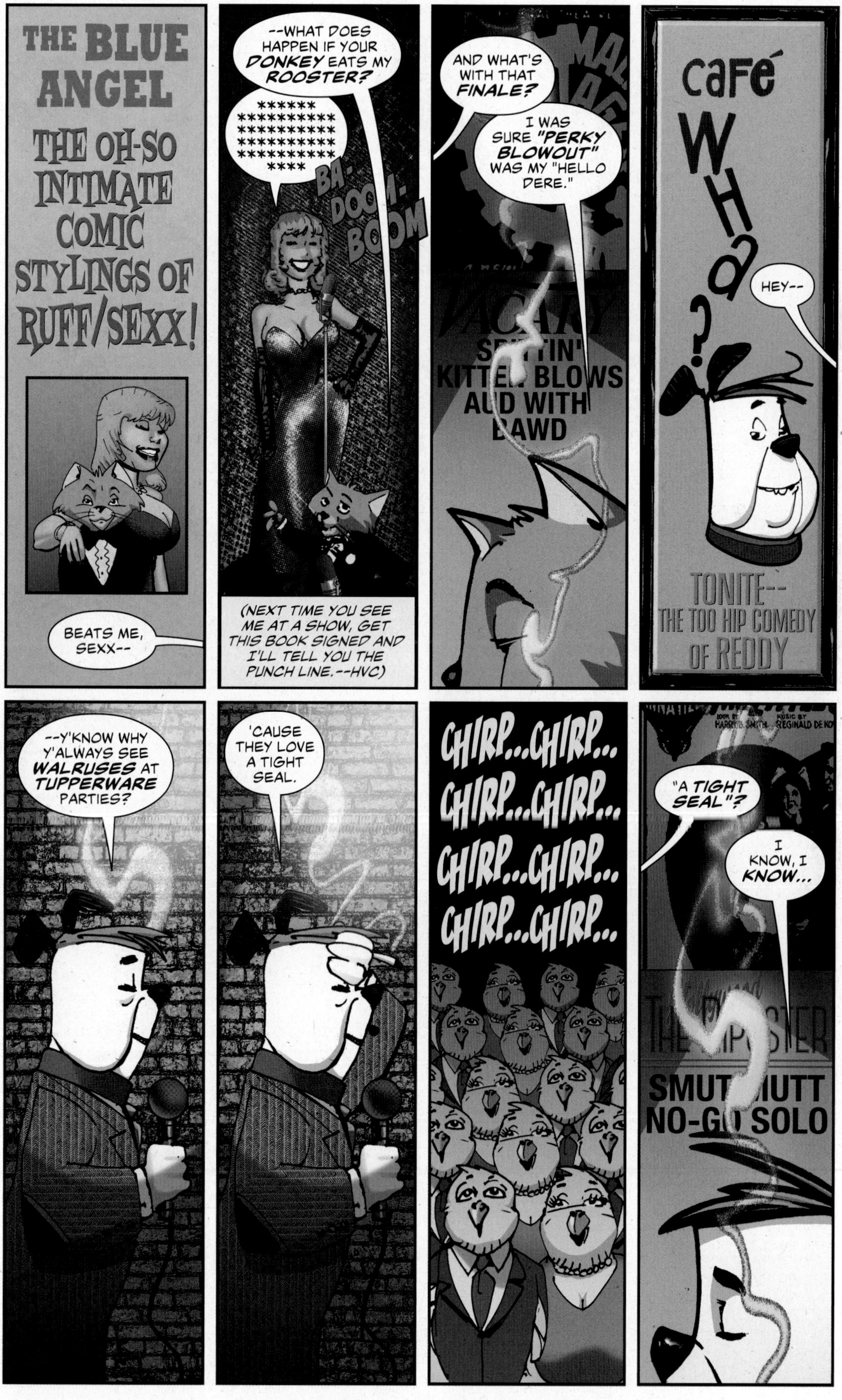
THE BLUE ANGEL
THE OH-SO INTIMATE COMIC STYLINGS OF RUFF/SEXX!
BEATS ME, SEXX--
--WHAT DOES HAPPEN IF YOUR *DONKEY* EATS MY *ROOSTER?*
****
BA-DOOM-BOOM
(NEXT TIME YOU SEE ME AT A SHOW, GET THIS BOOK SIGNED AND I'LL TELL YOU THE PUNCH LINE.--HVC)
AND WHAT'S WITH THAT *FINALE?*
I WAS SURE *"PERKY BLOWOUT"* WAS MY "HELLO DERE."
SPITTIN' KITTEN BLOWS AUD WITH BAWD
CAFÉ WHA?
HEY--
TONITE-- THE TOO HIP COMEDY OF REDDY
--Y'KNOW WHY Y'ALWAYS SEE *WALRUSES* AT *TUPPERWARE* PARTIES?
'CAUSE THEY LOVE A TIGHT SEAL.
CHIRP...CHIRP...
CHIRP...CHIRP...
CHIRP...CHIRP...
CHIRP...CHIRP...
"A *TIGHT SEAL*"?
I KNOW, I *KNOW*...
SMUTT MUTT NO-GO SOLO

THE ED SULLIVAN THEATER

LEW'S GETTIN' ME *BUPKIS.*

SAME HERE-- SID'S GOT *NADA.*

I MEAN, NOT REALLY *NOTHING* NOTHING...

SORRY, PALLY...

LET'S HAVE A *REALLY* BIG HAND FOR THE *HILARIOUS* NEW COMEDY DUO--

...I DON'T CALL A *SUPERMARKET* OPENING IN HUMPSTEAD A *GIG.*

HEY--IT'S A *PAYCHECK--*PLUS ALL THE *KIBBLE* I CAN CARRY.

I JUST KEEP THINKING WHAT IF TUMBL *HADN'T* DIED...

ME, I'M JEALOUS OF *ANYBODY* WITH A *DEAD* PARTNER...

--DOWN 'N' DIRTY!

...I WAKE UP EVERY MORNING *PRAYING* WILLING 'N' ABEL *BOTH* BURST INTO FLA--

...WELL THAT SURE ANSWERS THAT QUESTION!

HEY, DOWN, Y'KNOW WHY Y'ALWAYS SEE *WALRUSES* AT *TUPPERWARE* PARTIES?

SHUT THE *DUCK?!!*

GOOD EATS here

Sparkling Cascade GINGER ALE

MALTS 25¢

GOES GREAT WITH A SANDWICH
HAND PAC
VAN
STRA
MA
PI
ICE C
N
P

THE ED SULLIVAN THEATER

THAT *CAT'S* DOING A *DOG--*

--AND THE *DOG'S* MAKING LIKE A *CAT--*

--AND THAT'S OUR MATERIAL!

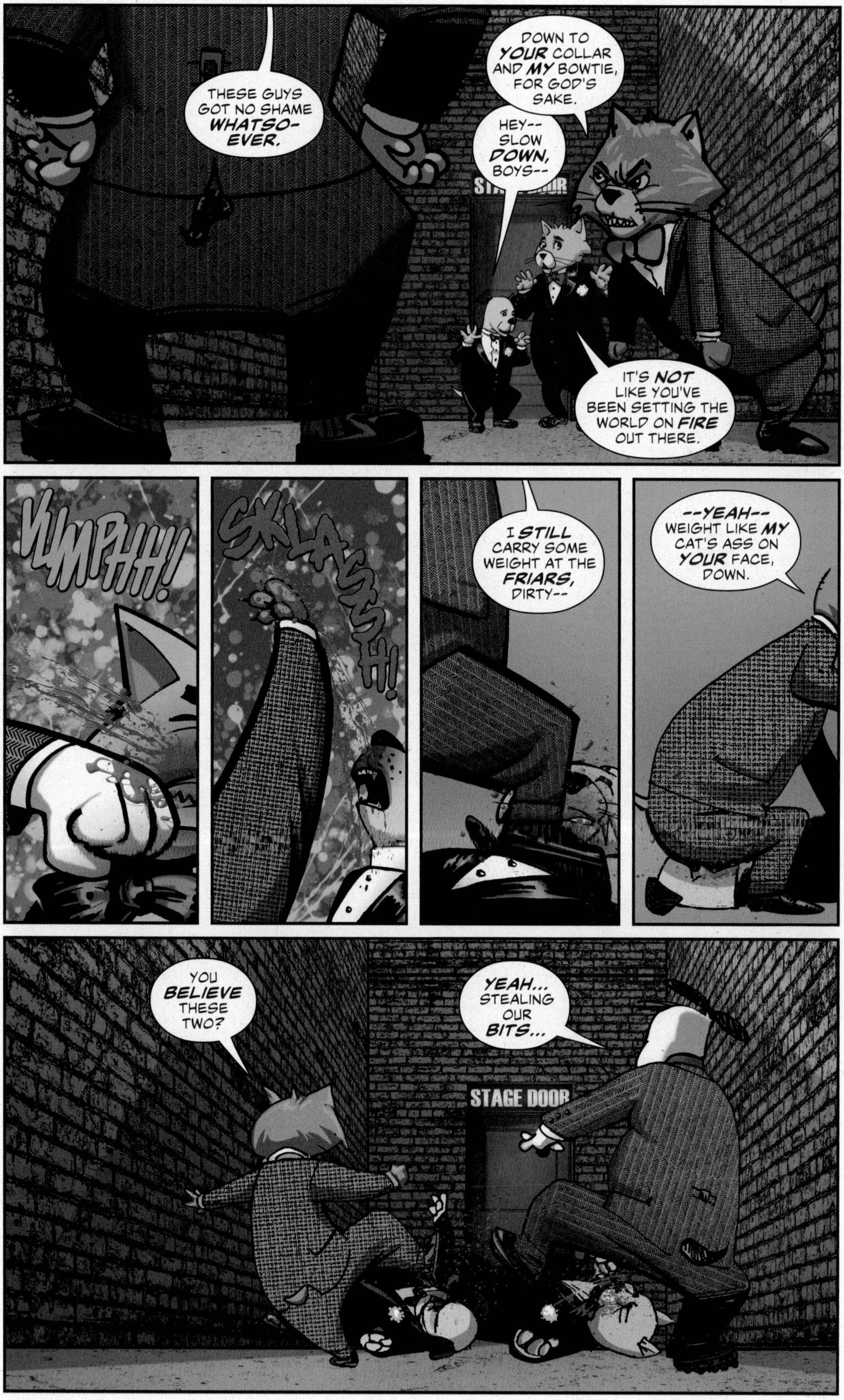
THESE GUYS GOT NO SHAME WHATSO-EVER.
DOWN TO YOUR COLLAR AND MY BOWTIE, FOR GOD'S SAKE.
HEY-- SLOW DOWN, BOYS--
STAGE DOOR
IT'S NOT LIKE YOU'VE BEEN SETTING THE WORLD ON FIRE OUT THERE.
VUMPHH!
SKLASSH!
I STILL CARRY SOME WEIGHT AT THE FRIARS, DIRTY--
--YEAH-- WEIGHT LIKE MY CAT'S ASS ON YOUR FACE, DOWN.
YOU BELIEVE THESE TWO?
YEAH... STEALING OUR BITS...
STAGE DOOR

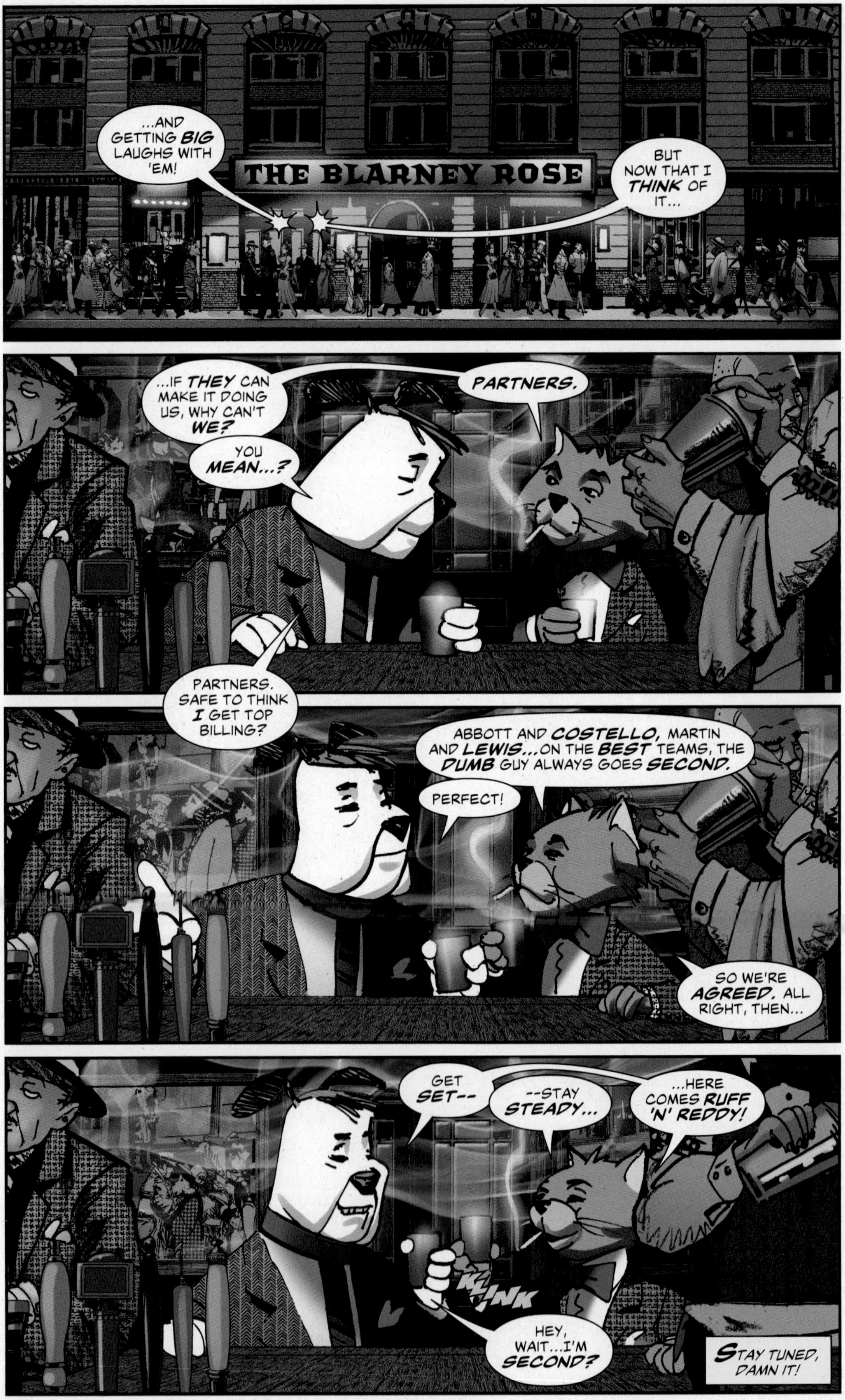

...AND GETTING BIG LAUGHS WITH 'EM!
THE BLARNEY ROSE
BUT NOW THAT I THINK OF IT...
...IF THEY CAN MAKE IT DOING US, WHY CAN'T WE?
PARTNERS.
YOU MEAN...?
PARTNERS. SAFE TO THINK I GET TOP BILLING?
ABBOTT AND COSTELLO, MARTIN AND LEWIS...ON THE BEST TEAMS, THE DUMB GUY ALWAYS GOES SECOND.
PERFECT!
SO WE'RE AGREED. ALL RIGHT, THEN...
GET SET--
--STAY STEADY...
...HERE COMES RUFF 'N' REDDY!
KLINK
HEY, WAIT...I'M SECOND?
STAY TUNED, DAMN IT!

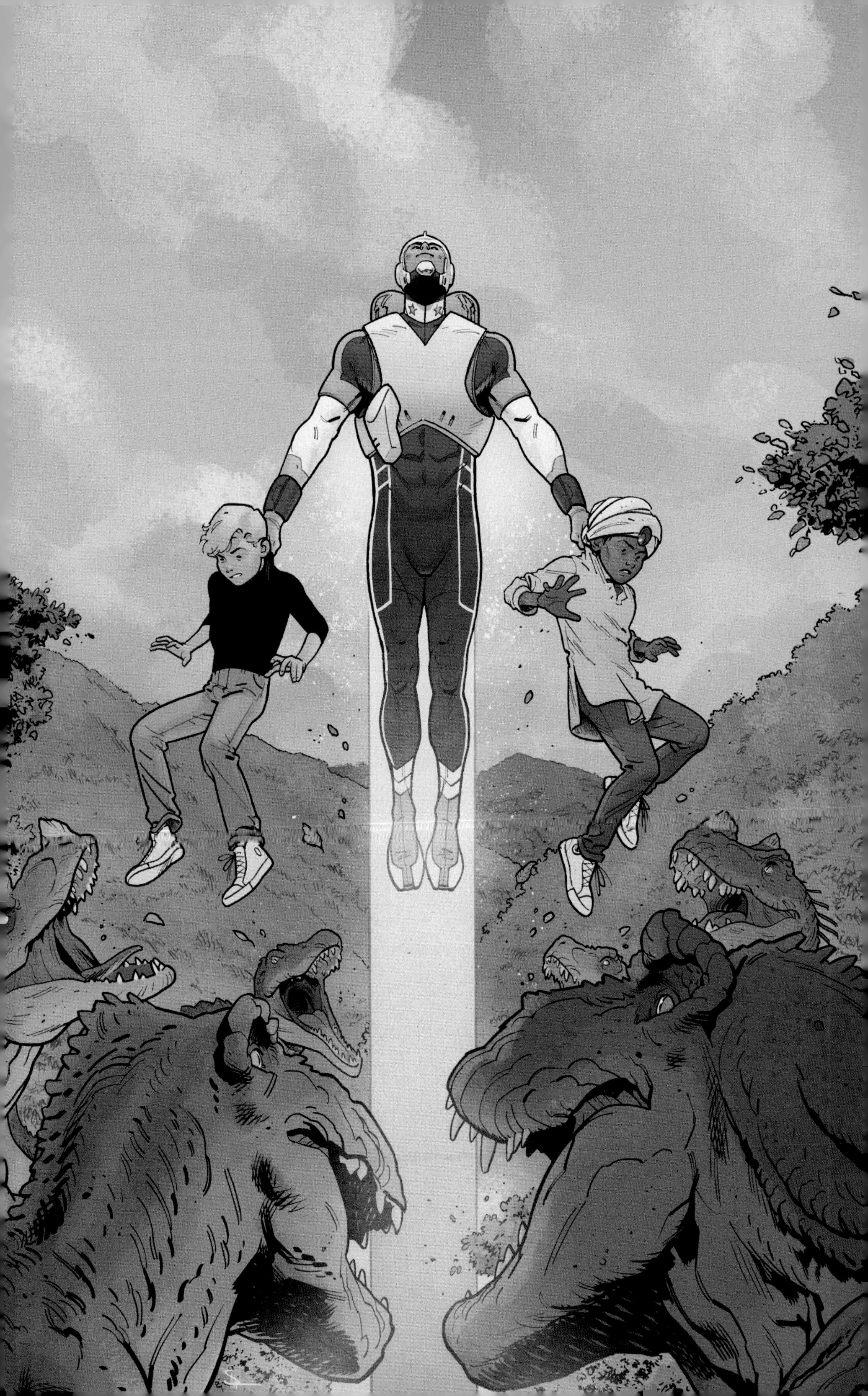

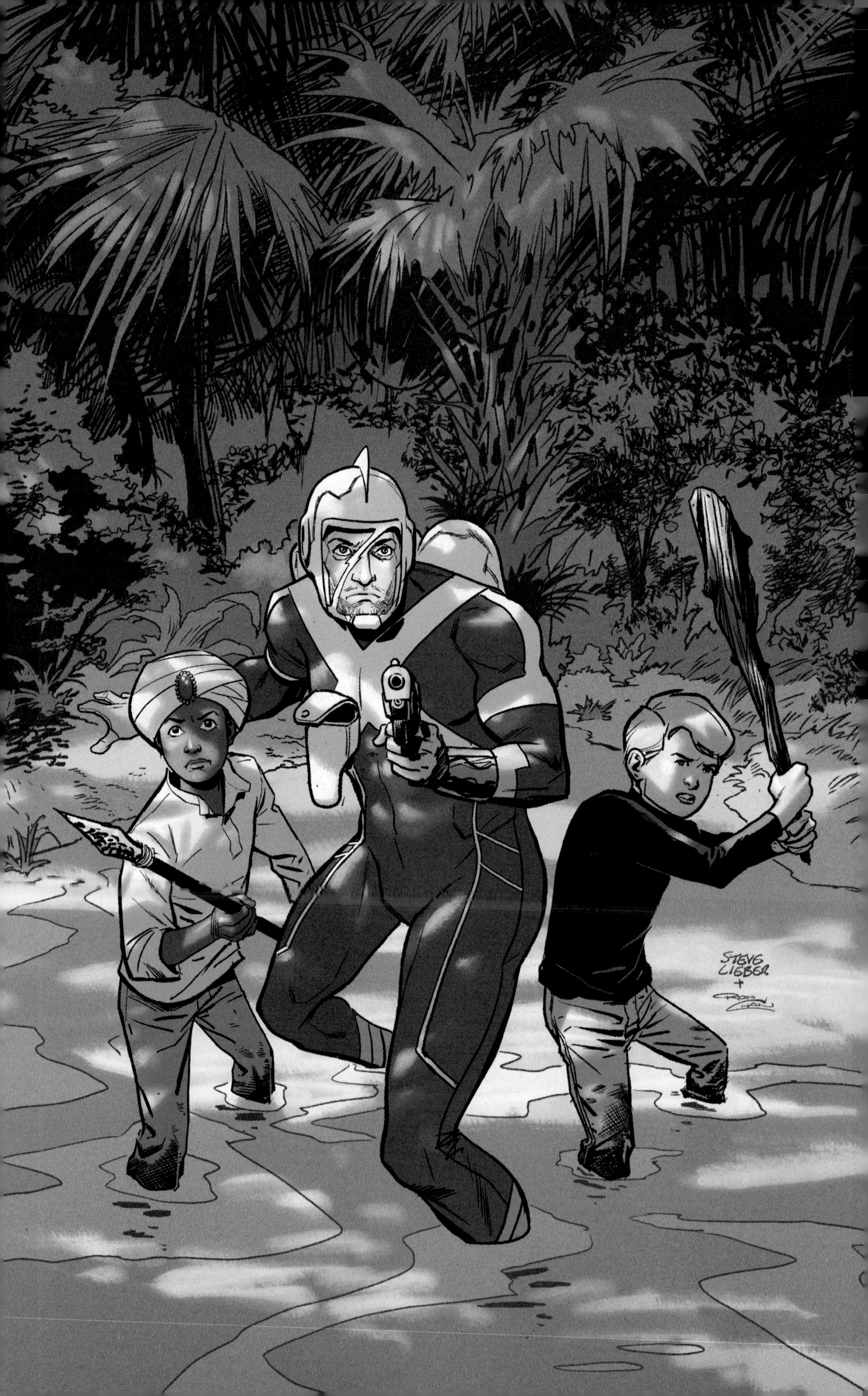
STEVE LIEBER + RON CHAN

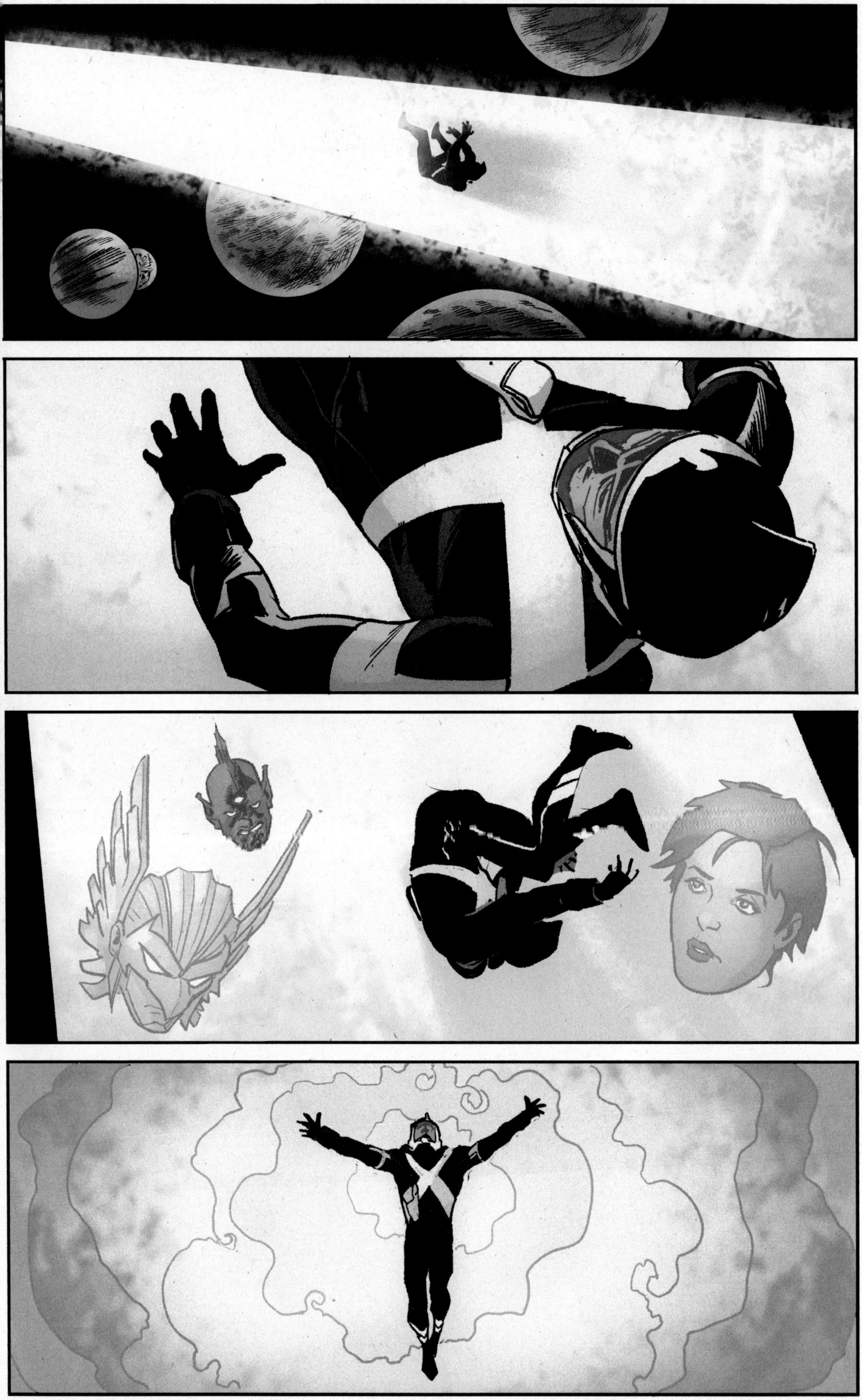

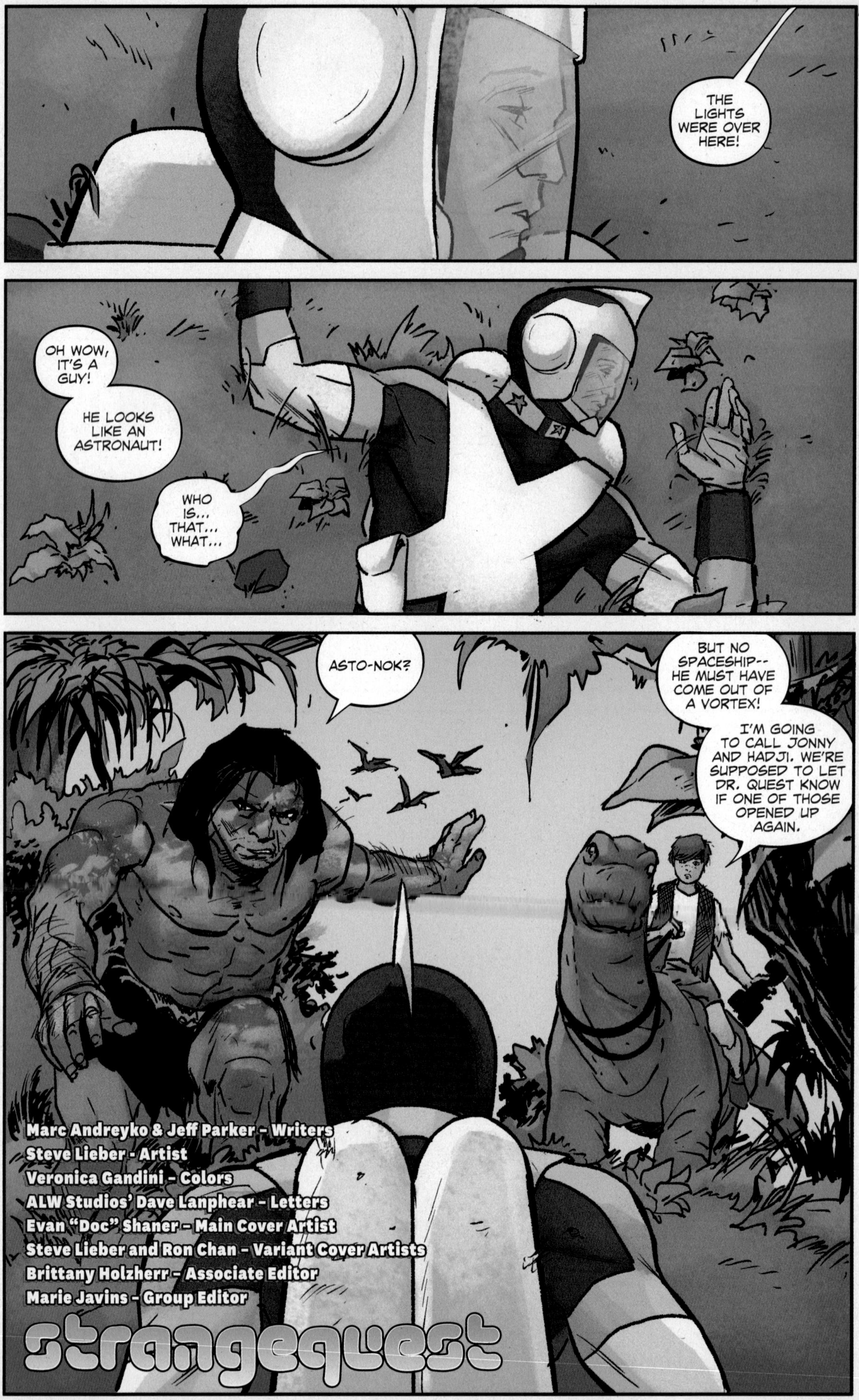
THE LIGHTS WERE OVER HERE!
OH WOW, IT'S A GUY!
HE LOOKS LIKE AN ASTRONAUT!
WHO IS... THAT... WHAT...
ASTO-NOK?
BUT NO SPACESHIP-- HE MUST HAVE COME OUT OF A VORTEX!
I'M GOING TO CALL JONNY AND HADJI. WE'RE SUPPOSED TO LET DR. QUEST KNOW IF ONE OF THOSE OPENED UP AGAIN.
Marc Andreyko & Jeff Parker - Writers
Steve Lieber - Artist
Veronica Gandini - Colors
ALW Studios' Dave Lanphear - Letters
Evan "Doc" Shaner - Main Cover Artist
Steve Lieber and Ron Chan - Variant Cover Artists
Brittany Holzherr - Associate Editor
Marie Javins - Group Editor
strangequest

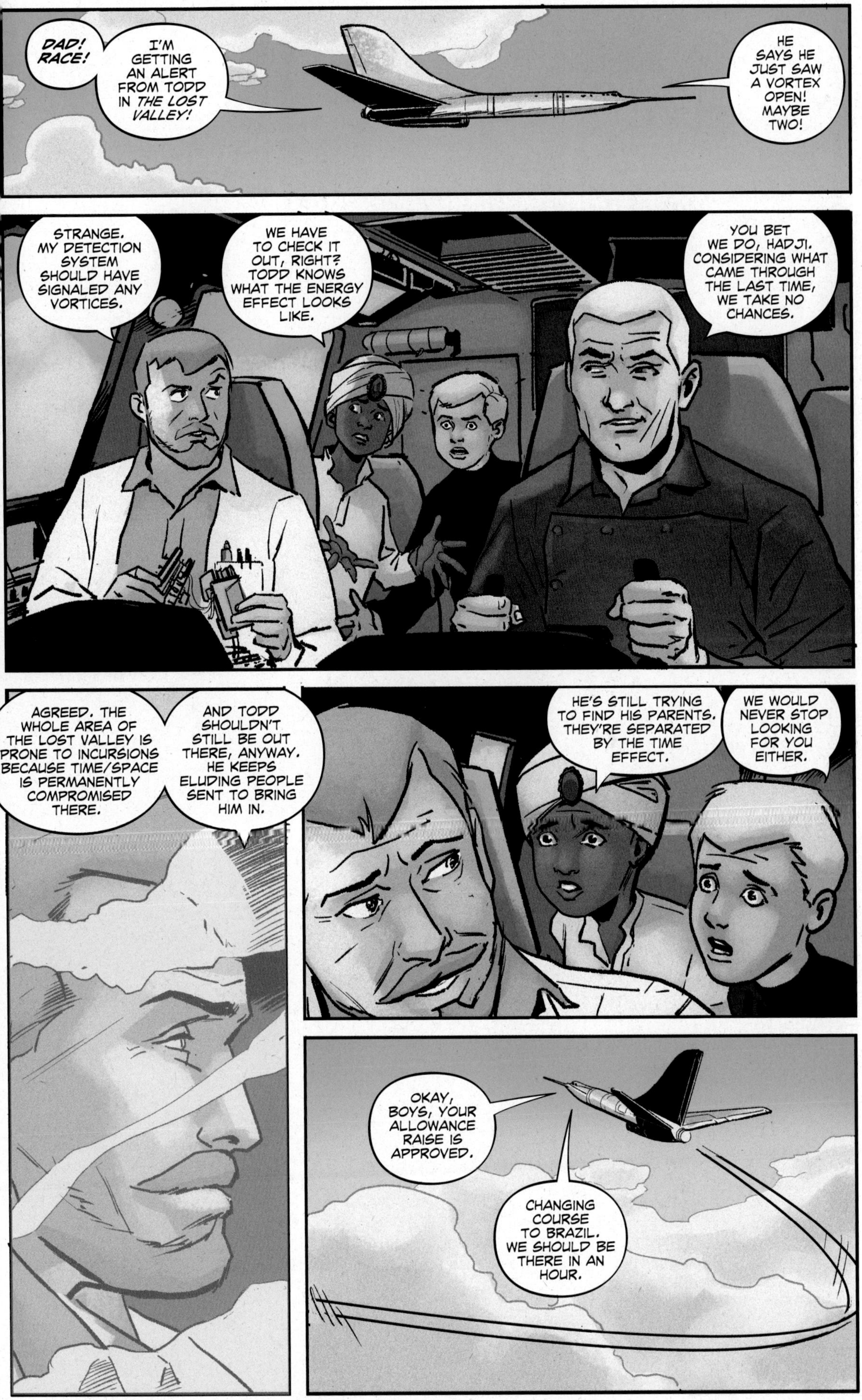

DAD! RACE!
I'M GETTING AN ALERT FROM TODD IN THE LOST VALLEY!
HE SAYS HE JUST SAW A VORTEX OPEN! MAYBE TWO!
STRANGE. MY DETECTION SYSTEM SHOULD HAVE SIGNALED ANY VORTICES.
WE HAVE TO CHECK IT OUT, RIGHT? TODD KNOWS WHAT THE ENERGY EFFECT LOOKS LIKE.
YOU BET WE DO, HADJI. CONSIDERING WHAT CAME THROUGH THE LAST TIME, WE TAKE NO CHANCES.
AGREED. THE WHOLE AREA OF THE LOST VALLEY IS PRONE TO INCURSIONS BECAUSE TIME/SPACE IS PERMANENTLY COMPROMISED THERE.
AND TODD SHOULDN'T STILL BE OUT THERE, ANYWAY. HE KEEPS ELUDING PEOPLE SENT TO BRING HIM IN.
HE'S STILL TRYING TO FIND HIS PARENTS. THEY'RE SEPARATED BY THE TIME EFFECT.
WE WOULD NEVER STOP LOOKING FOR YOU EITHER.
OKAY, BOYS, YOUR ALLOWANCE RAISE IS APPROVED.
CHANGING COURSE TO BRAZIL. WE SHOULD BE THERE IN AN HOUR.

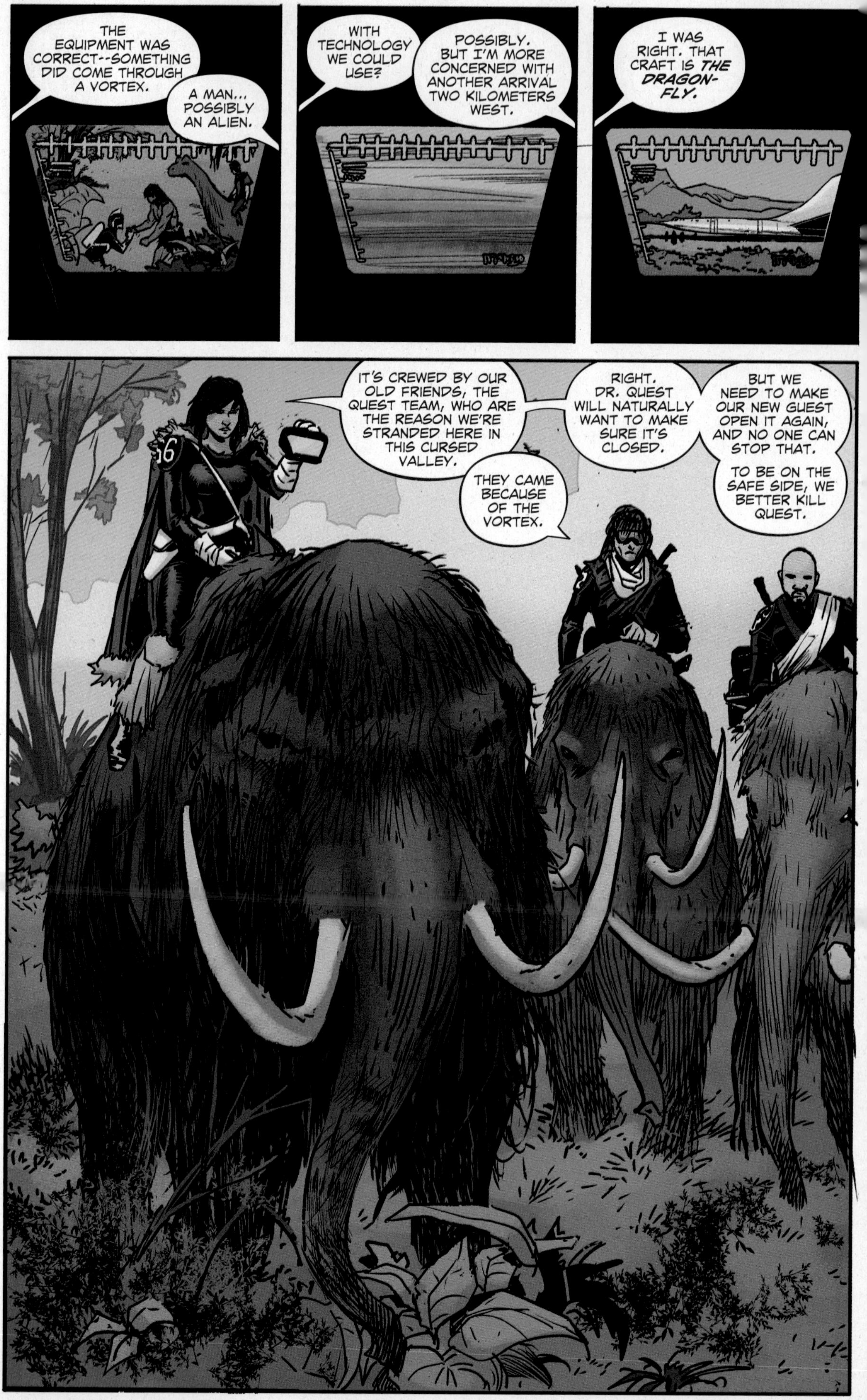
THE EQUIPMENT WAS CORRECT--SOMETHING DID COME THROUGH A VORTEX.
A MAN... POSSIBLY AN ALIEN.
WITH TECHNOLOGY WE COULD USE?
POSSIBLY. BUT I'M MORE CONCERNED WITH ANOTHER ARRIVAL TWO KILOMETERS WEST.
I WAS RIGHT. THAT CRAFT IS THE DRAGON-FLY.
IT'S CREWED BY OUR OLD FRIENDS, THE QUEST TEAM, WHO ARE THE REASON WE'RE STRANDED HERE IN THIS CURSED VALLEY.
THEY CAME BECAUSE OF THE VORTEX.
RIGHT. DR. QUEST WILL NATURALLY WANT TO MAKE SURE IT'S CLOSED.
BUT WE NEED TO MAKE OUR NEW GUEST OPEN IT AGAIN, AND NO ONE CAN STOP THAT.
TO BE ON THE SAFE SIDE, WE BETTER KILL QUEST.

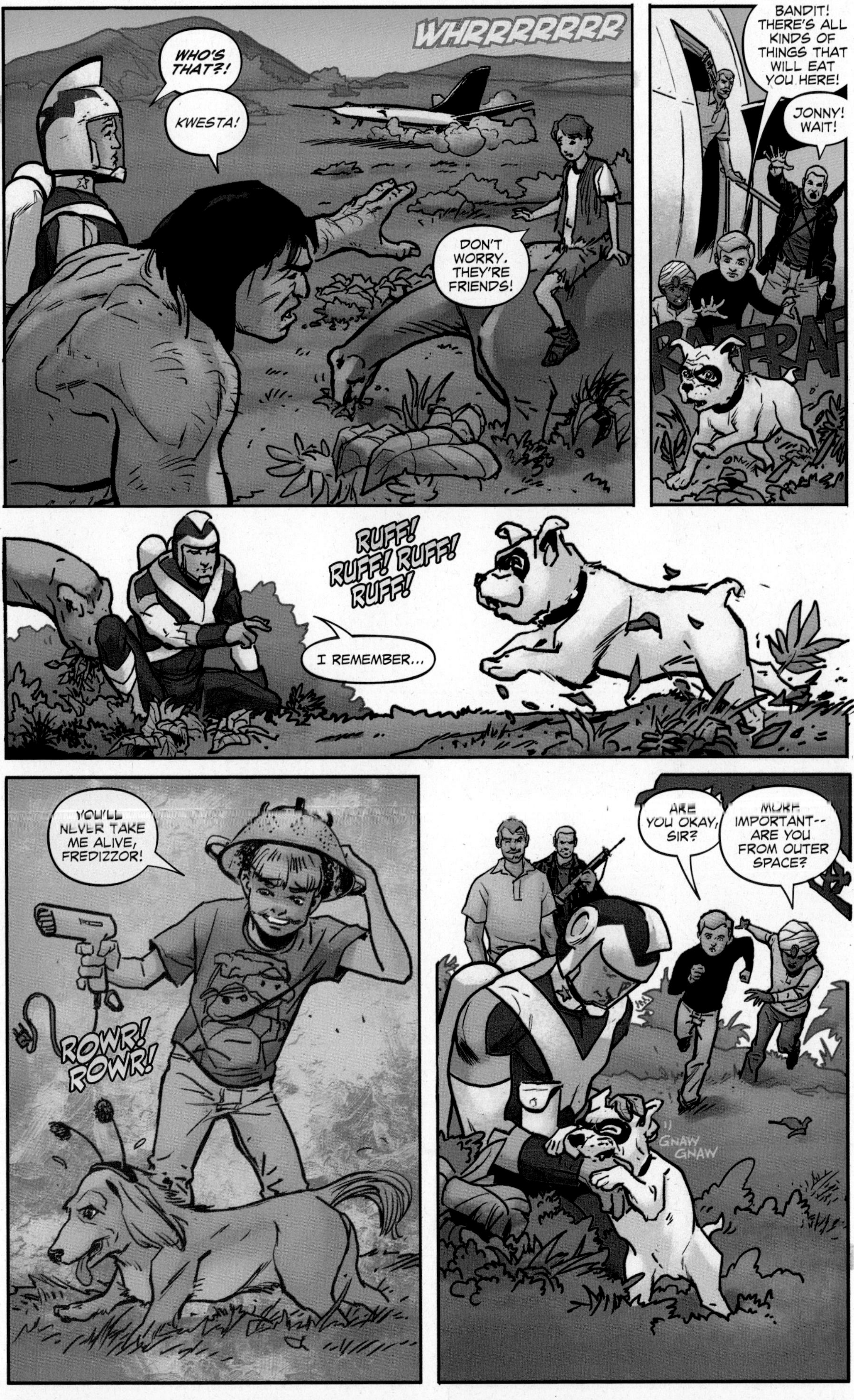
WHRRRRRRR
WHO'S THAT?!
KWESTA!
DON'T WORRY. THEY'RE FRIENDS!
BANDIT! THERE'S ALL KINDS OF THINGS THAT WILL EAT YOU HERE!
JONNY! WAIT!
RUFF! RUFF! RUFF! RUFF!
I REMEMBER...
YOU'LL NEVER TAKE ME ALIVE, FREDIZZOR!
ROWR! ROWR!
ARE YOU OKAY, SIR?
MORE IMPORTANT-- ARE YOU FROM OUTER SPACE?
GNAW GNAW

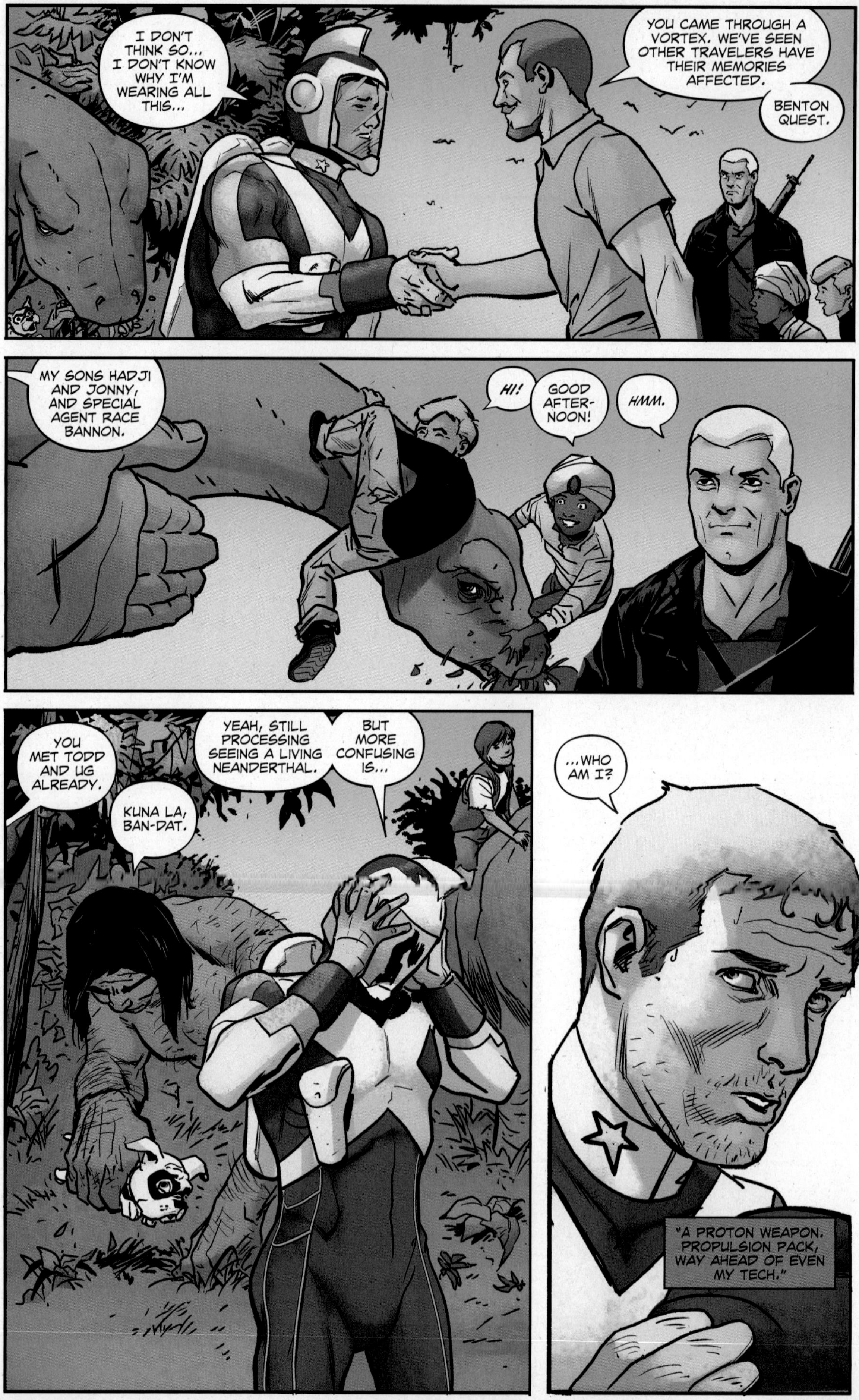

I DON'T THINK SO... I DON'T KNOW WHY I'M WEARING ALL THIS...
YOU CAME THROUGH A VORTEX. WE'VE SEEN OTHER TRAVELERS HAVE THEIR MEMORIES AFFECTED.
BENTON QUEST.
MY SONS HADJI AND JONNY, AND SPECIAL AGENT RACE BANNON.
HI!
GOOD AFTER-NOON!
HMM.
YOU MET TODD AND UG ALREADY.
KUNA LA, BAN-DAT.
YEAH, STILL PROCESSING SEEING A LIVING NEANDERTHAL.
BUT MORE CONFUSING IS...
...WHO AM I?
"A PROTON WEAPON. PROPULSION PACK, WAY AHEAD OF EVEN MY TECH."

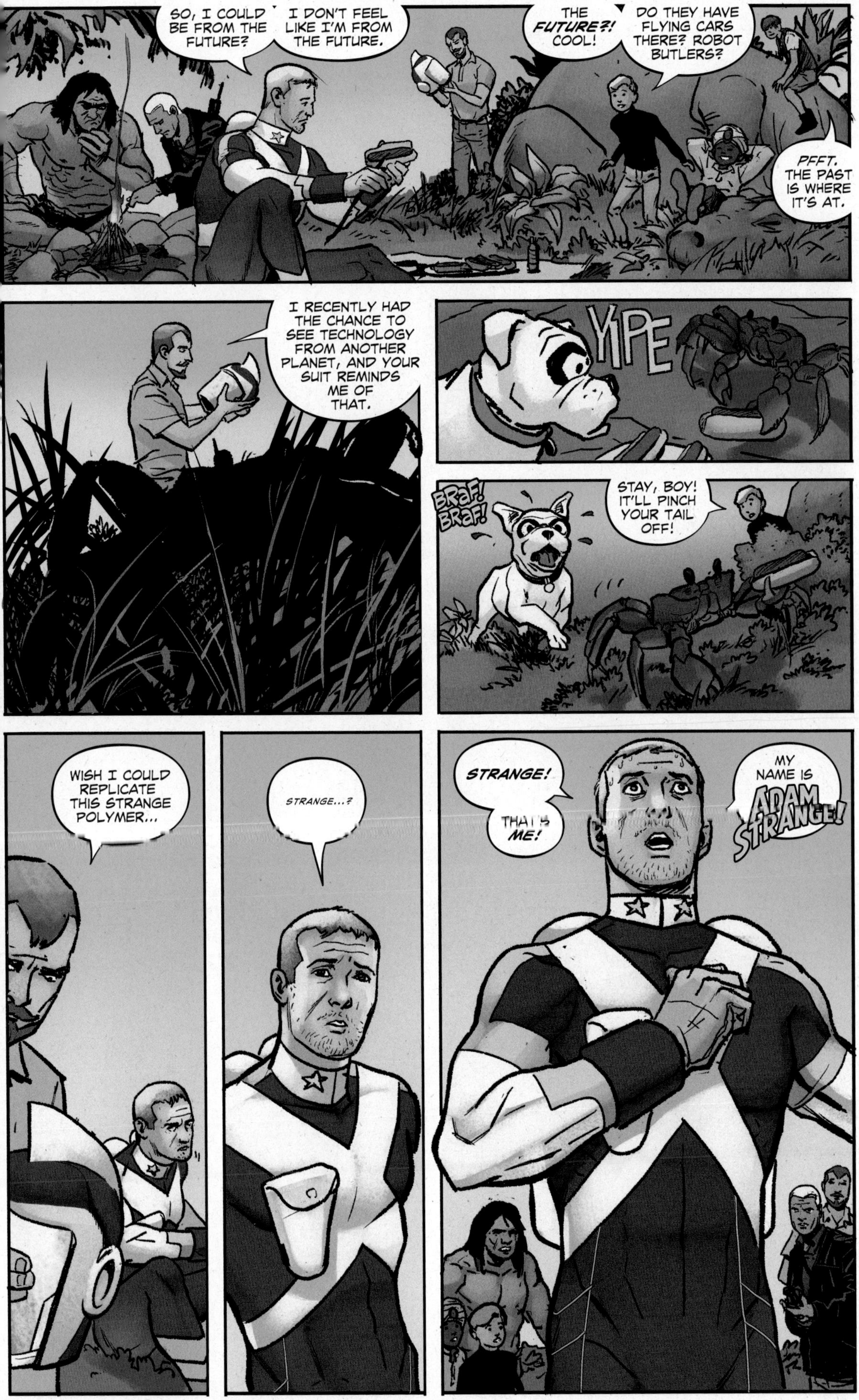

SO, I COULD BE FROM THE FUTURE?
I DON'T FEEL LIKE I'M FROM THE FUTURE.
THE FUTURE?! COOL!
DO THEY HAVE FLYING CARS THERE? ROBOT BUTLERS?
PFFT. THE PAST IS WHERE IT'S AT.
I RECENTLY HAD THE CHANCE TO SEE TECHNOLOGY FROM ANOTHER PLANET, AND YOUR SUIT REMINDS ME OF THAT.
YIPE
BRAF! BRAF!
STAY, BOY! IT'LL PINCH YOUR TAIL OFF!
WISH I COULD REPLICATE THIS STRANGE POLYMER...
STRANGE...?
STRANGE!
THAT'S ME!
MY NAME IS
ADAM STRANGE!

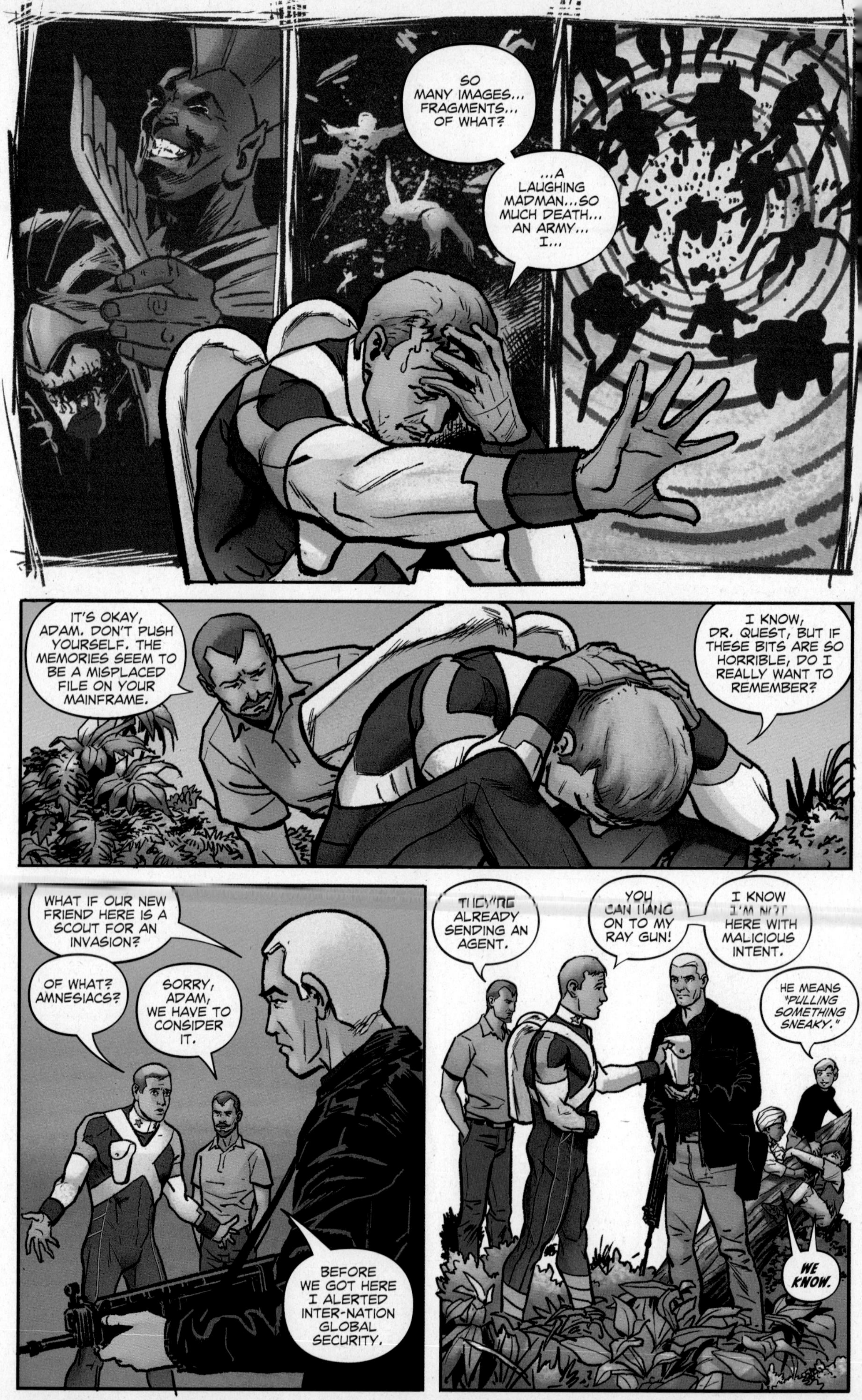

SO MANY IMAGES... FRAGMENTS... OF WHAT?
...A LAUGHING MADMAN...SO MUCH DEATH... AN ARMY... I...
IT'S OKAY, ADAM. DON'T PUSH YOURSELF. THE MEMORIES SEEM TO BE A MISPLACED FILE ON YOUR MAINFRAME.
I KNOW, DR. QUEST, BUT IF THESE BITS ARE SO HORRIBLE, DO I REALLY WANT TO REMEMBER?
WHAT IF OUR NEW FRIEND HERE IS A SCOUT FOR AN INVASION?
OF WHAT? AMNESIACS?
SORRY, ADAM, WE HAVE TO CONSIDER IT.
BEFORE WE GOT HERE I ALERTED INTER-NATION GLOBAL SECURITY.
THEY'RE ALREADY SENDING AN AGENT.
YOU CAN HANG ON TO MY RAY GUN!
I KNOW I'M NOT HERE WITH MALICIOUS INTENT.
HE MEANS *"PULLING SOMETHING SNEAKY."*
WE KNOW.

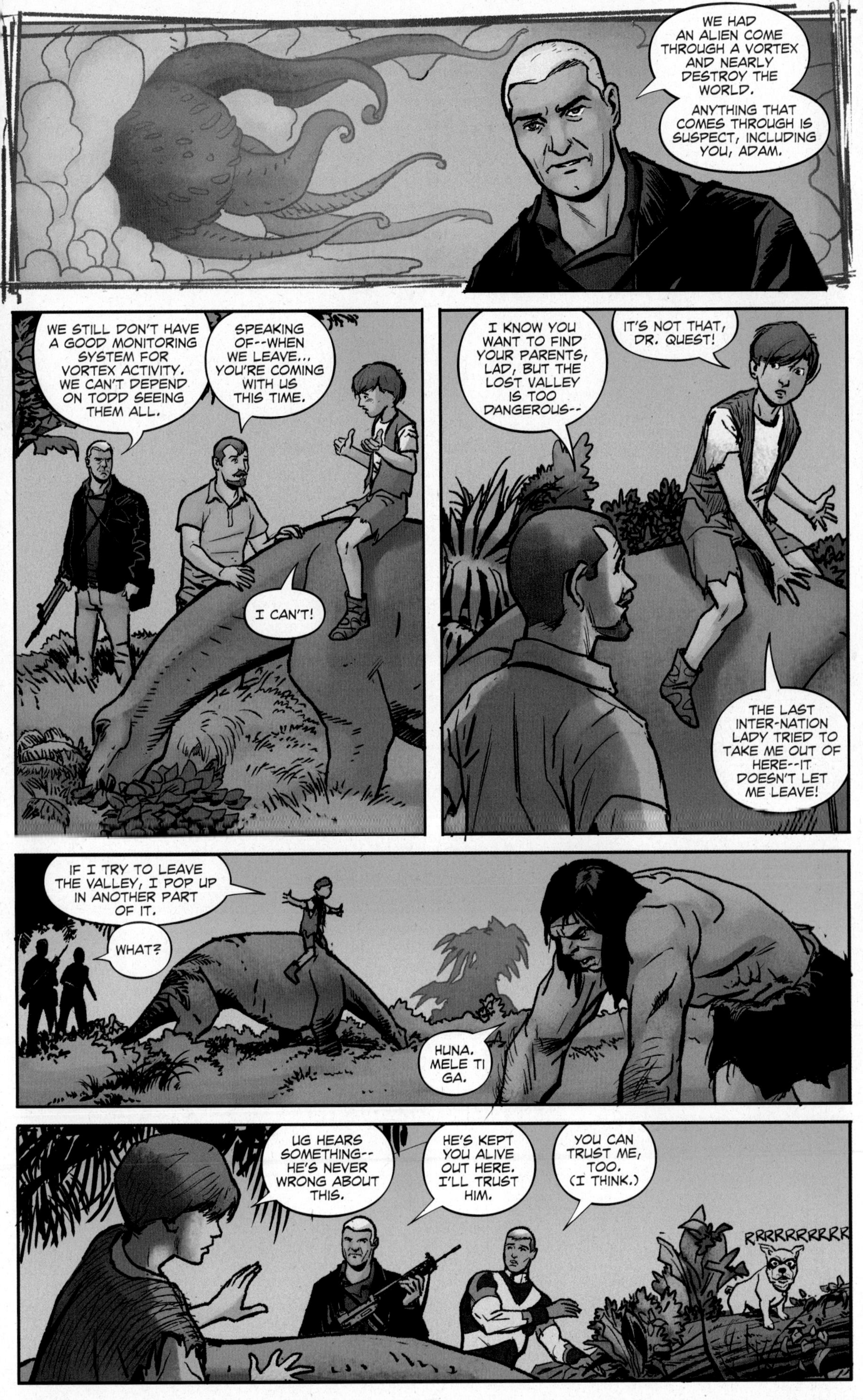

WE HAD AN ALIEN COME THROUGH A VORTEX AND NEARLY DESTROY THE WORLD.
ANYTHING THAT COMES THROUGH IS SUSPECT, INCLUDING YOU, ADAM.
WE STILL DON'T HAVE A GOOD MONITORING SYSTEM FOR VORTEX ACTIVITY. WE CAN'T DEPEND ON TODD SEEING THEM ALL.
SPEAKING OF--WHEN WE LEAVE... YOU'RE COMING WITH US THIS TIME.
I CAN'T!
I KNOW YOU WANT TO FIND YOUR PARENTS, LAD, BUT THE LOST VALLEY IS TOO DANGEROUS--
IT'S NOT THAT, DR. QUEST!
THE LAST INTER-NATION LADY TRIED TO TAKE ME OUT OF HERE--IT DOESN'T LET ME LEAVE!
IF I TRY TO LEAVE THE VALLEY, I POP UP IN ANOTHER PART OF IT.
WHAT?
HUNA. MELE TI GA.
UG HEARS SOMETHING-- HE'S NEVER WRONG ABOUT THIS.
HE'S KEPT YOU ALIVE OUT HERE. I'LL TRUST HIM.
YOU CAN TRUST ME, TOO. (I THINK.)
RRRRRRRRRR

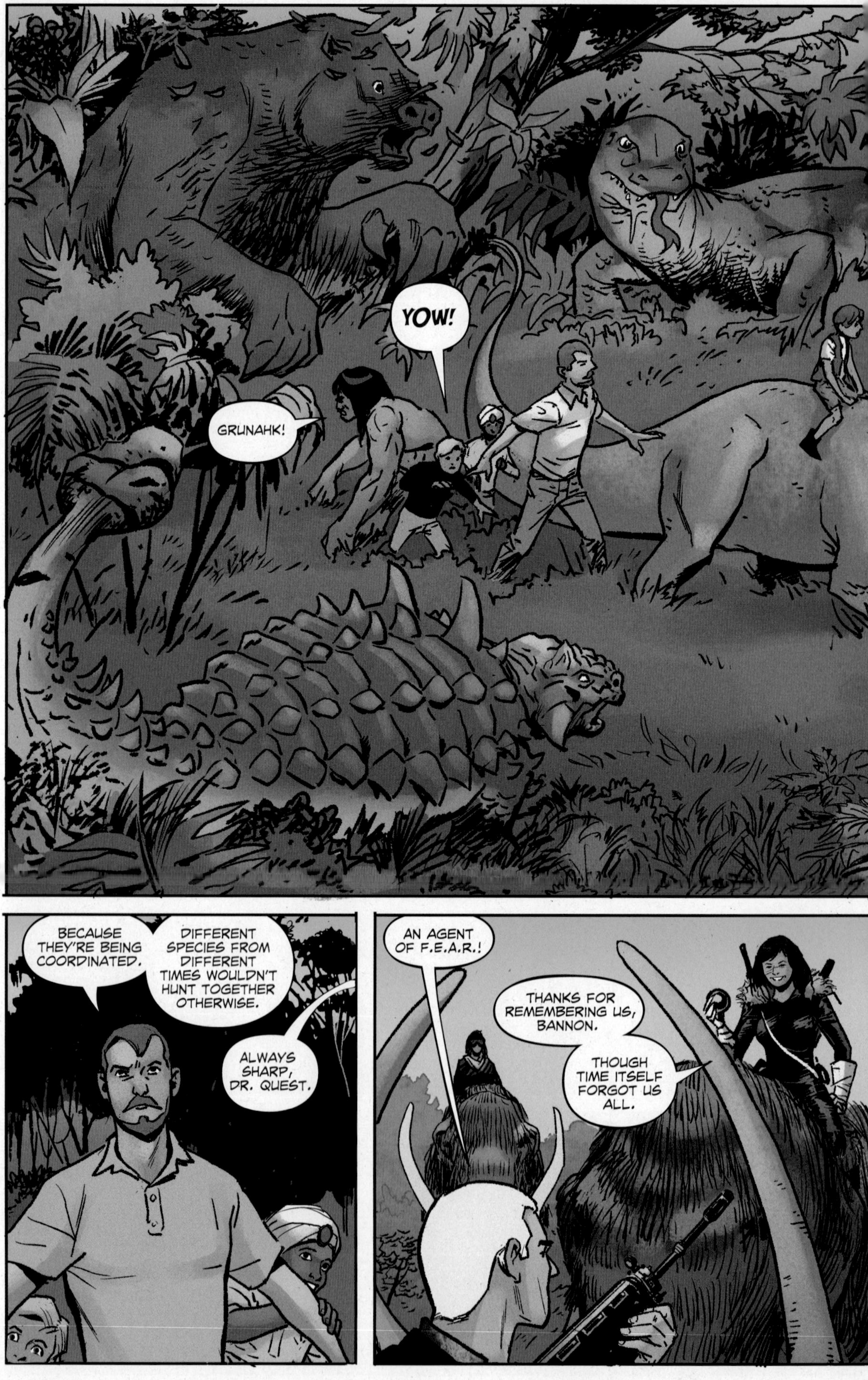
YOW!
GRUNAHK!
BECAUSE THEY'RE BEING COORDINATED.
DIFFERENT SPECIES FROM DIFFERENT TIMES WOULDN'T HUNT TOGETHER OTHERWISE.
ALWAYS SHARP, DR. QUEST.
AN AGENT OF F.E.A.R.!
THANKS FOR REMEMBERING US, BANNON.
THOUGH TIME ITSELF FORGOT US ALL.

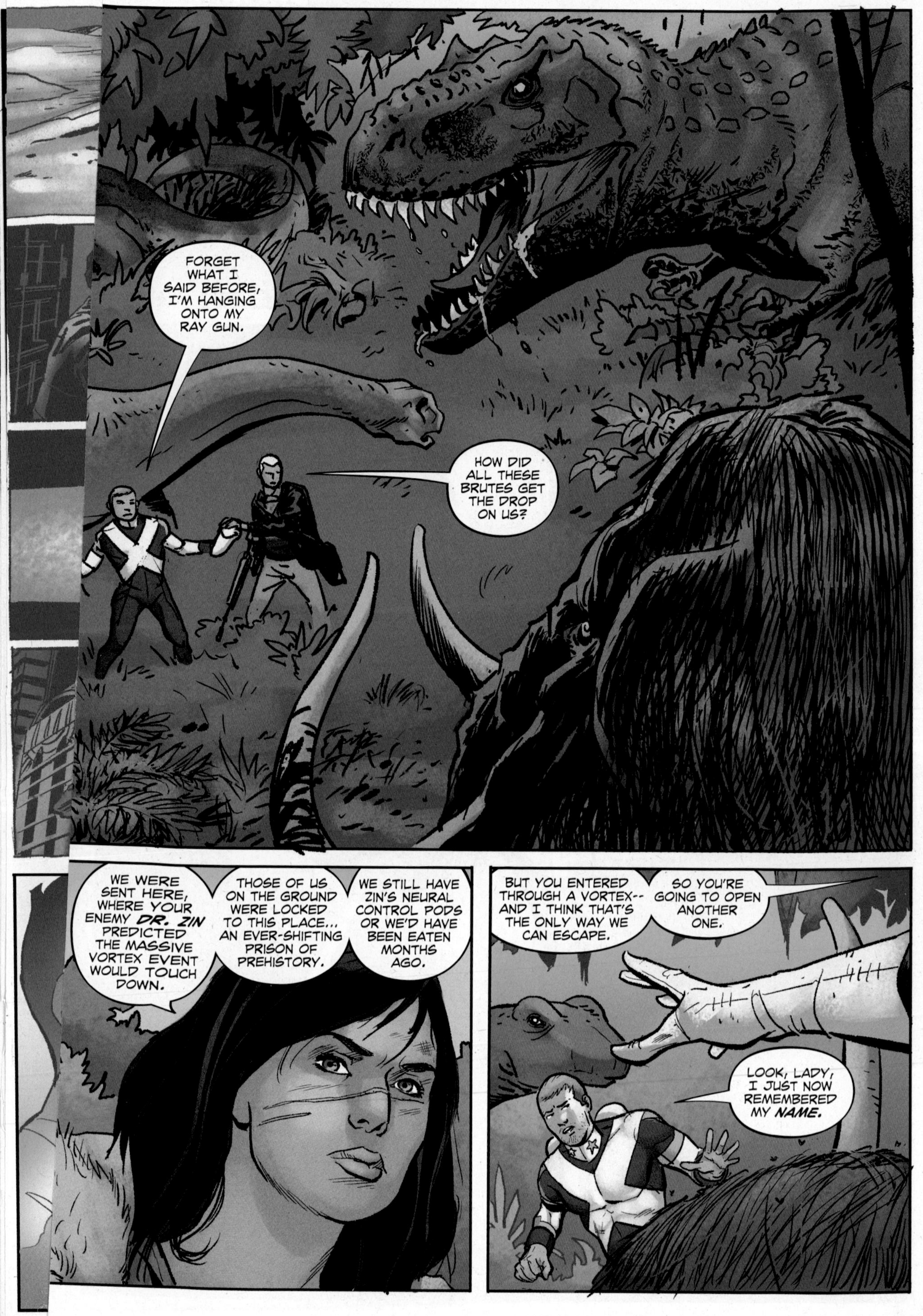
FORGET WHAT I SAID BEFORE, I'M HANGING ONTO MY RAY GUN.
HOW DID ALL THESE BRUTES GET THE DROP ON US?
WE WERE SENT HERE, WHERE YOUR ENEMY **DR. ZIN** PREDICTED THE MASSIVE VORTEX EVENT WOULD TOUCH DOWN.
THOSE OF US ON THE GROUND WERE LOCKED TO THIS PLACE... AN EVER-SHIFTING PRISON OF PREHISTORY.
WE STILL HAVE ZIN'S NEURAL CONTROL PODS OR WE'D HAVE BEEN EATEN MONTHS AGO.
BUT YOU ENTERED THROUGH A VORTEX-- AND I THINK THAT'S THE ONLY WAY WE CAN ESCAPE.
SO YOU'RE GOING TO OPEN ANOTHER ONE.
LOOK, LADY, I JUST NOW REMEMBERED MY ***NAME.***

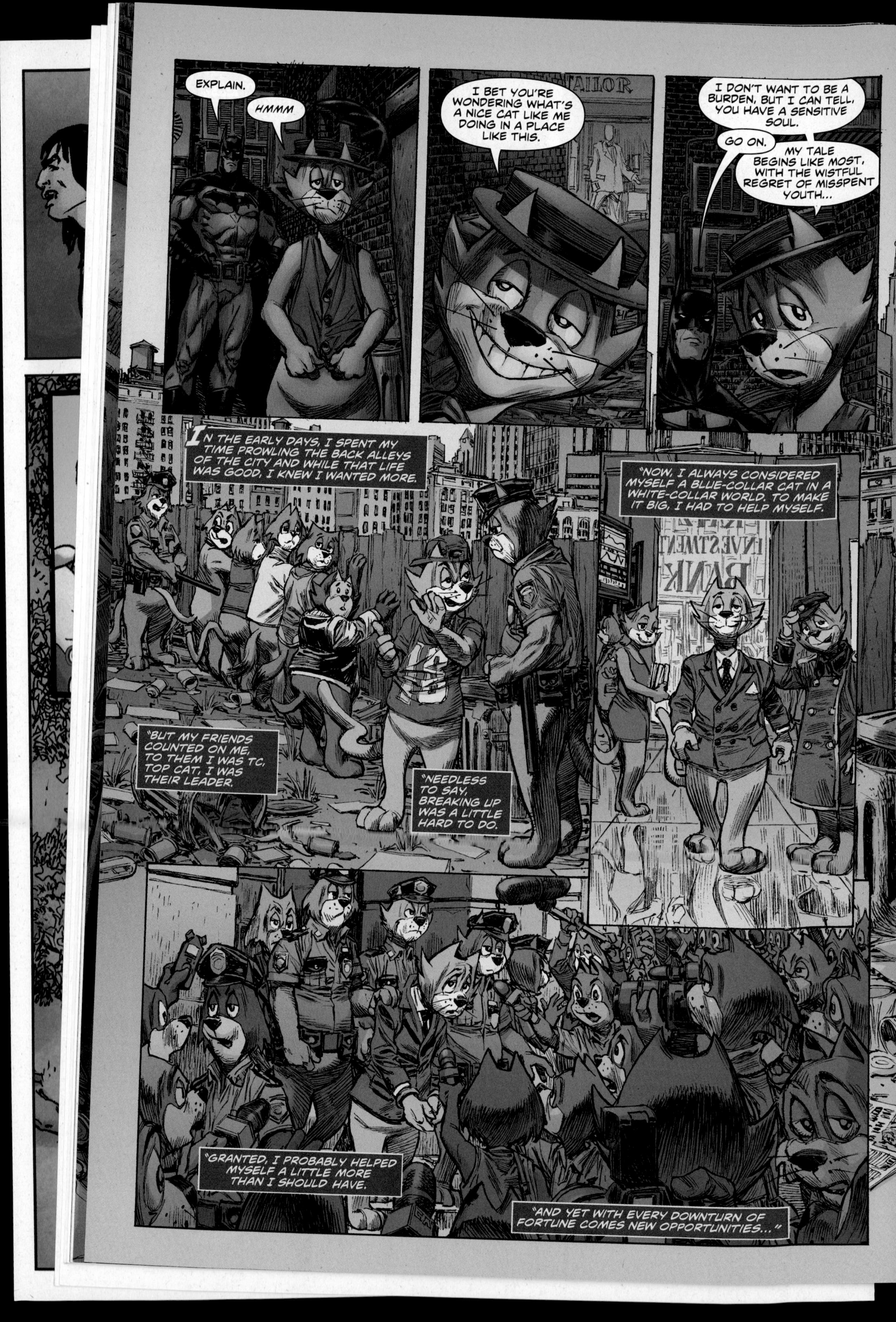
EXPLAIN.
HMMM
I BET YOU'RE WONDERING WHAT'S A NICE CAT LIKE ME DOING IN A PLACE LIKE THIS.
I DON'T WANT TO BE A BURDEN, BUT I CAN TELL, YOU HAVE A SENSITIVE SOUL.
GO ON.
MY TALE BEGINS LIKE MOST, WITH THE WISTFUL REGRET OF MISSPENT YOUTH...
IN THE EARLY DAYS, I SPENT MY TIME PROWLING THE BACK ALLEYS OF THE CITY AND WHILE THAT LIFE WAS GOOD, I KNEW I WANTED MORE.
"BUT MY FRIENDS COUNTED ON ME, TO THEM I WAS TC, TOP CAT, I WAS THEIR LEADER.
"NEEDLESS TO SAY, BREAKING UP WAS A LITTLE HARD TO DO.
"NOW, I ALWAYS CONSIDERED MYSELF A BLUE-COLLAR CAT IN A WHITE-COLLAR WORLD. TO MAKE IT BIG, I HAD TO HELP MYSELF.
INVESTMENT BANK
"GRANTED, I PROBABLY HELPED MYSELF A LITTLE MORE THAN I SHOULD HAVE.
"AND YET WITH EVERY DOWNTURN OF FORTUNE COMES NEW OPPORTUNITIES..."

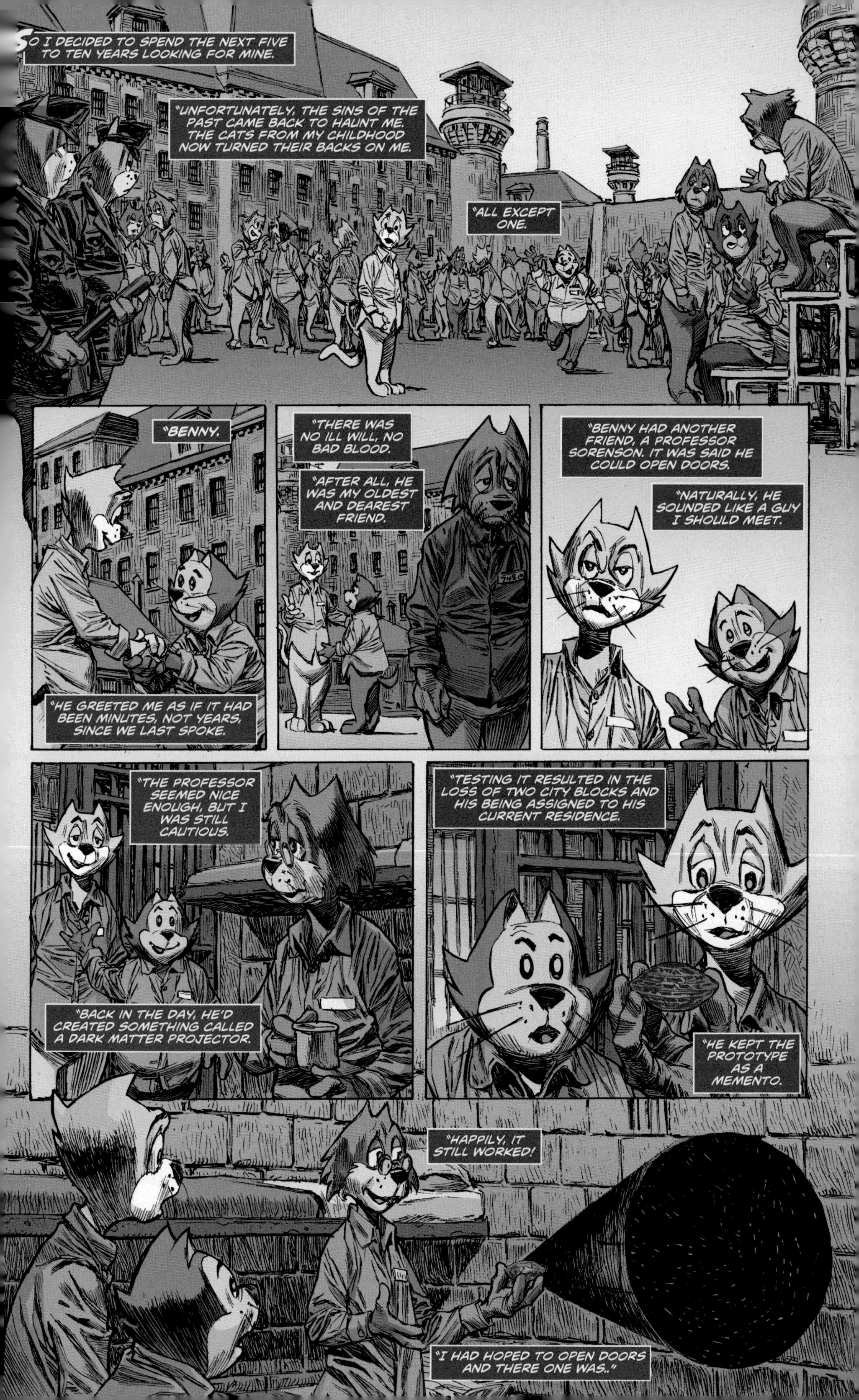
SO I DECIDED TO SPEND THE NEXT FIVE TO TEN YEARS LOOKING FOR MINE.
"UNFORTUNATELY, THE SINS OF THE PAST CAME BACK TO HAUNT ME. THE CATS FROM MY CHILDHOOD NOW TURNED THEIR BACKS ON ME.
"ALL EXCEPT ONE.
"BENNY.
"HE GREETED ME AS IF IT HAD BEEN MINUTES, NOT YEARS, SINCE WE LAST SPOKE.
"THERE WAS NO ILL WILL, NO BAD BLOOD.
"AFTER ALL, HE WAS MY OLDEST AND DEAREST FRIEND.
"BENNY HAD ANOTHER FRIEND, A PROFESSOR SORENSON. IT WAS SAID HE COULD OPEN DOORS.
"NATURALLY, HE SOUNDED LIKE A GUY I SHOULD MEET.
"THE PROFESSOR SEEMED NICE ENOUGH, BUT I WAS STILL CAUTIOUS.
"BACK IN THE DAY, HE'D CREATED SOMETHING CALLED A DARK MATTER PROJECTOR.
"TESTING IT RESULTED IN THE LOSS OF TWO CITY BLOCKS AND HIS BEING ASSIGNED TO HIS CURRENT RESIDENCE.
"HE KEPT THE PROTOTYPE AS A MEMENTO.
"HAPPILY, IT STILL WORKED!
"I HAD HOPED TO OPEN DOORS AND THERE ONE WAS."

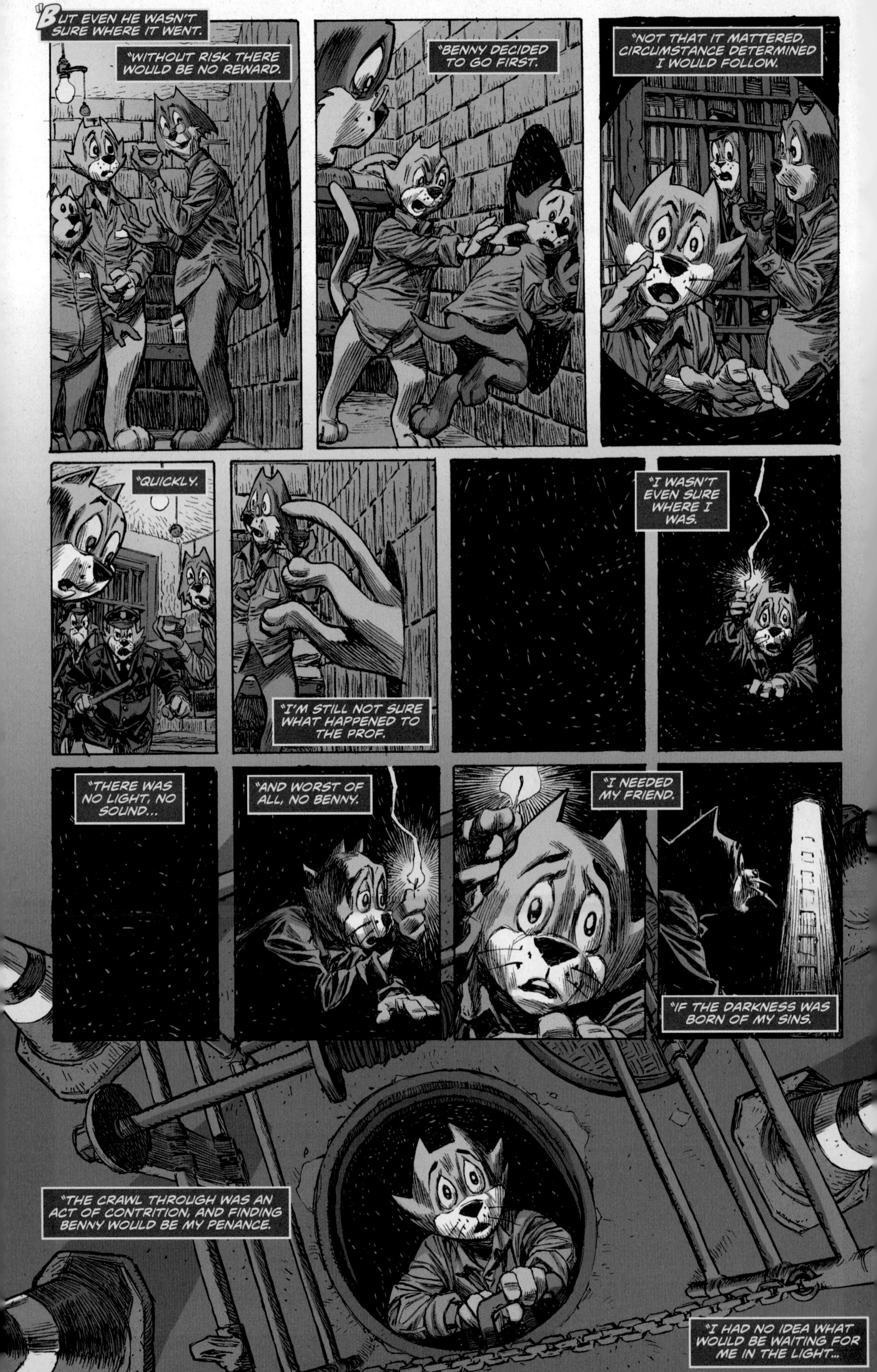
"BUT EVEN HE WASN'T SURE WHERE IT WENT.
"WITHOUT RISK THERE WOULD BE NO REWARD.
"BENNY DECIDED TO GO FIRST.
"NOT THAT IT MATTERED, CIRCUMSTANCE DETERMINED I WOULD FOLLOW.
"QUICKLY.
"I'M STILL NOT SURE WHAT HAPPENED TO THE PROF.
"I WASN'T EVEN SURE WHERE I WAS.
"THERE WAS NO LIGHT, NO SOUND...
"AND WORST OF ALL, NO BENNY.
"I NEEDED MY FRIEND.
"IF THE DARKNESS WAS BORN OF MY SINS.
"THE CRAWL THROUGH WAS AN ACT OF CONTRITION, AND FINDING BENNY WOULD BE MY PENANCE.
"I HAD NO IDEA WHAT WOULD BE WAITING FOR ME IN THE LIGHT...

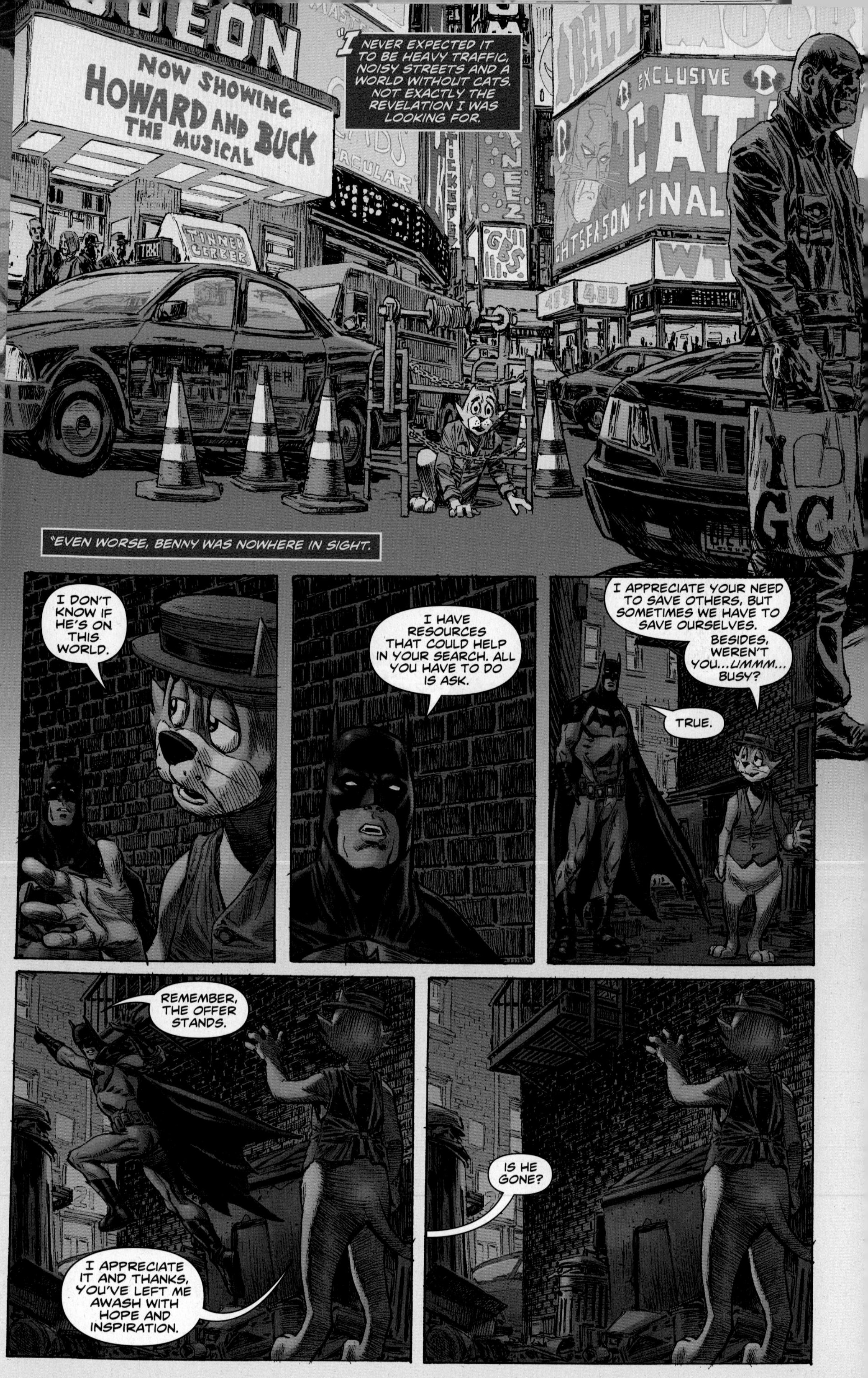
NOW SHOWING
HOWARD AND BUCK
THE MUSICAL
TINNED GERBER
EXCLUSIVE
"I NEVER EXPECTED IT TO BE HEAVY TRAFFIC, NOISY STREETS AND A WORLD WITHOUT CATS. NOT EXACTLY THE REVELATION I WAS LOOKING FOR.
"EVEN WORSE, BENNY WAS NOWHERE IN SIGHT.
I DON'T KNOW IF HE'S ON THIS WORLD.
I HAVE RESOURCES THAT COULD HELP IN YOUR SEARCH. ALL YOU HAVE TO DO IS ASK.
I APPRECIATE YOUR NEED TO SAVE OTHERS, BUT SOMETIMES WE HAVE TO SAVE OURSELVES.
BESIDES, WEREN'T YOU...UMMM... BUSY?
TRUE.
REMEMBER, THE OFFER STANDS.
I APPRECIATE IT AND THANKS, YOU'VE LEFT ME AWASH WITH HOPE AND INSPIRATION.
IS HE GONE?

=A-HEM= LET US FOCUS ON THE TASK AT HAND.
WE MUST LEVEL THAT ROBOT FACTORY, BUT THEY ARE HOLDING COLONEL FLAG INSIDE.
AW, RICKY, I'M GONNA MISS YA...
NO, HARLEY. WE FREE FLAG, THEN BLOW IT UP.
BUT HOW DO WE FIND HIM? MIGHT BE A FREAKIN' MAZE IN THERE, AND IT'S CRAWLING WITH TWERPINATORS.
OOOH! LET'S REPROGRAM ONE TO BE MY SIDEKICK!
HONK
HONKWHEEZE
KBRAPT
BRP
HMM...
NOT A BAD PLAN, BIG GUY.
WHAT PLAN? WHAT THE HELL ARE YOU PEOPLE UP TO?
I'LL TELL YA, MS. WALLER. JUST DON'T BACKSEAT-DRIVE THIS...

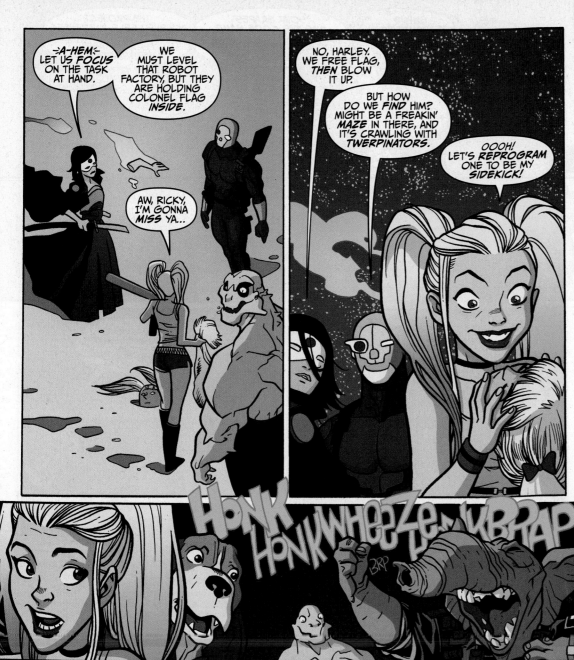

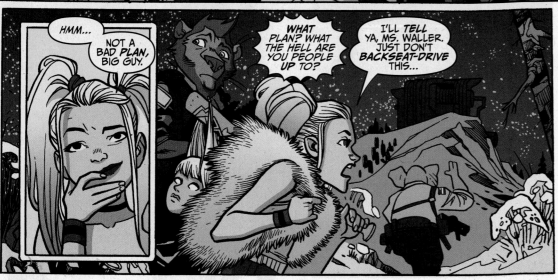

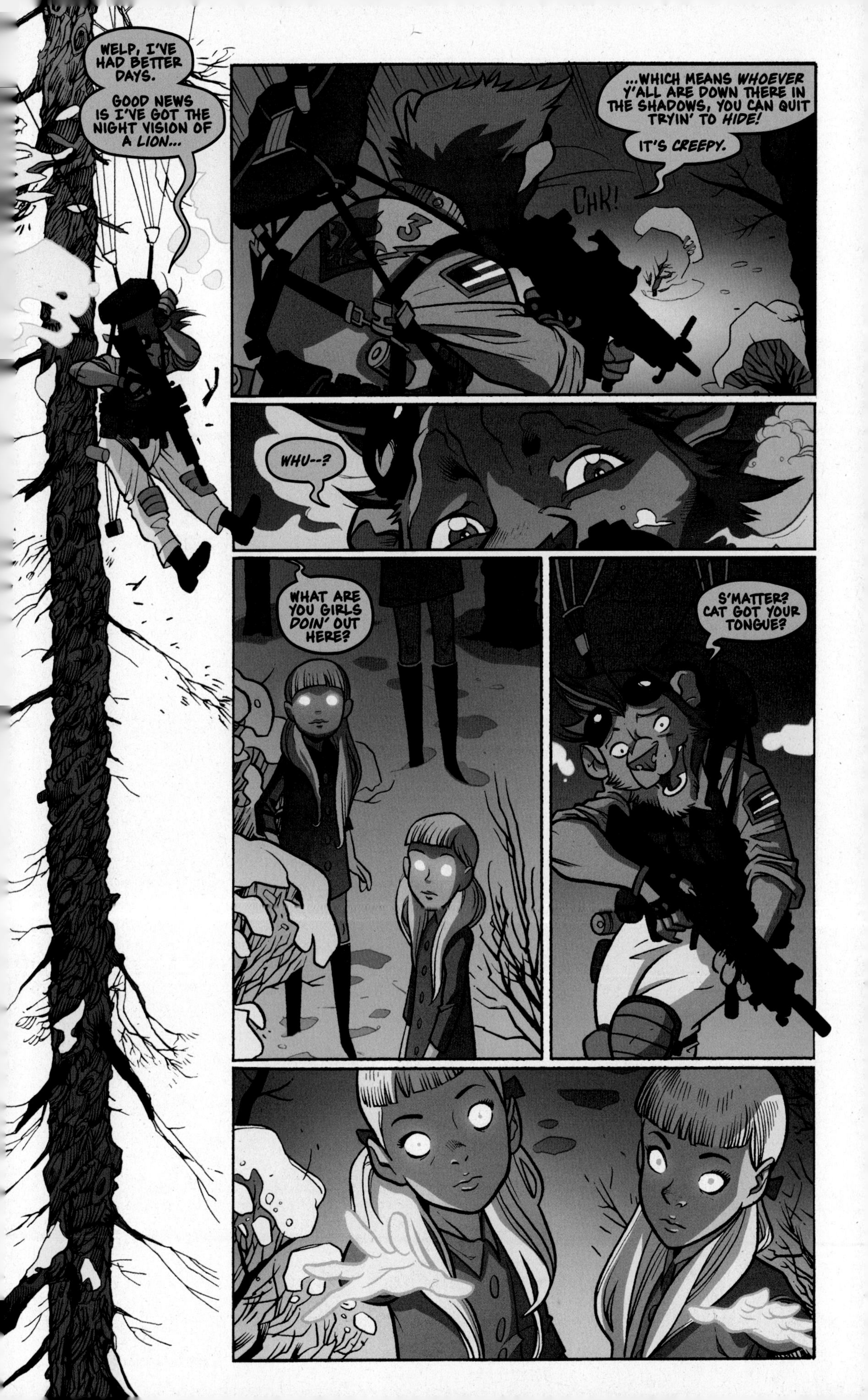
WELP, I'VE HAD BETTER DAYS.
GOOD NEWS IS I'VE GOT THE NIGHT VISION OF A LION...
...WHICH MEANS WHOEVER Y'ALL ARE DOWN THERE IN THE SHADOWS, YOU CAN QUIT TRYIN' TO HIDE!
IT'S CREEPY.
CHK!
WHU--?
WHAT ARE YOU GIRLS DOIN' OUT HERE?
S'MATTER? CAT GOT YOUR TONGUE?

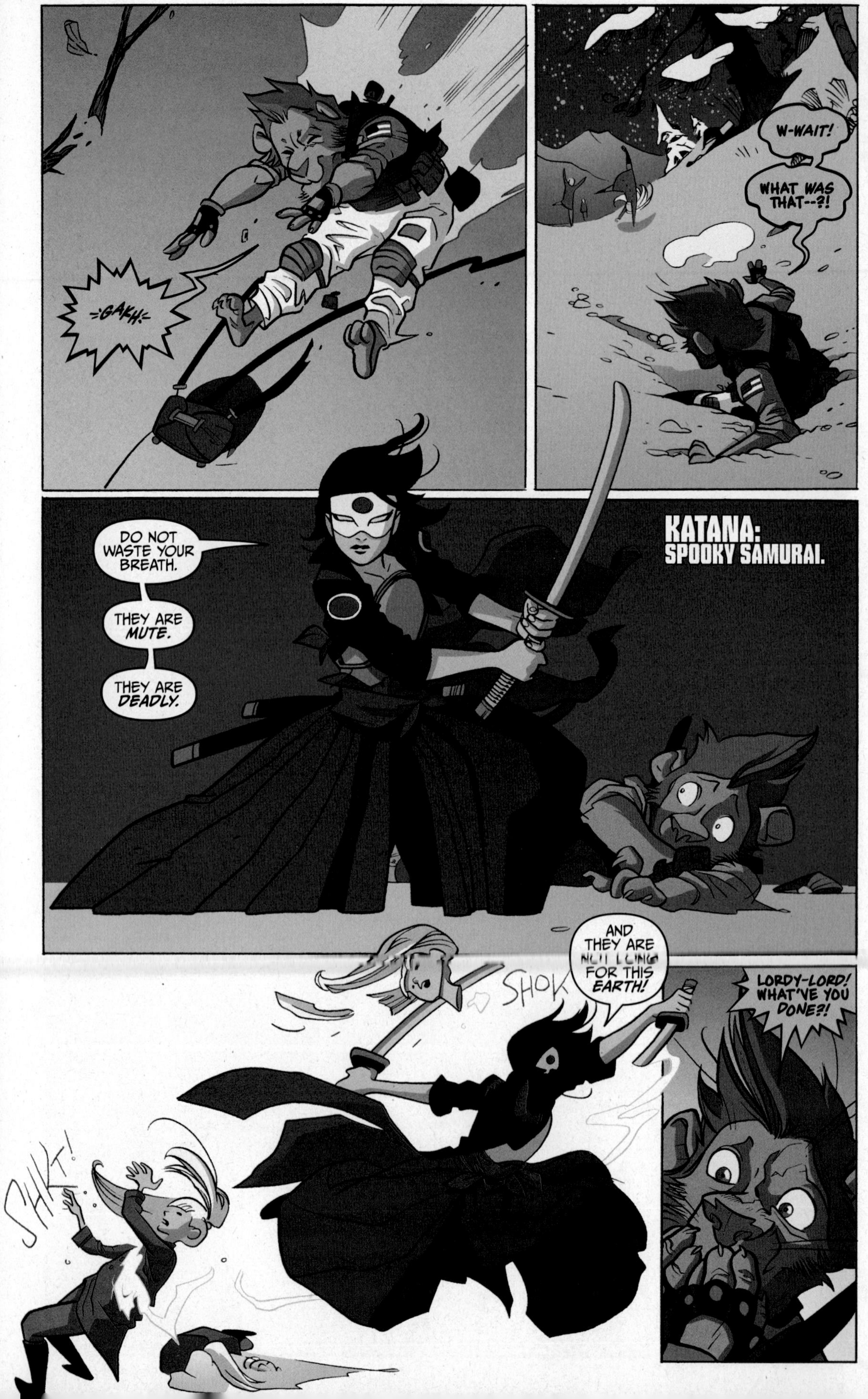
=GAKH=
W-WAIT!
WHAT WAS THAT--?!
KATANA: SPOOKY SAMURAI.
DO NOT WASTE YOUR BREATH.
THEY ARE *MUTE.*
THEY ARE *DEADLY.*
SHOK
AND THEY ARE NOT LONG FOR THIS *EARTH!*
SHKT!
LORDY-LORD! WHAT'VE YOU DONE?!

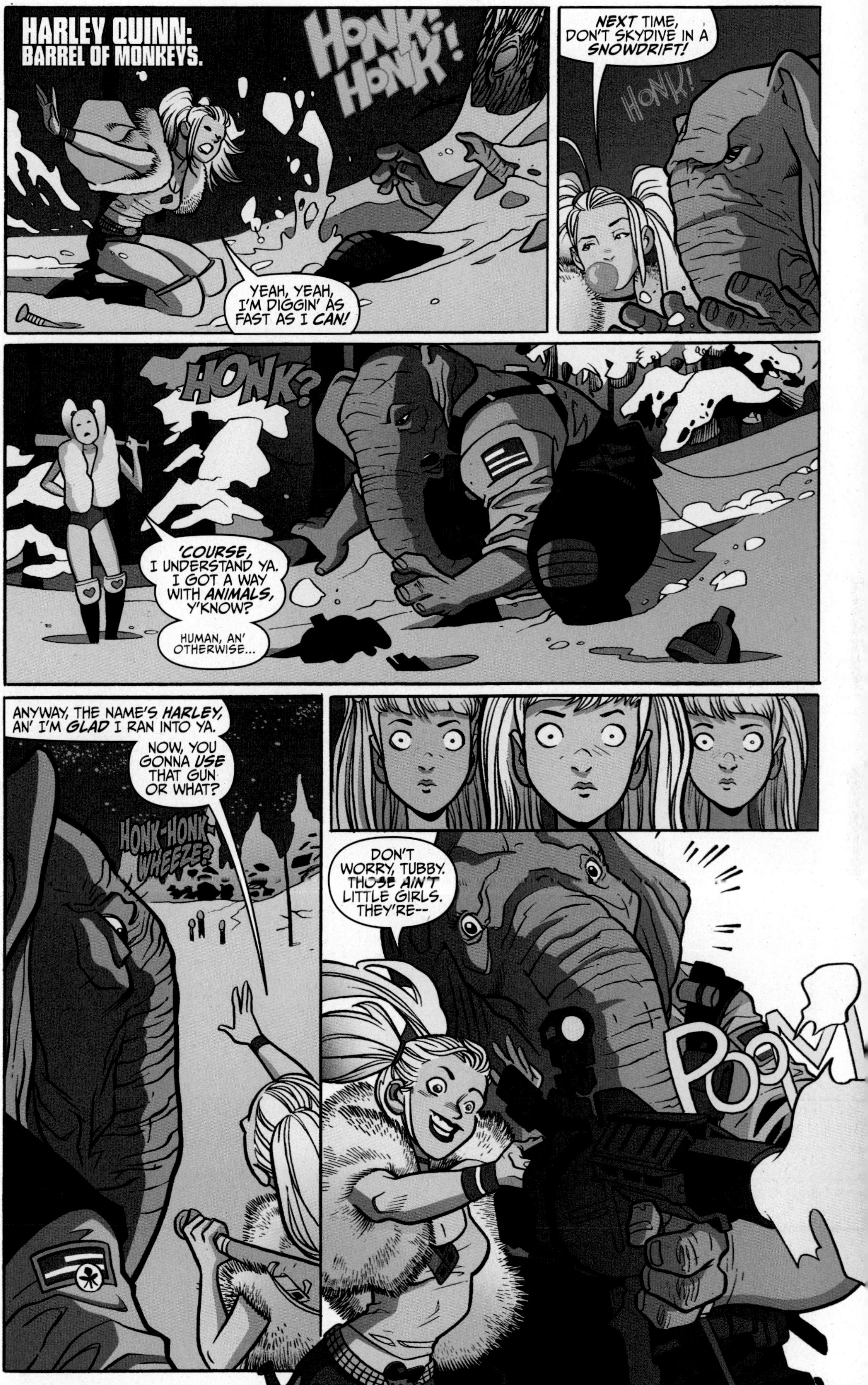
HARLEY QUINN:
BARREL OF MONKEYS.
HONK-HONK!
YEAH, YEAH, I'M DIGGIN' AS FAST AS I CAN!
NEXT TIME, DON'T SKYDIVE IN A SNOWDRIFT!
HONK!
HONK?
'COURSE, I UNDERSTAND YA. I GOT A WAY WITH ANIMALS, Y'KNOW?
HUMAN, AN' OTHERWISE...
ANYWAY, THE NAME'S HARLEY, AN' I'M GLAD I RAN INTO YA.
NOW, YOU GONNA USE THAT GUN OR WHAT?
HONK-HONK-WHEEZE?
DON'T WORRY, TUBBY. THOSE AIN'T LITTLE GIRLS. THEY'RE--
POOM

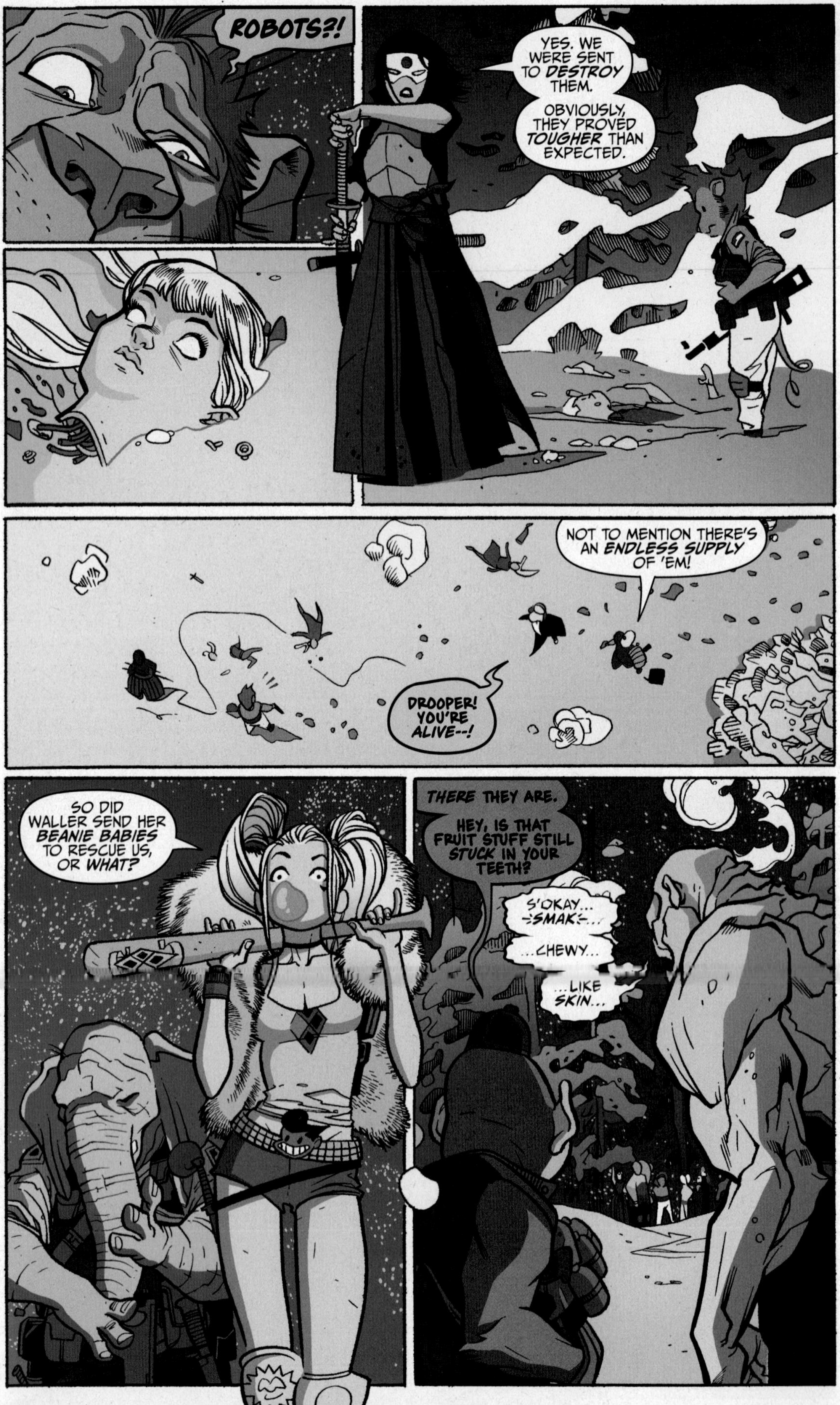
ROBOTS?!
YES. WE WERE SENT TO DESTROY THEM.
OBVIOUSLY, THEY PROVED TOUGHER THAN EXPECTED.
NOT TO MENTION THERE'S AN ENDLESS SUPPLY OF 'EM!
DROOPER! YOU'RE ALIVE--!
SO DID WALLER SEND HER BEANIE BABIES TO RESCUE US, OR WHAT?
THERE THEY ARE.
HEY, IS THAT FRUIT STUFF STILL STUCK IN YOUR TEETH?
S'OKAY... -SMAK-...
...CHEWY...
...LIKE SKIN...

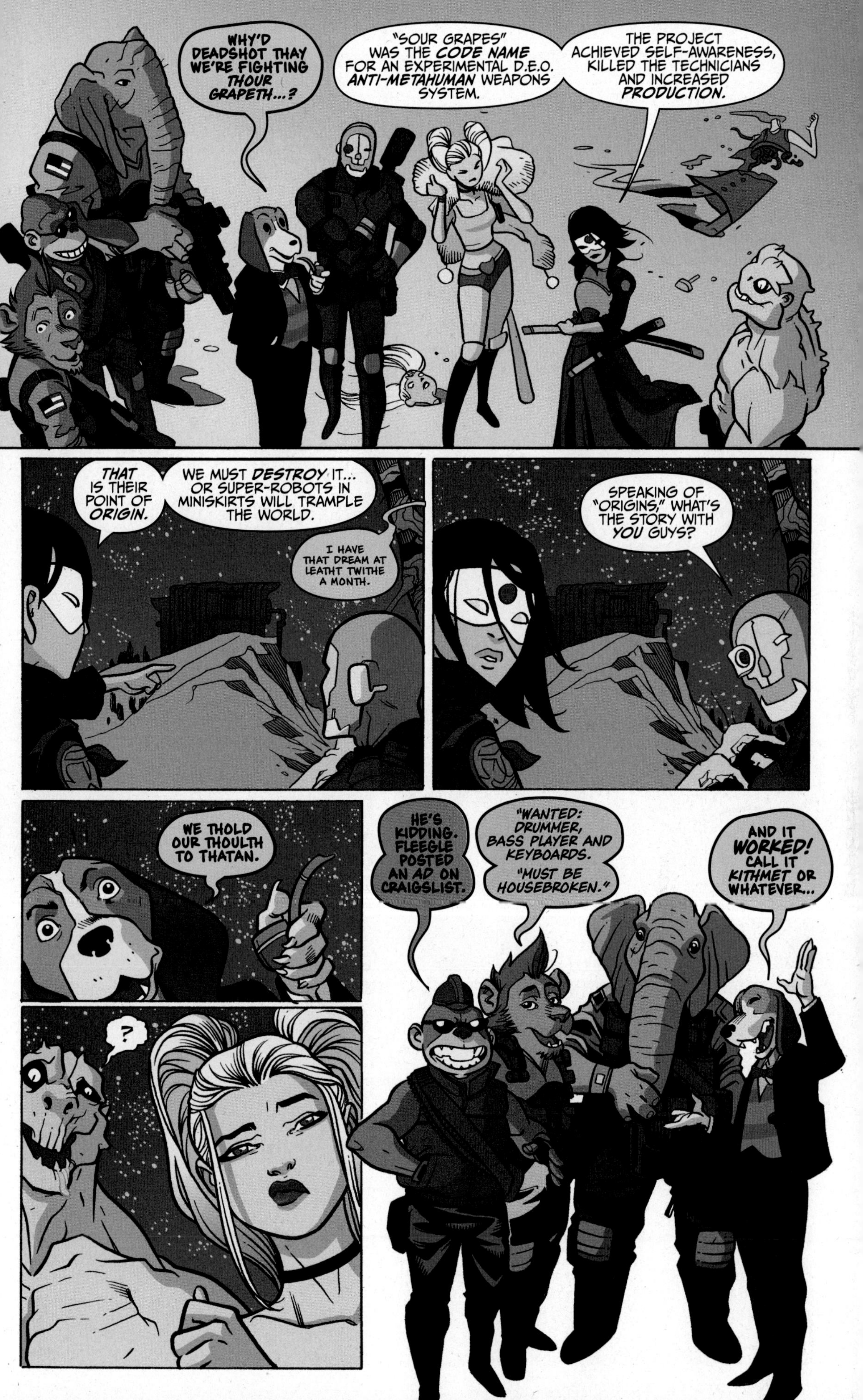
WHY'D DEADSHOT THAY WE'RE FIGHTING THOUR GRAPETH...?
"SOUR GRAPES" WAS THE CODE NAME FOR AN EXPERIMENTAL D.E.O. ANTI-METAHUMAN WEAPONS SYSTEM.
THE PROJECT ACHIEVED SELF-AWARENESS, KILLED THE TECHNICIANS AND INCREASED PRODUCTION.
THAT IS THEIR POINT OF ORIGIN.
WE MUST DESTROY IT... OR SUPER-ROBOTS IN MINISKIRTS WILL TRAMPLE THE WORLD.
I HAVE THAT DREAM AT LEATHT TWITHE A MONTH.
SPEAKING OF "ORIGINS," WHAT'S THE STORY WITH YOU GUYS?
WE THOLD OUR THOULTH TO THATAN.
?
HE'S KIDDING. FLEEGLE POSTED AN AD ON CRAIGSLIST.
"WANTED: DRUMMER, BASS PLAYER AND KEYBOARDS. "MUST BE HOUSEBROKEN."
AND IT WORKED! CALL IT KITHMET OR WHATEVER...

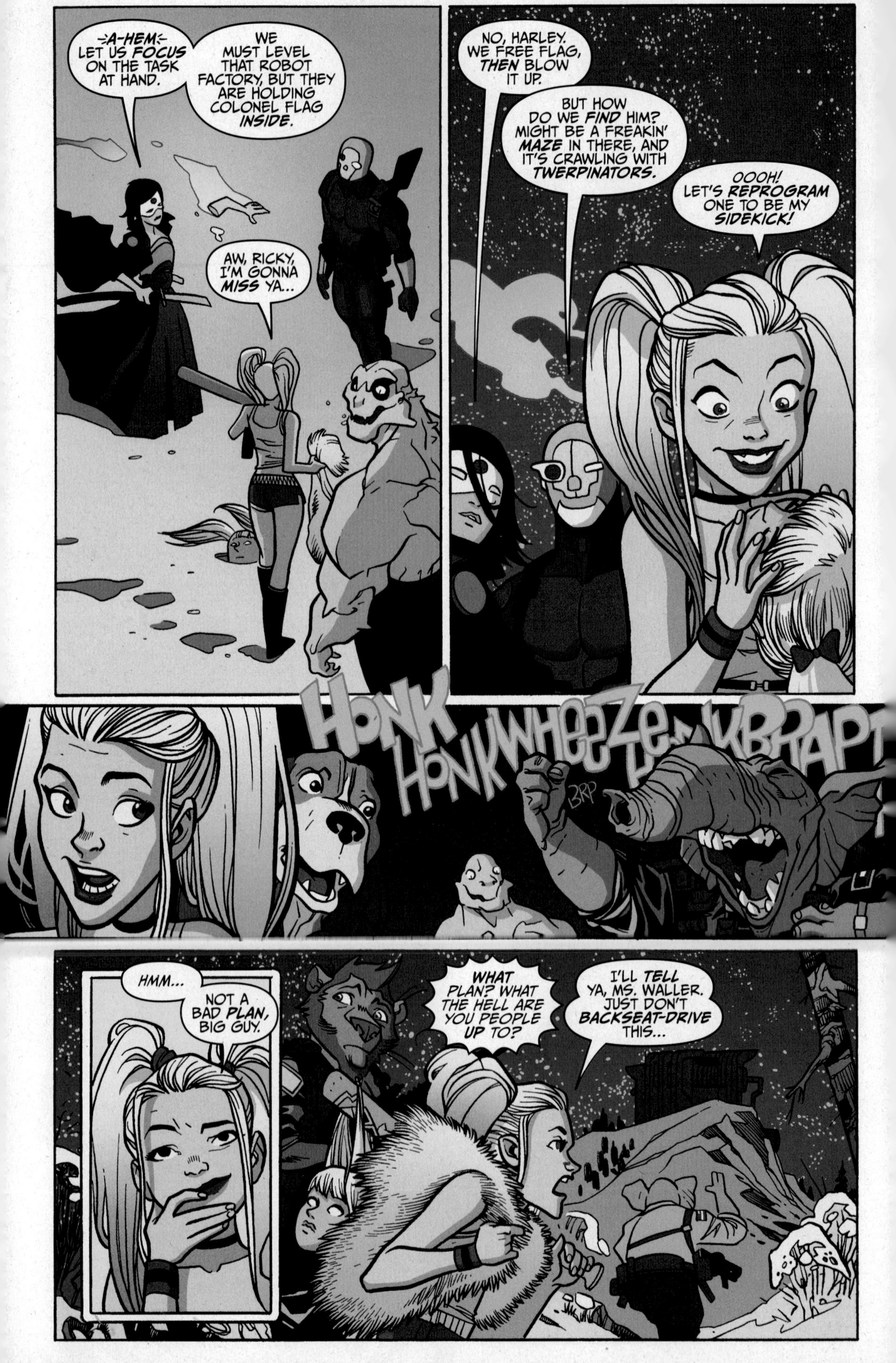

-A-HEM- LET US FOCUS ON THE TASK AT HAND.
WE MUST LEVEL THAT ROBOT FACTORY, BUT THEY ARE HOLDING COLONEL FLAG INSIDE.
AW, RICKY, I'M GONNA MISS YA...
NO, HARLEY. WE FREE FLAG, THEN BLOW IT UP.
BUT HOW DO WE FIND HIM? MIGHT BE A FREAKIN' MAZE IN THERE, AND IT'S CRAWLING WITH TWERPINATORS.
OOOH! LET'S REPROGRAM ONE TO BE MY SIDEKICK!
HONK
HONKWHEEZE
BRP
HMM...
NOT A BAD PLAN, BIG GUY.
WHAT PLAN? WHAT THE HELL ARE YOU PEOPLE UP TO?
I'LL TELL YA, MS. WALLER. JUST DON'T BACKSEAT-DRIVE THIS...

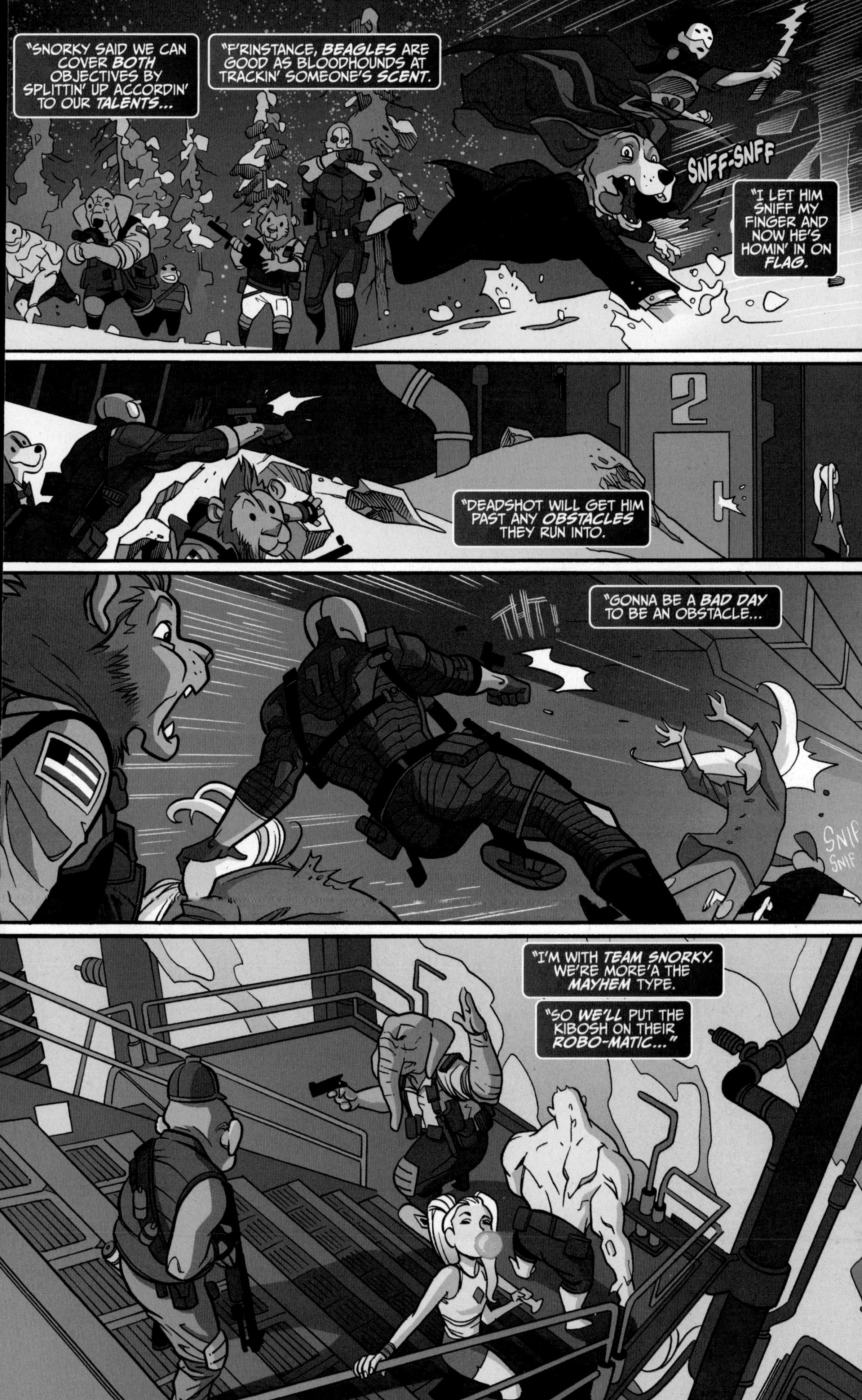
"SNORKY SAID WE CAN COVER BOTH OBJECTIVES BY SPLITTIN' UP ACCORDIN' TO OUR TALENTS...
"F'RINSTANCE, BEAGLES ARE GOOD AS BLOODHOUNDS AT TRACKIN' SOMEONE'S SCENT.
SNFF-SNFF
"I LET HIM SNIFF MY FINGER AND NOW HE'S HOMIN' IN ON FLAG.
2
"DEADSHOT WILL GET HIM PAST ANY OBSTACLES THEY RUN INTO.
THT!
"GONNA BE A BAD DAY TO BE AN OBSTACLE...
SNIF SNIF
"I'M WITH TEAM SNORKY. WE'RE MORE'A THE MAYHEM TYPE.
"SO WE'LL PUT THE KIBOSH ON THEIR ROBO-MATIC..."

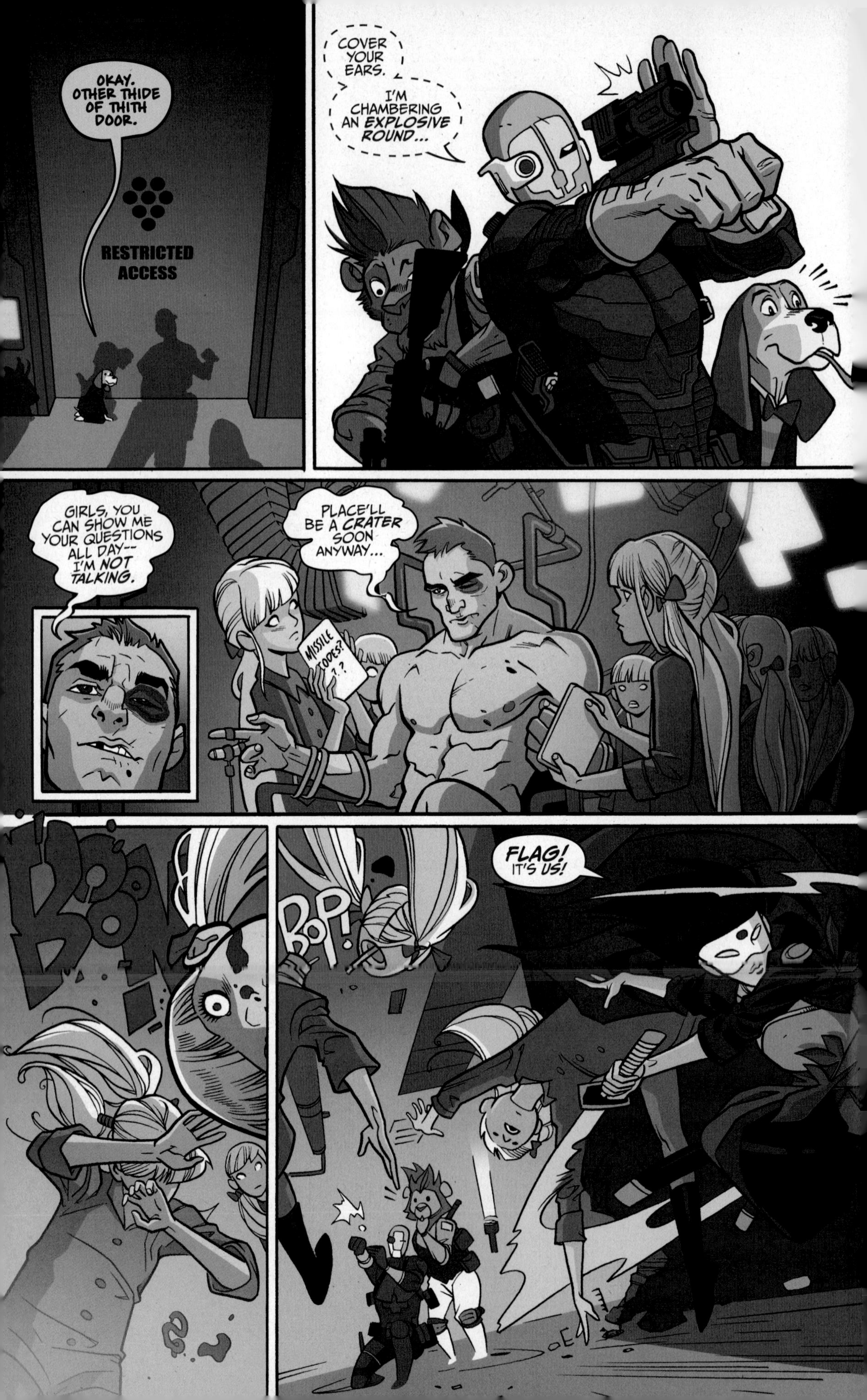
OKAY. OTHER THIDE OF THITH DOOR.
RESTRICTED ACCESS
COVER YOUR EARS.
I'M CHAMBERING AN *EXPLOSIVE ROUND...*
GIRLS, YOU CAN SHOW ME YOUR QUESTIONS ALL DAY-- I'M *NOT TALKING.*
PLACE'LL BE A *CRATER* SOON ANYWAY...
MISSILE CODES? ?.?
BOOM
BOP!
FLAG! IT'S US!

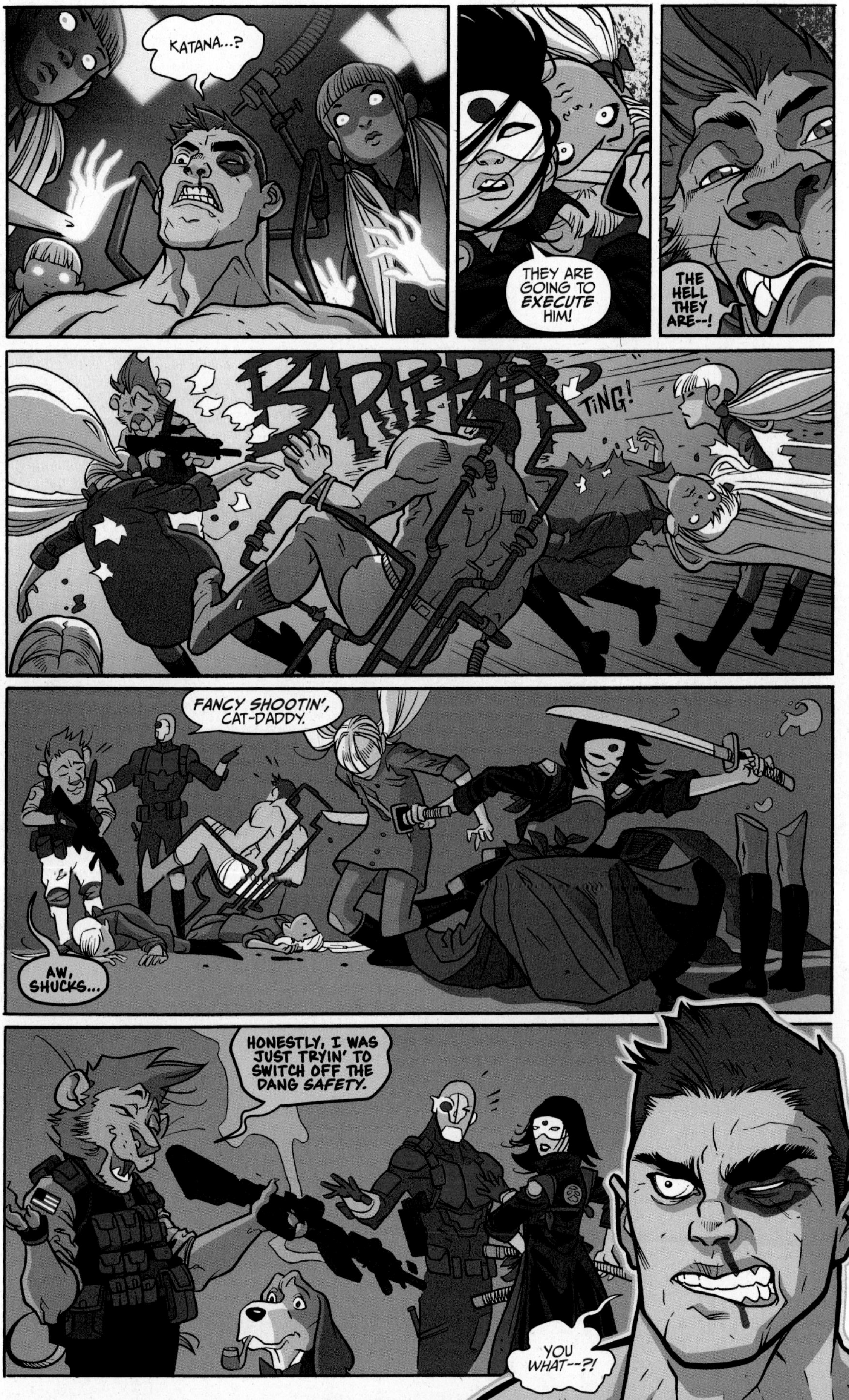
KATANA...?
THEY ARE GOING TO EXECUTE HIM!
THE HELL THEY ARE--!
BARRRRRRRRP
TING!
FANCY SHOOTIN', CAT-DADDY.
AW, SHUCKS...
HONESTLY, I WAS JUST TRYIN' TO SWITCH OFF THE DANG SAFETY.
YOU WHAT--?!

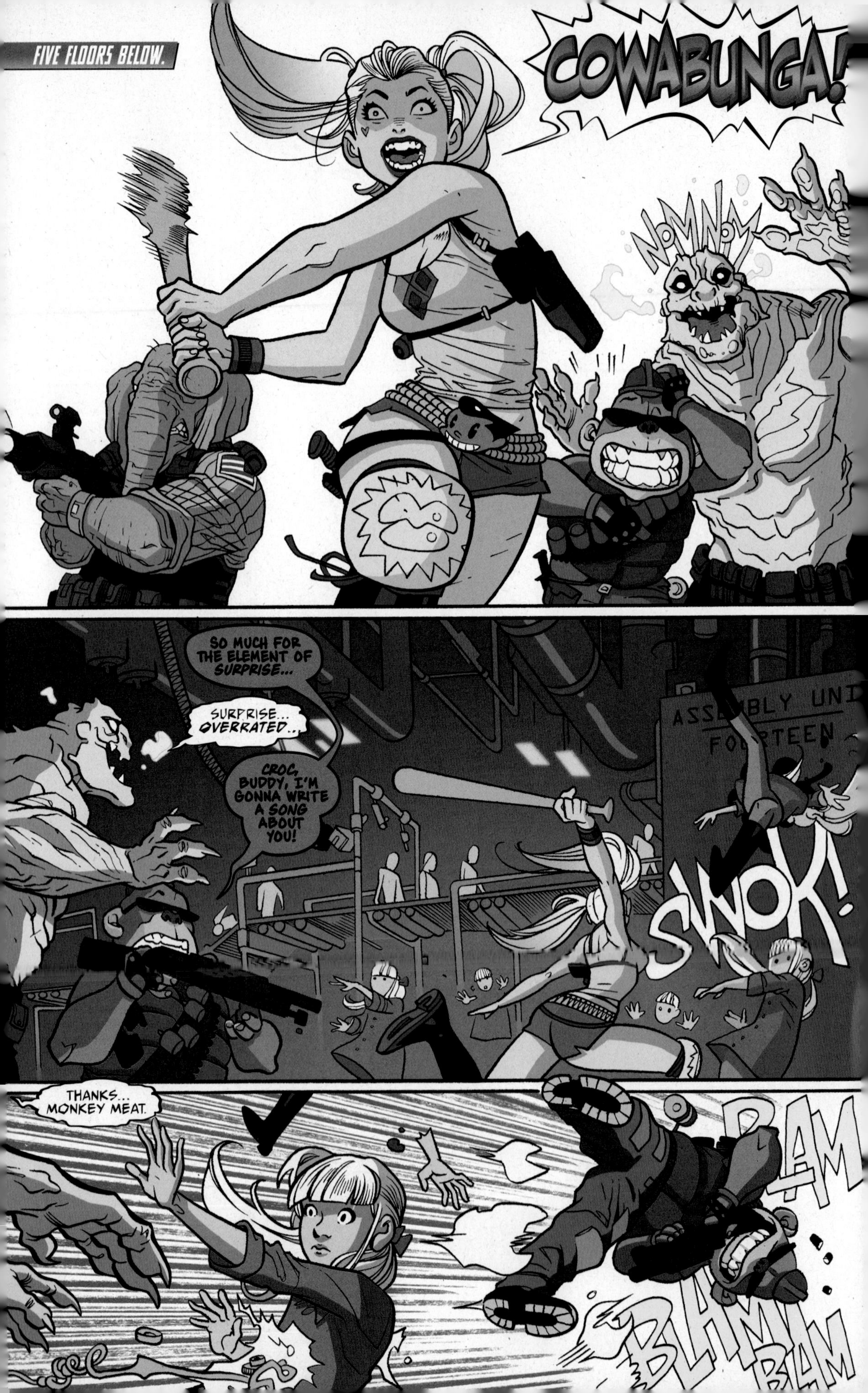
FIVE FLOORS BELOW.
COWABUNGA!
NOMNOM
SO MUCH FOR THE ELEMENT OF SURPRISE...
SURPRISE... OVERRATED...
CROC, BUDDY, I'M GONNA WRITE A SONG ABOUT YOU!
ASSEMBLY UNI
FOURTEEN
SWOK!
THANKS... MONKEY MEAT.
BAM
BLAM
BAM

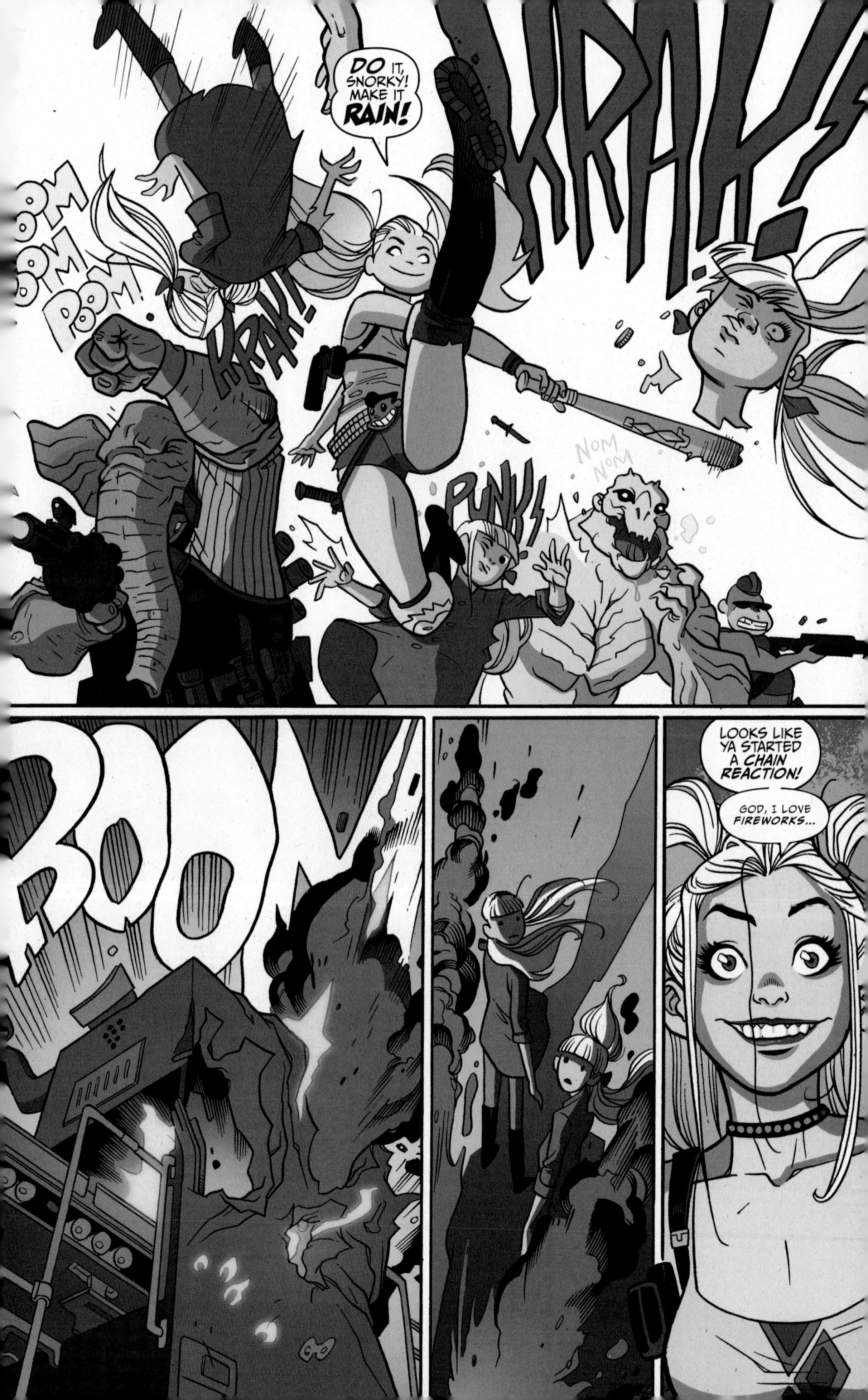
DO IT, SNORKY! MAKE IT RAIN!
KRAK!
BOOM BOOM BOOM!
KRAK!
NOM NOM
PUNK!
BOOM
LOOKS LIKE YA STARTED A CHAIN REACTION!
GOD, I LOVE FIREWORKS...

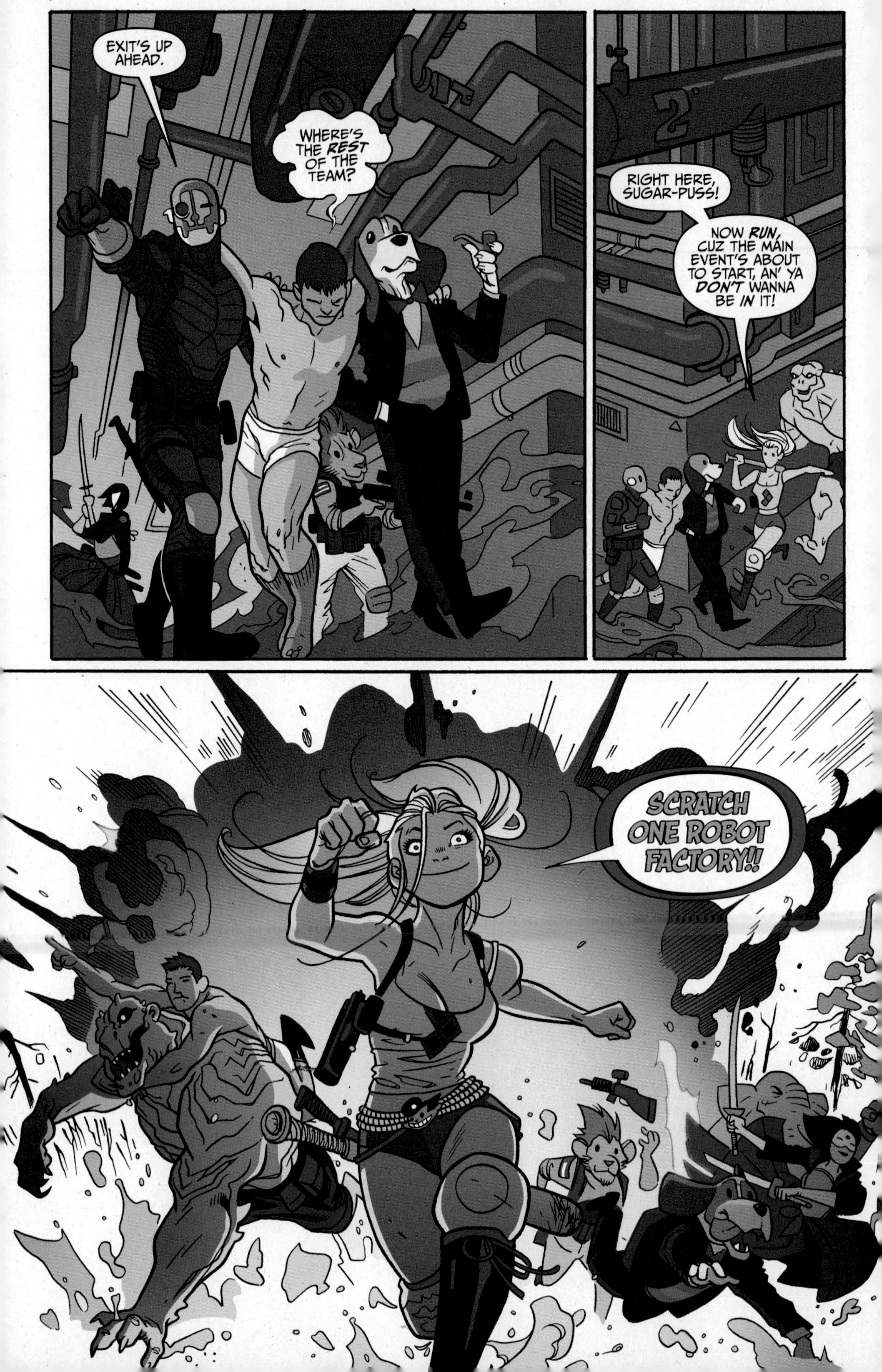
EXIT'S UP AHEAD.
WHERE'S THE REST OF THE TEAM?
RIGHT HERE, SUGAR-PUSS!
NOW RUN, CUZ THE MAIN EVENT'S ABOUT TO START, AN' YA DON'T WANNA BE IN IT!
SCRATCH ONE ROBOT FACTORY!!

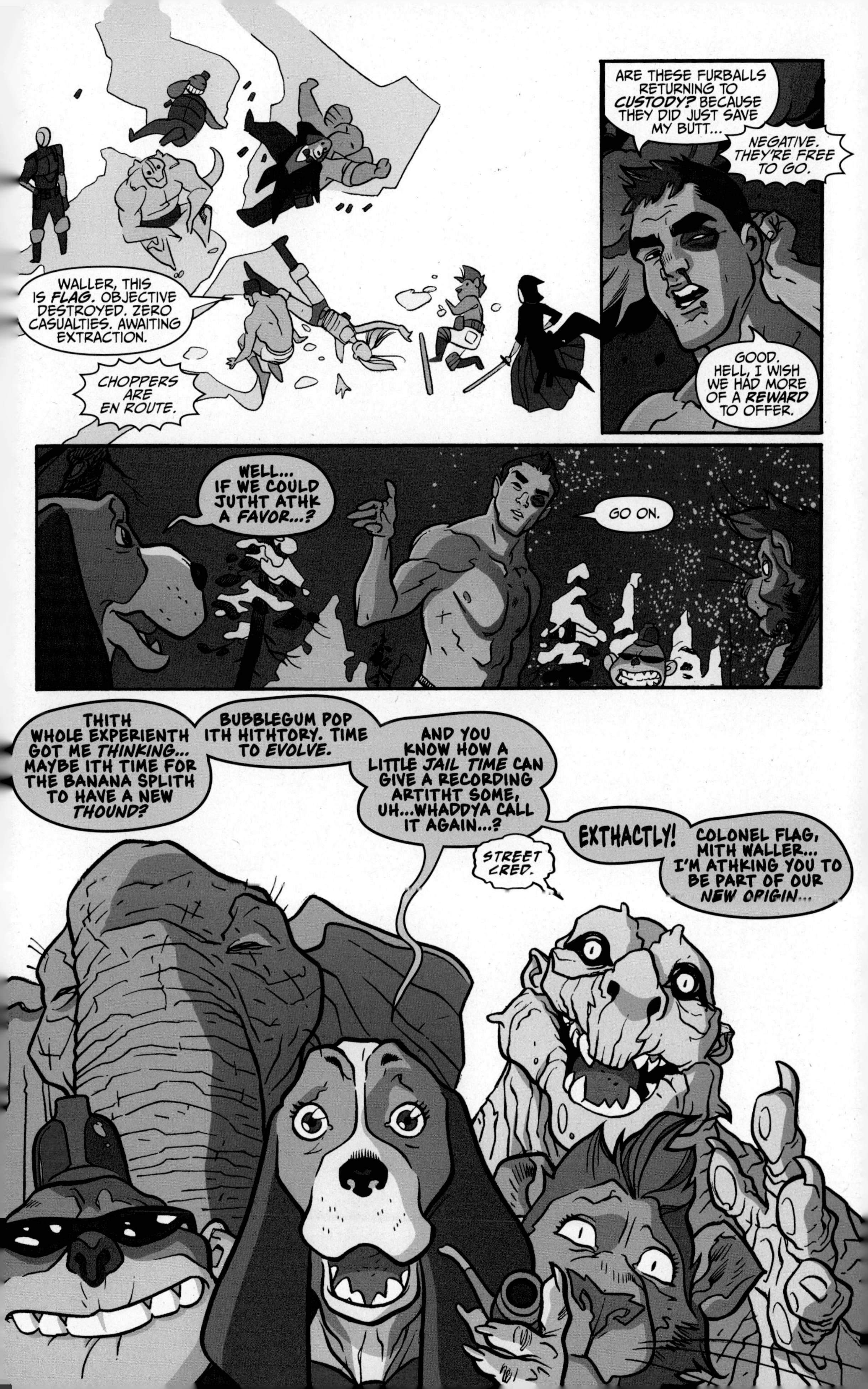
WALLER, THIS IS FLAG. OBJECTIVE DESTROYED. ZERO CASUALTIES. AWAITING EXTRACTION.
CHOPPERS ARE EN ROUTE.
ARE THESE FURBALLS RETURNING TO CUSTODY? BECAUSE THEY DID JUST SAVE MY BUTT...
NEGATIVE. THEY'RE FREE TO GO.
GOOD. HELL, I WISH WE HAD MORE OF A REWARD TO OFFER.
WELL... IF WE COULD JUTHT ATHK A FAVOR...?
GO ON.
THITH WHOLE EXPERIENTH GOT ME THINKING... MAYBE ITH TIME FOR THE BANANA SPLITH TO HAVE A NEW THOUND?
BUBBLEGUM POP ITH HITHTORY. TIME TO EVOLVE.
AND YOU KNOW HOW A LITTLE JAIL TIME CAN GIVE A RECORDING ARTITHT SOME, UH...WHADDYA CALL IT AGAIN...?
STREET CRED.
EXTHACTLY!
COLONEL FLAG, MITH WALLER... I'M ATHKING YOU TO BE PART OF OUR NEW ORIGIN...

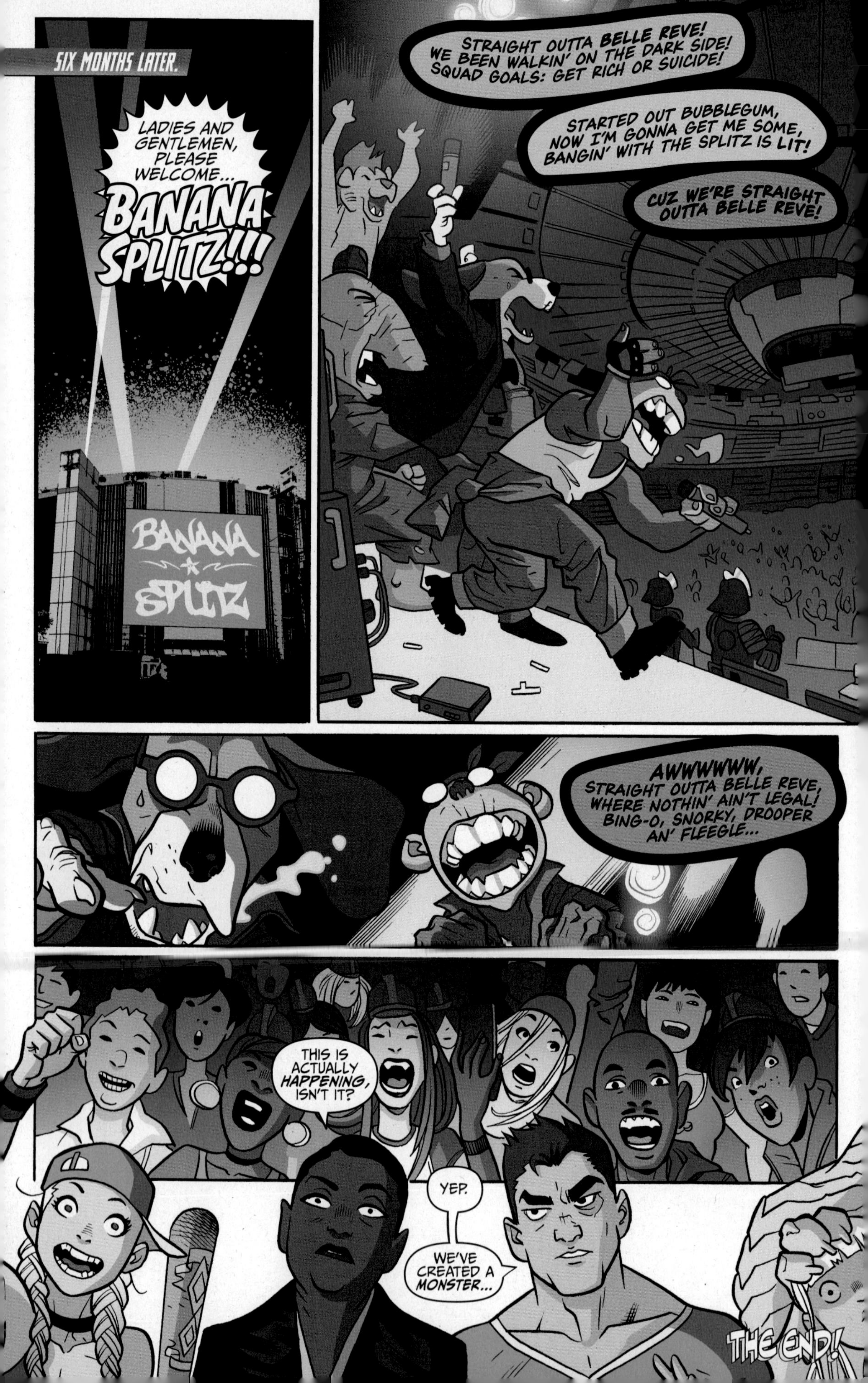
SIX MONTHS LATER.
LADIES AND GENTLEMEN, PLEASE WELCOME...
BANANA SPLITZ!!!
BANANA SPLITZ
STRAIGHT OUTTA BELLE REVE! WE BEEN WALKIN' ON THE DARK SIDE! SQUAD GOALS: GET RICH OR SUICIDE!
STARTED OUT BUBBLEGUM, NOW I'M GONNA GET ME SOME, BANGIN' WITH THE SPLITZ IS LIT!
CUZ WE'RE STRAIGHT OUTTA BELLE REVE!
AWWWWWW, STRAIGHT OUTTA BELLE REVE, WHERE NOTHIN' AIN'T LEGAL! BING-O, SNORKY, DROOPER AN' FLEEGLE...
THIS IS ACTUALLY HAPPENING, ISN'T IT?
YEP.
WE'VE CREATED A MONSTER...
THE END!

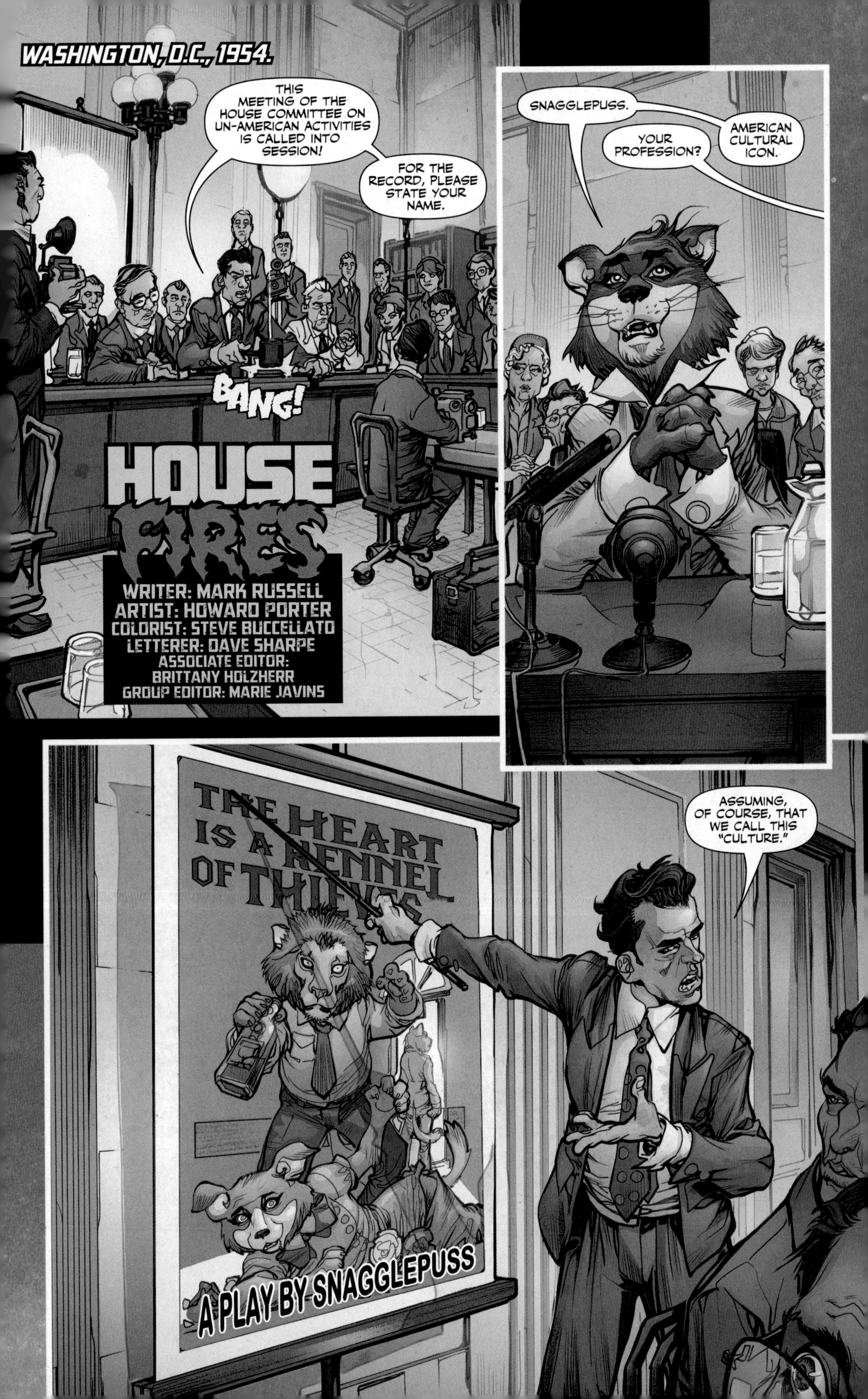
WASHINGTON, D.C., 1954.
THIS MEETING OF THE HOUSE COMMITTEE ON UN-AMERICAN ACTIVITIES IS CALLED INTO SESSION!
FOR THE RECORD, PLEASE STATE YOUR NAME.
BANG!
HOUSE FIRES
WRITER: MARK RUSSELL
ARTIST: HOWARD PORTER
COLORIST: STEVE BUCCELLATO
LETTERER: DAVE SHARPE
ASSOCIATE EDITOR: BRITTANY HOLZHERR
GROUP EDITOR: MARIE JAVINS
SNAGGLEPUSS.
YOUR PROFESSION?
AMERICAN CULTURAL ICON.
ASSUMING, OF COURSE, THAT WE CALL THIS "CULTURE."
THE HEART IS A KENNEL OF THIEVES
A PLAY BY SNAGGLEPUSS

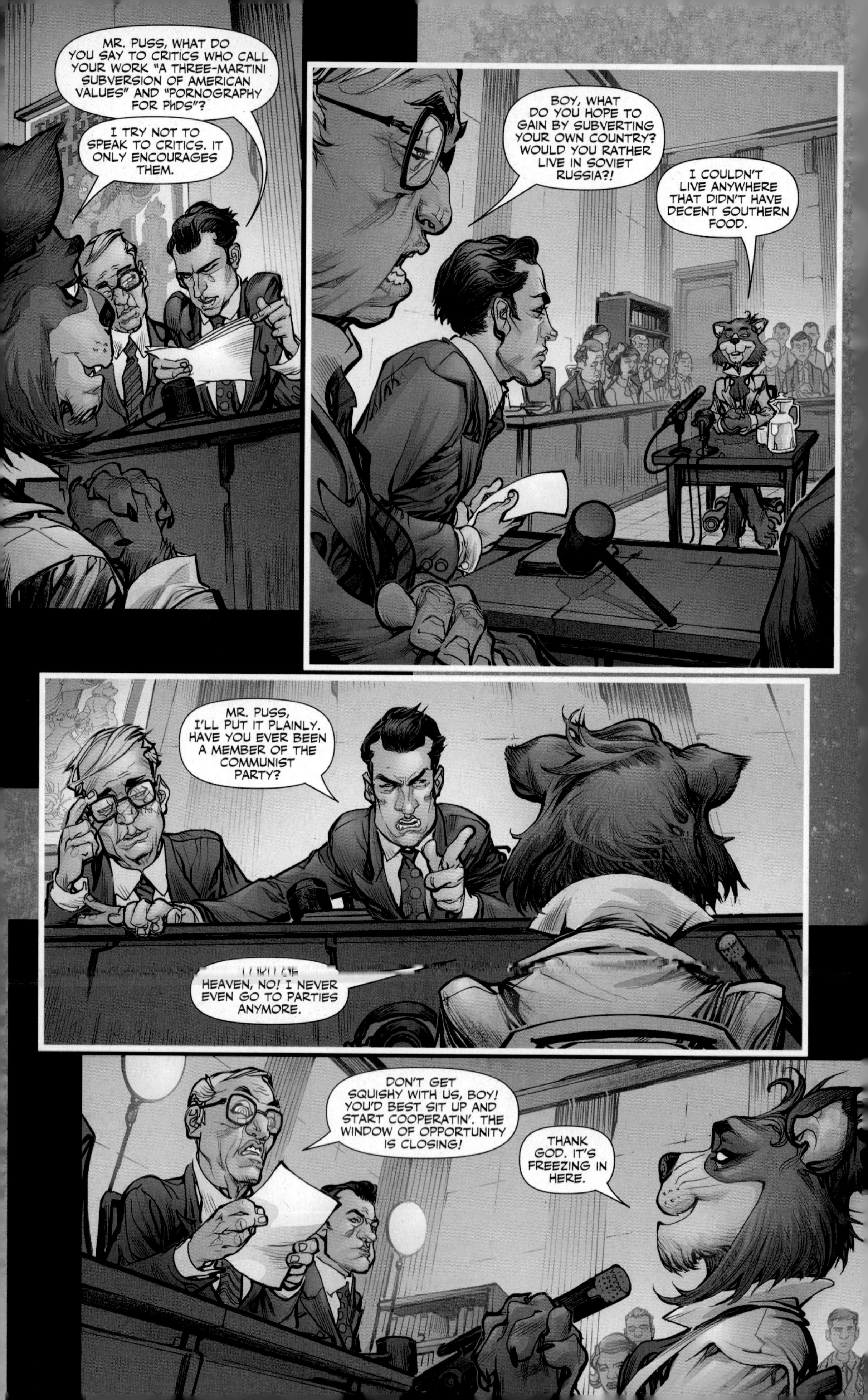
MR. PUSS, WHAT DO YOU SAY TO CRITICS WHO CALL YOUR WORK "A THREE-MARTINI SUBVERSION OF AMERICAN VALUES" AND "PORNOGRAPHY FOR PhDS"?
I TRY NOT TO SPEAK TO CRITICS. IT ONLY ENCOURAGES THEM.
BOY, WHAT DO YOU HOPE TO GAIN BY SUBVERTING YOUR OWN COUNTRY? WOULD YOU RATHER LIVE IN SOVIET RUSSIA?!
I COULDN'T LIVE ANYWHERE THAT DIDN'T HAVE DECENT SOUTHERN FOOD.
MR. PUSS, I'LL PUT IT PLAINLY. HAVE YOU EVER BEEN A MEMBER OF THE COMMUNIST PARTY?
HEAVEN, NO! I NEVER EVEN GO TO PARTIES ANYMORE.
DON'T GET SQUISHY WITH US, BOY! YOU'D BEST SIT UP AND START COOPERATIN'. THE WINDOW OF OPPORTUNITY IS CLOSING!
THANK GOD. IT'S FREEZING IN HERE.

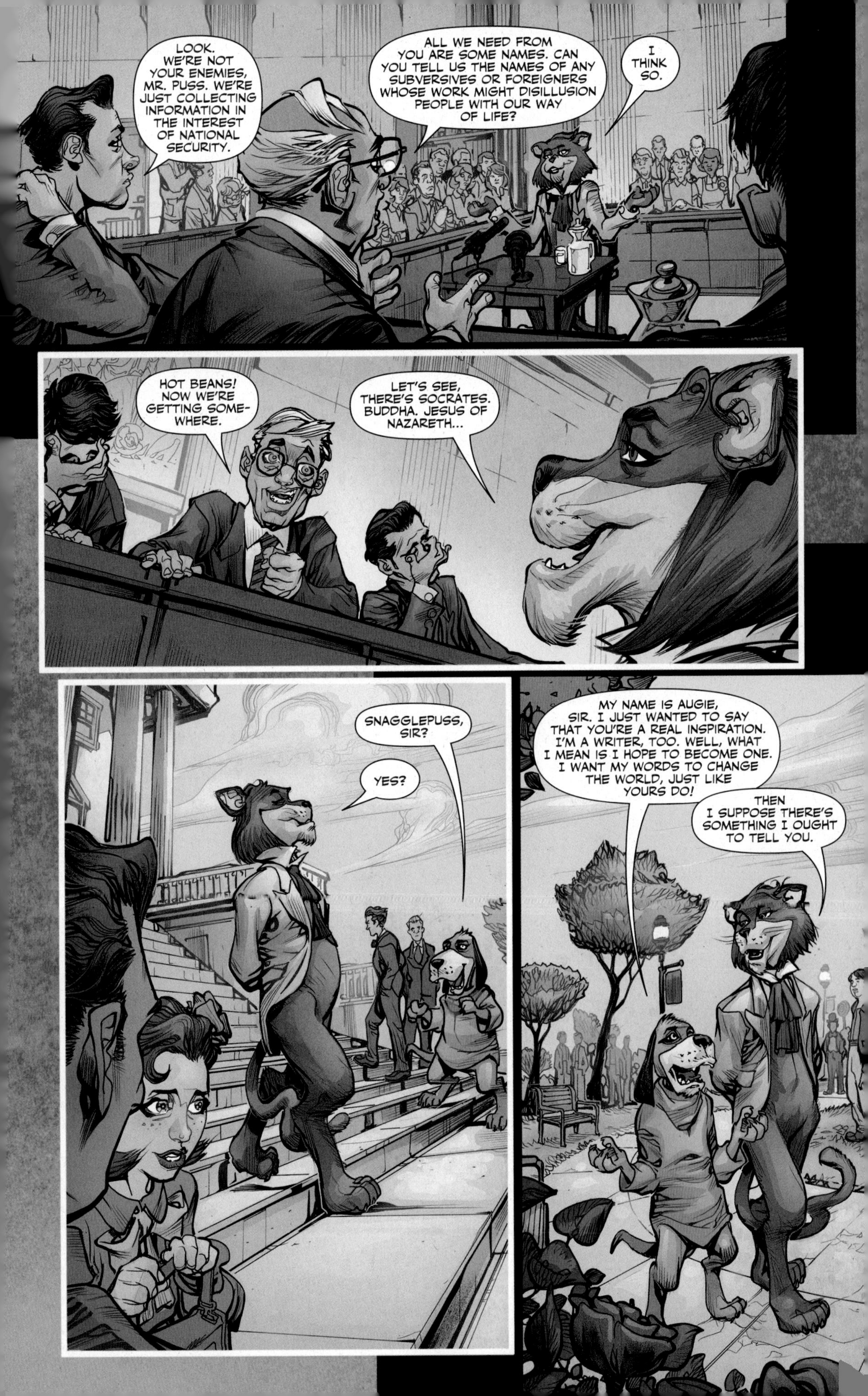
LOOK. WE'RE NOT YOUR ENEMIES, MR. PUSS. WE'RE JUST COLLECTING INFORMATION IN THE INTEREST OF NATIONAL SECURITY.
ALL WE NEED FROM YOU ARE SOME NAMES. CAN YOU TELL US THE NAMES OF ANY SUBVERSIVES OR FOREIGNERS WHOSE WORK MIGHT DISILLUSION PEOPLE WITH OUR WAY OF LIFE?
I THINK SO.
HOT BEANS! NOW WE'RE GETTING SOME-WHERE.
LET'S SEE, THERE'S SOCRATES. BUDDHA. JESUS OF NAZARETH...
SNAGGLEPUSS, SIR?
YES?
MY NAME IS AUGIE, SIR. I JUST WANTED TO SAY THAT YOU'RE A REAL INSPIRATION. I'M A WRITER, TOO. WELL, WHAT I MEAN IS I HOPE TO BECOME ONE. I WANT MY WORDS TO CHANGE THE WORLD, JUST LIKE YOURS DO!
THEN I SUPPOSE THERE'S SOMETHING I OUGHT TO TELL YOU.

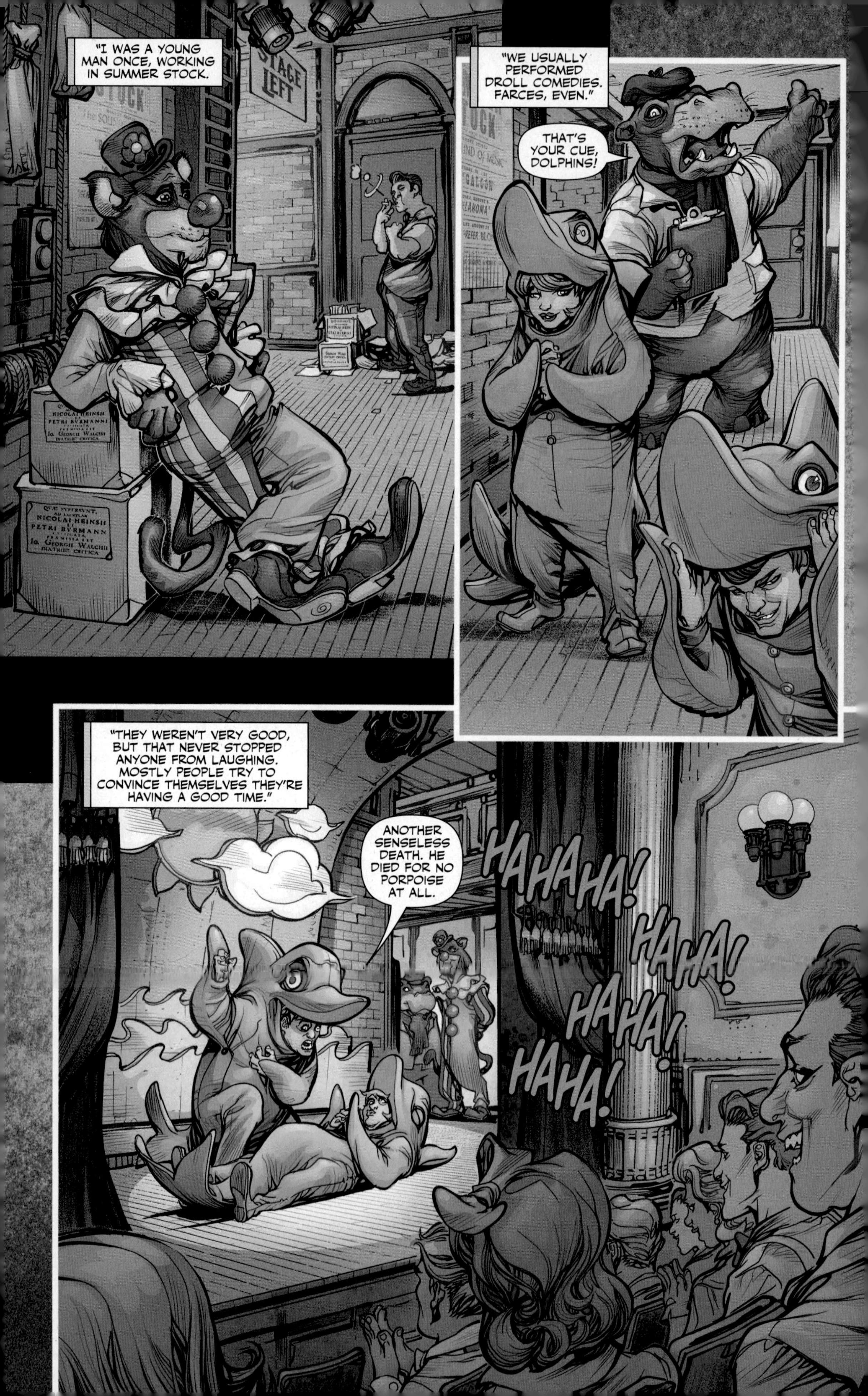
"I WAS A YOUNG MAN ONCE, WORKING IN SUMMER STOCK.
"WE USUALLY PERFORMED DROLL COMEDIES. FARCES, EVEN."
THAT'S YOUR CUE, DOLPHINS!
"THEY WEREN'T VERY GOOD, BUT THAT NEVER STOPPED ANYONE FROM LAUGHING. MOSTLY PEOPLE TRY TO CONVINCE THEMSELVES THEY'RE HAVING A GOOD TIME."
ANOTHER SENSELESS DEATH. HE DIED FOR NO PORPOISE AT ALL.
HAHAHA! HAHA! HAHA! HAHA!

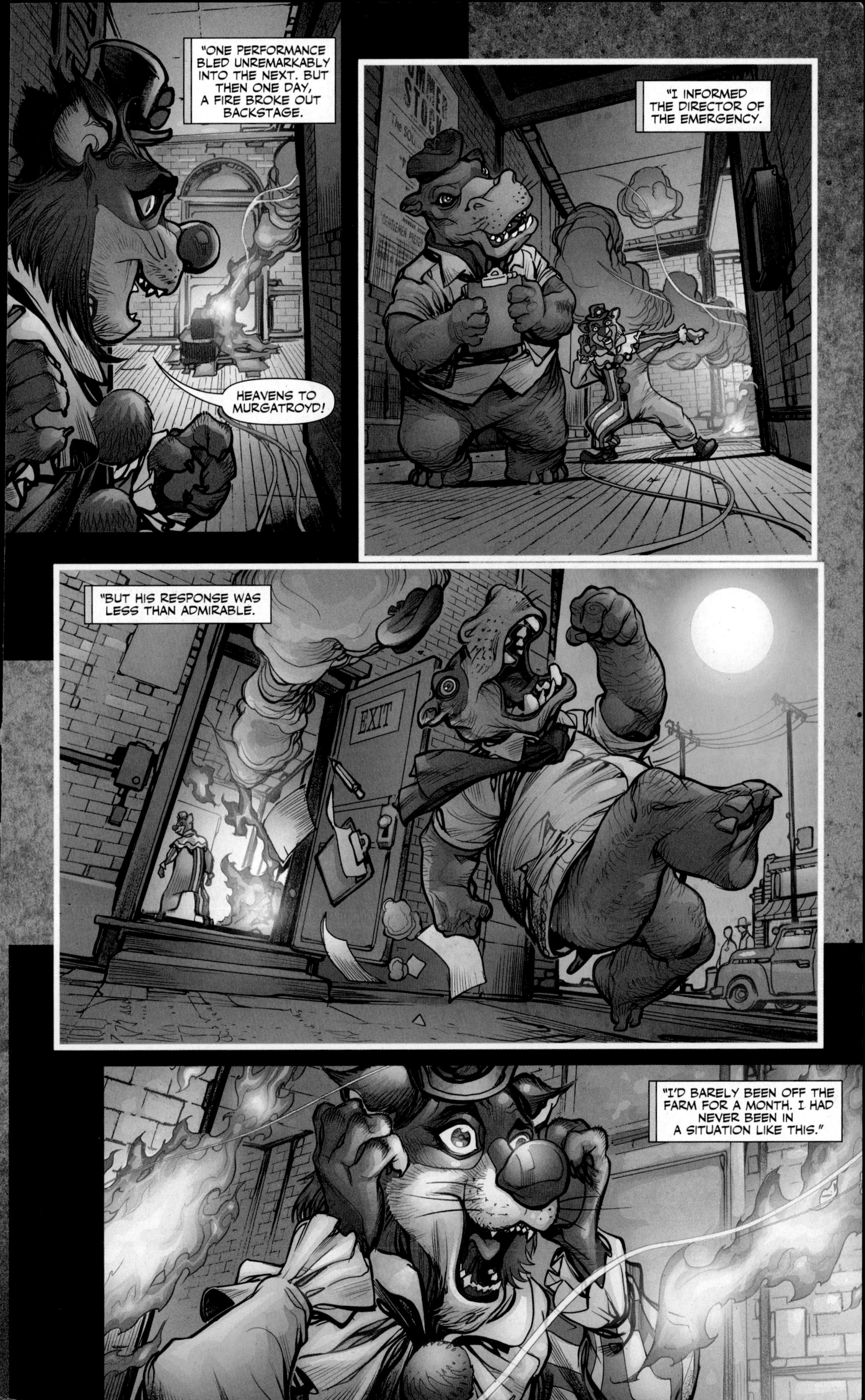
"ONE PERFORMANCE BLED UNREMARKABLY INTO THE NEXT. BUT THEN ONE DAY, A FIRE BROKE OUT BACKSTAGE.
HEAVENS TO MURGATROYD!
"I INFORMED THE DIRECTOR OF THE EMERGENCY.
"BUT HIS RESPONSE WAS LESS THAN ADMIRABLE.
EXIT
"I'D BARELY BEEN OFF THE FARM FOR A MONTH. I HAD NEVER BEEN IN A SITUATION LIKE THIS."

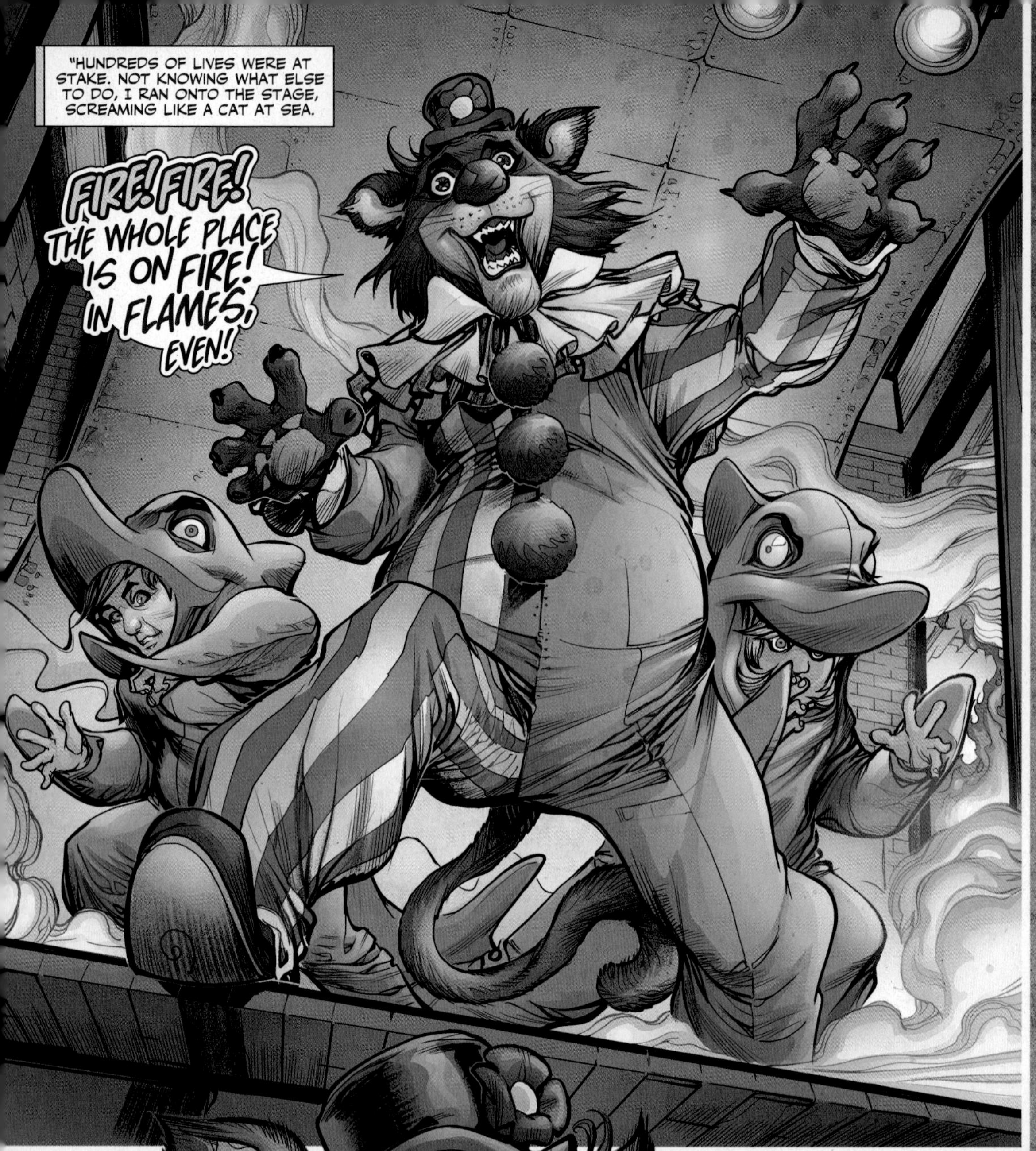
"HUNDREDS OF LIVES WERE AT STAKE. NOT KNOWING WHAT ELSE TO DO, I RAN ONTO THE STAGE, SCREAMING LIKE A CAT AT SEA.
FIRE! FIRE! THE WHOLE PLACE IS ON FIRE! IN FLAMES, EVEN!
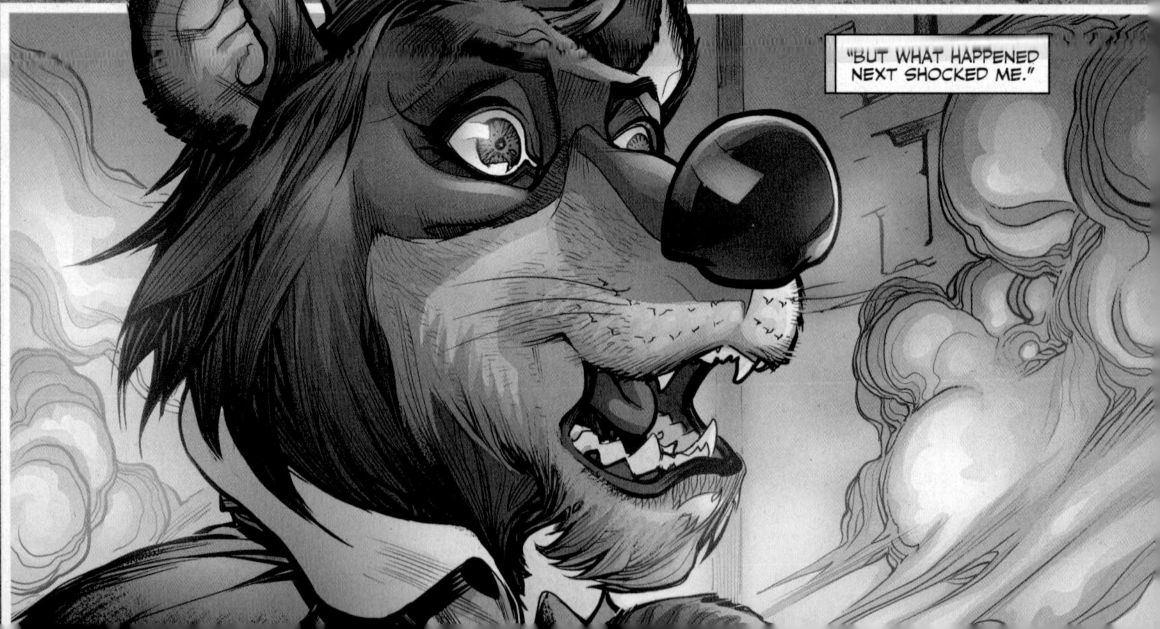
"BUT WHAT HAPPENED NEXT SHOCKED ME."

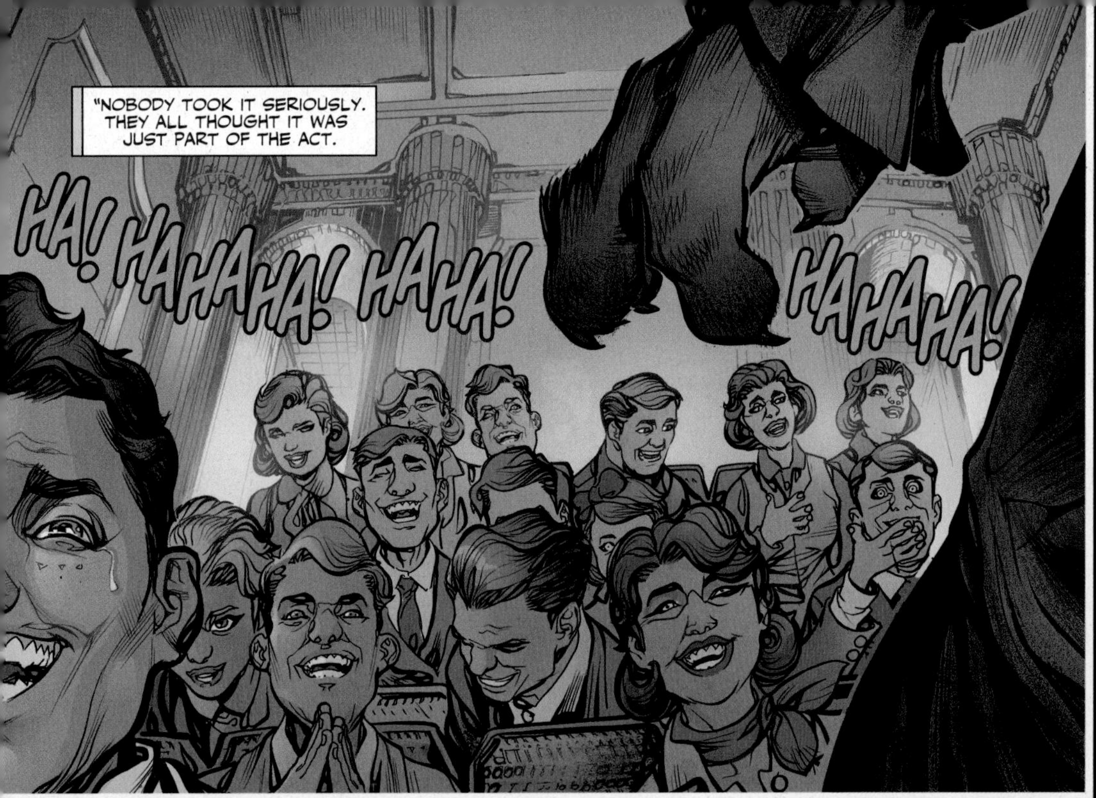
"NOBODY TOOK IT SERIOUSLY. THEY ALL THOUGHT IT WAS JUST PART OF THE ACT.
HA! HAHAHA! HAHA!
HAHAHA!

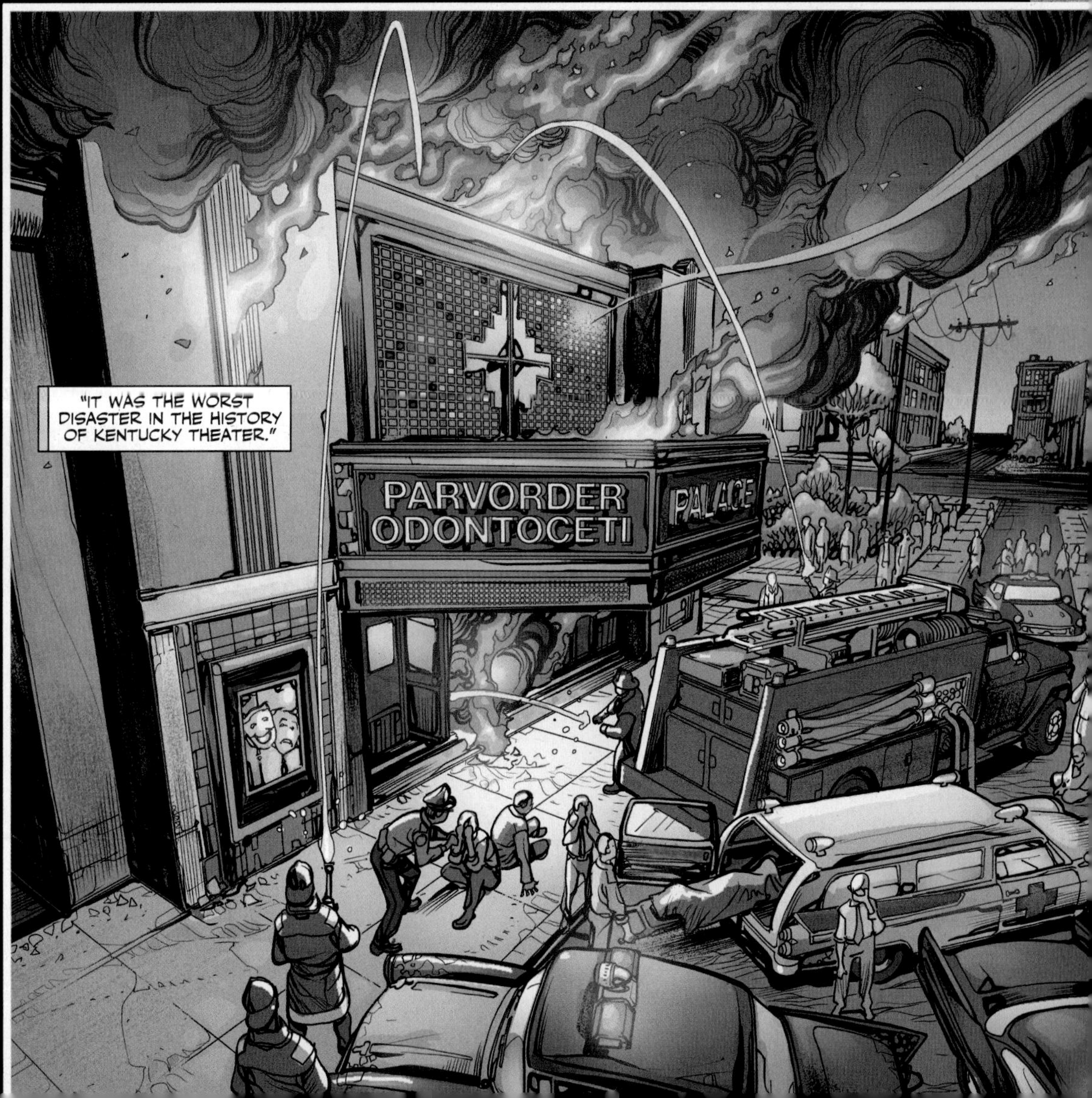
"IT WAS THE WORST DISASTER IN THE HISTORY OF KENTUCKY THEATER."
PARVORDER ODONTOCETI
PALACE

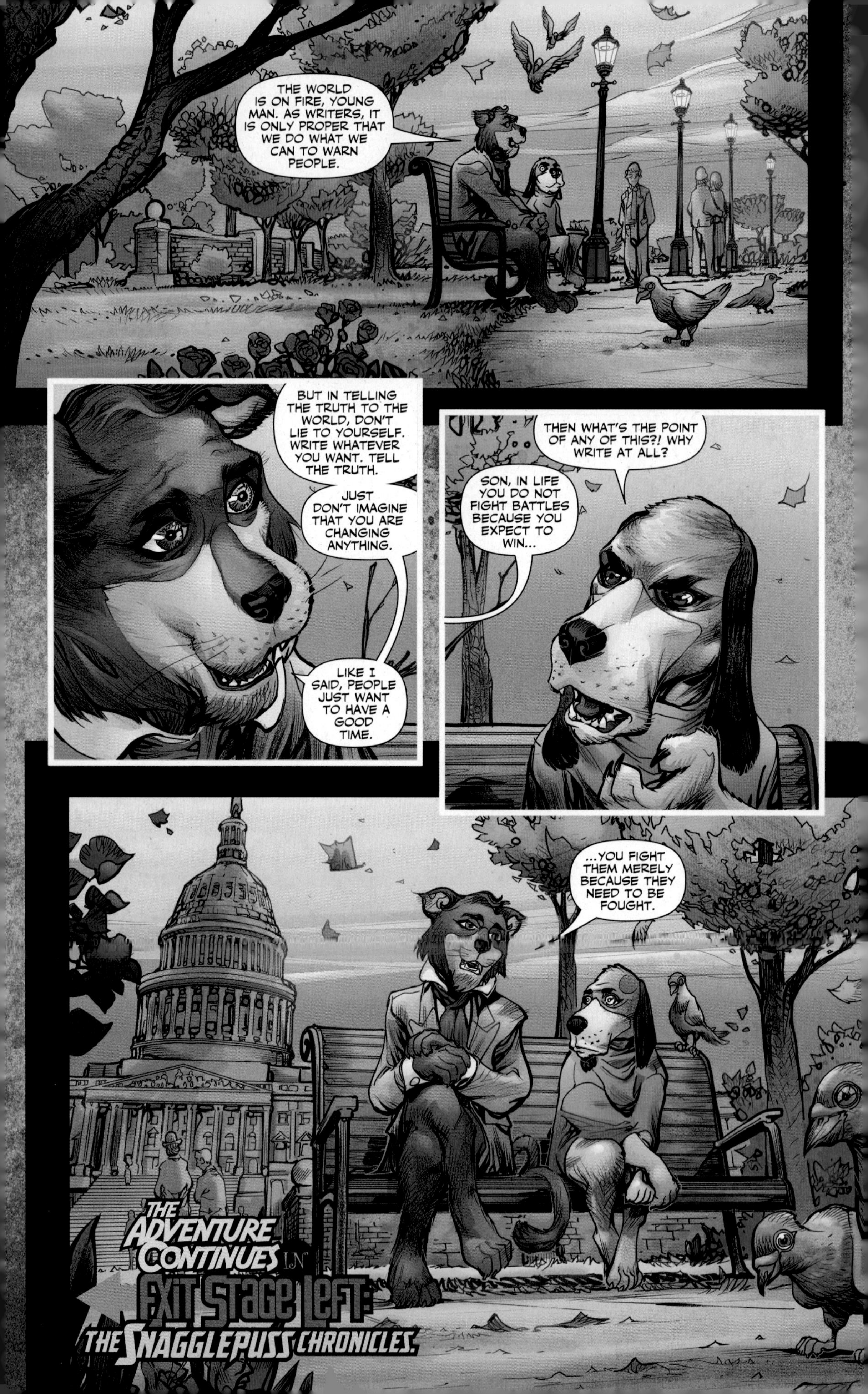
THE WORLD IS ON FIRE, YOUNG MAN. AS WRITERS, IT IS ONLY PROPER THAT WE DO WHAT WE CAN TO WARN PEOPLE.
BUT IN TELLING THE TRUTH TO THE WORLD, DON'T LIE TO YOURSELF. WRITE WHATEVER YOU WANT. TELL THE TRUTH.
JUST DON'T IMAGINE THAT YOU ARE CHANGING ANYTHING.
LIKE I SAID, PEOPLE JUST WANT TO HAVE A GOOD TIME.
THEN WHAT'S THE POINT OF ANY OF THIS?! WHY WRITE AT ALL?
SON, IN LIFE YOU DO NOT FIGHT BATTLES BECAUSE YOU EXPECT TO WIN...
...YOU FIGHT THEM MERELY BECAUSE THEY NEED TO BE FOUGHT.
THE ADVENTURE CONTINUES IN
EXIT STAGE LEFT:
THE SNAGGLEPUSS CHRONICLES.

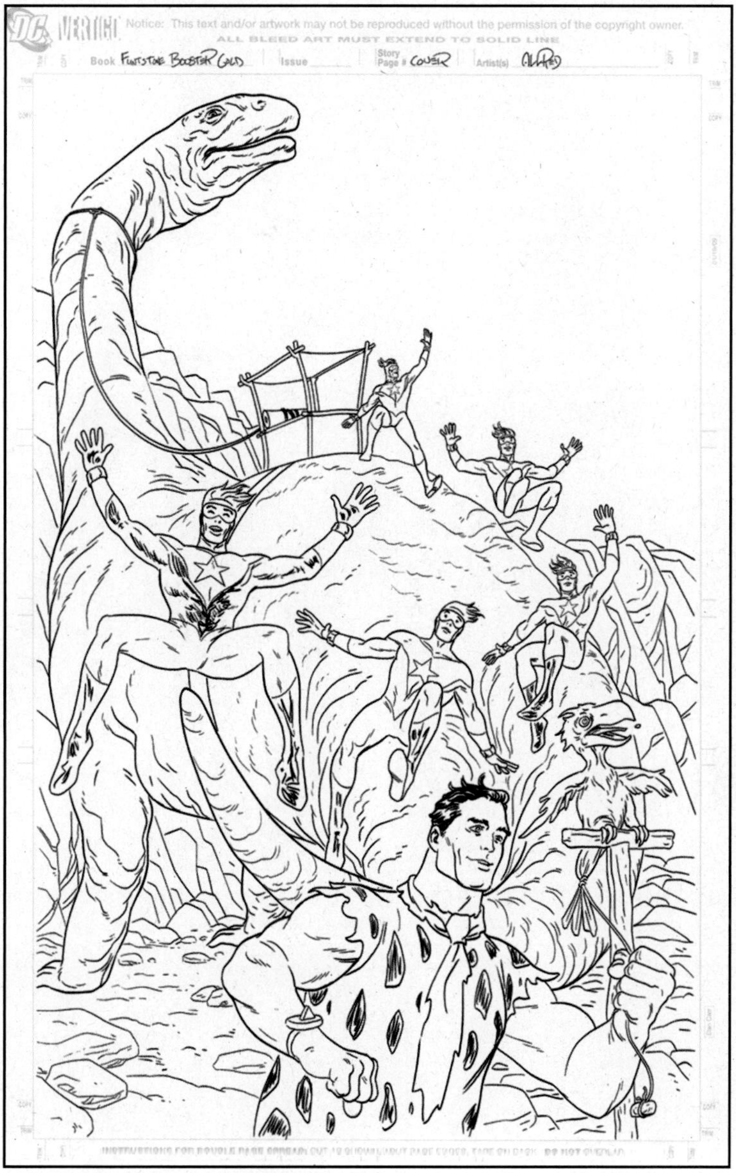
Notice: This text and/or artwork may not be reproduced without the permission of the copyright owner.
ALL BLEED ART MUST EXTEND TO SOLID LINE
Book FLINTSTONE BOOSTER GOLD
Issue
Story Page # COVER
Artist(s)

BOOSTER GOLD/THE FLINTSTONES SPECIAL #1 cover pencils by **MICHAEL ALLRED**

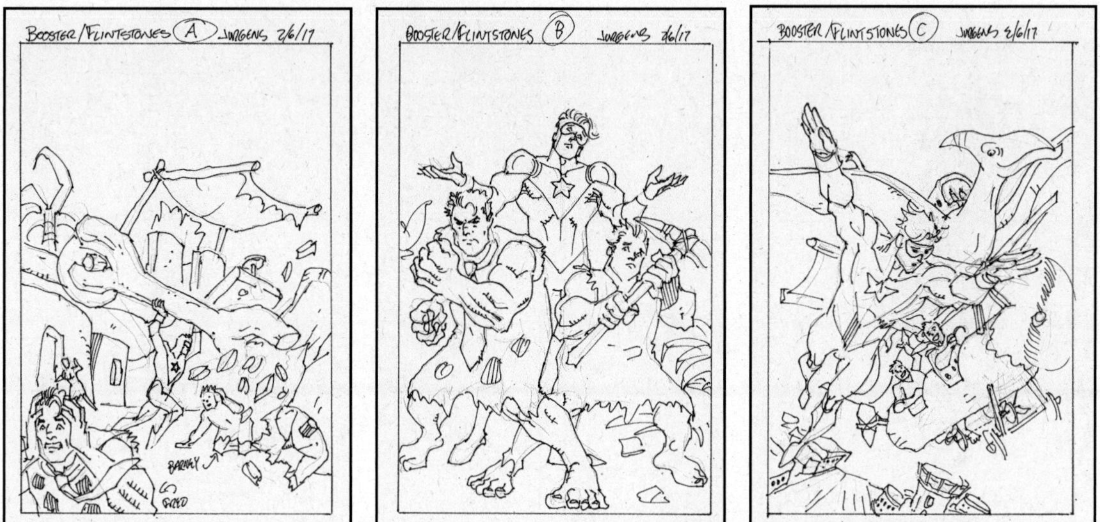
BOOSTER/FLINTSTONES A JURGENS 2/6/17
BARNEY
FRED
BOOSTER/FLINTSTONES B JURGENS 2/6/17
BOOSTER/FLINTSTONES C JURGENS 2/6/17

BOOSTER GOLD/THE FLINTSTONES SPECIAL #1 variant cover sketches by **DAN JURGENS**

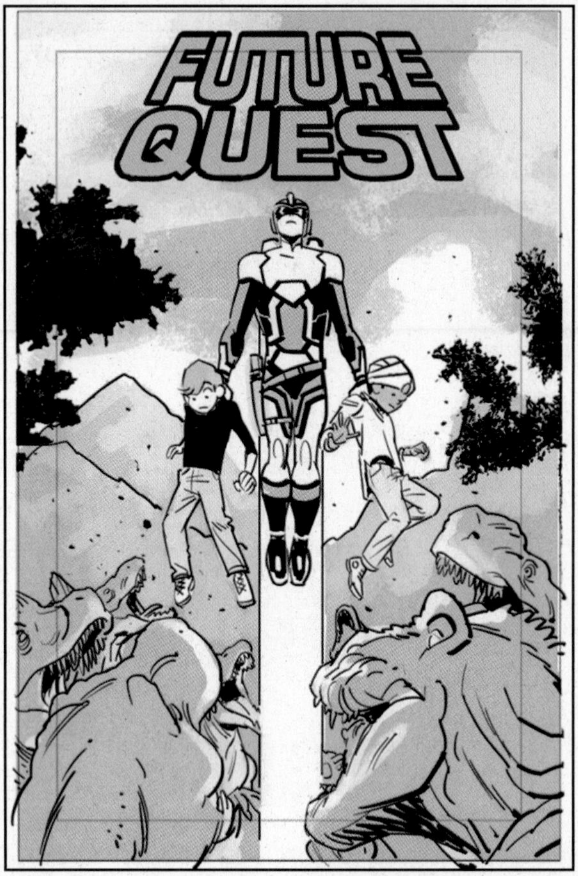
FUTURE
QUEST

ADAM STRANGE/FUTURE QUEST SPECIAL #1 cover rough by **EVAN "DOC" SHANER**

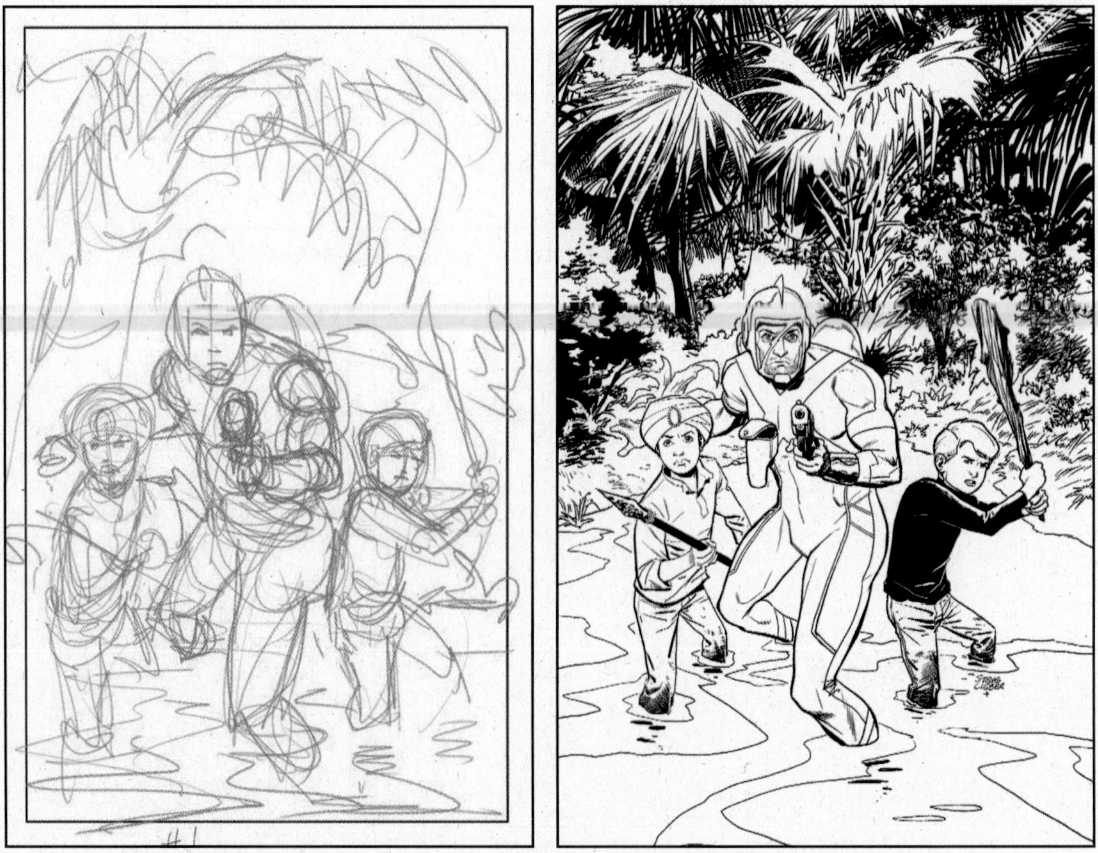
#1

ADAM STRANGE/FUTURE QUEST SPECIAL #1 variant cover sketch and inks by **STEVE LIEBER**

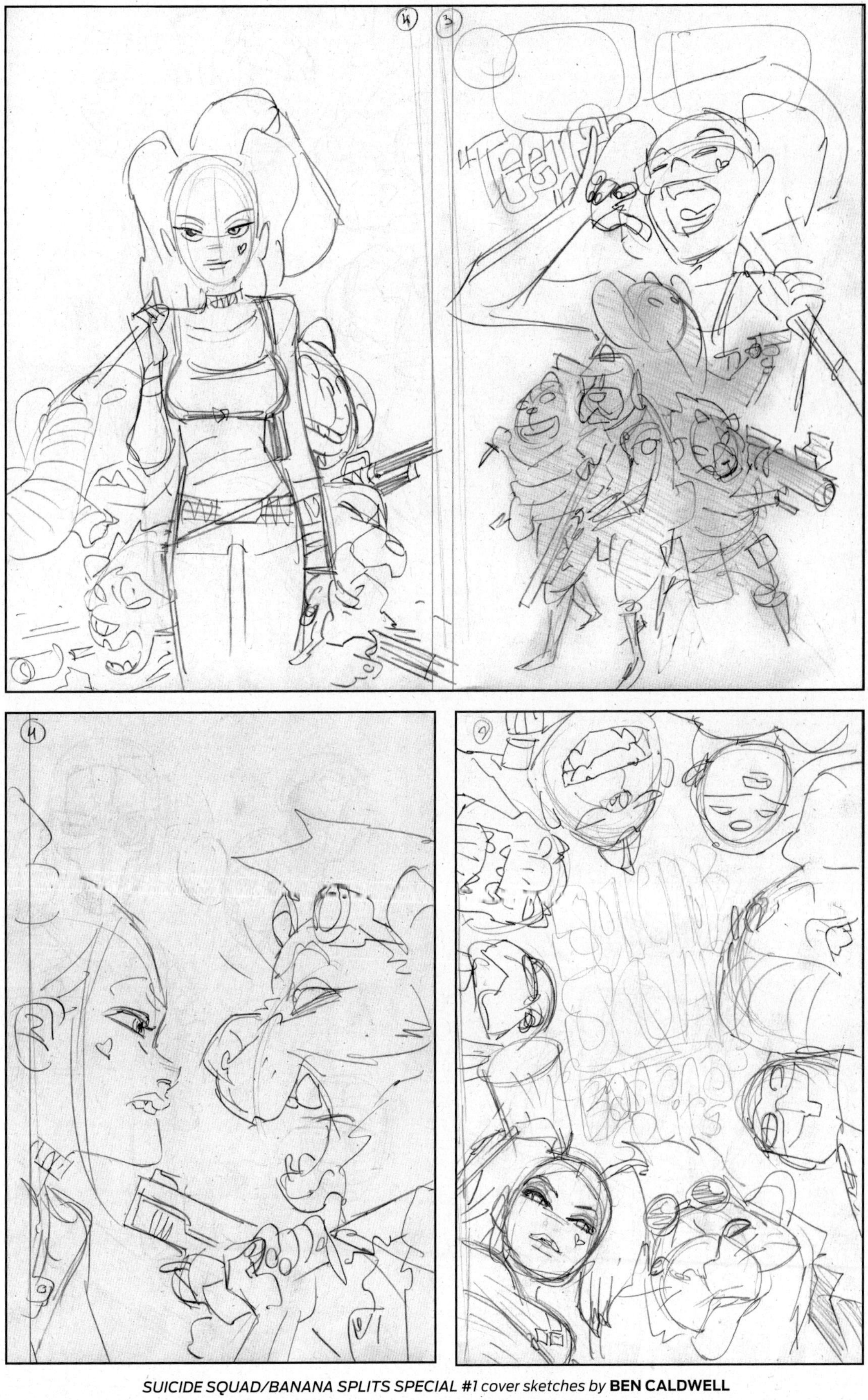

SUICIDE SQUAD/BANANA SPLITS SPECIAL #1 cover sketches by **BEN CALDWELL**

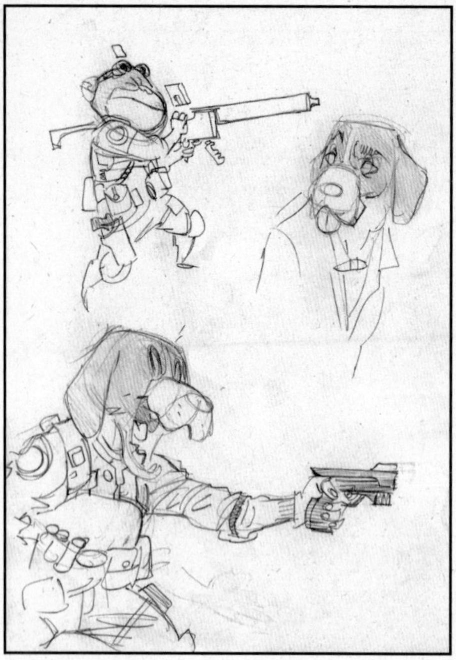

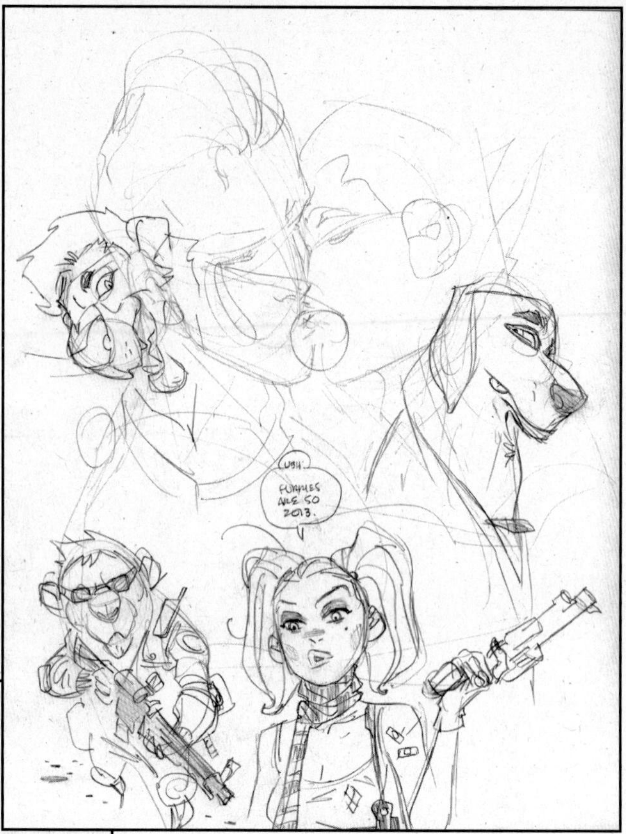
UGH.
FURRIES ARE SO 2013.

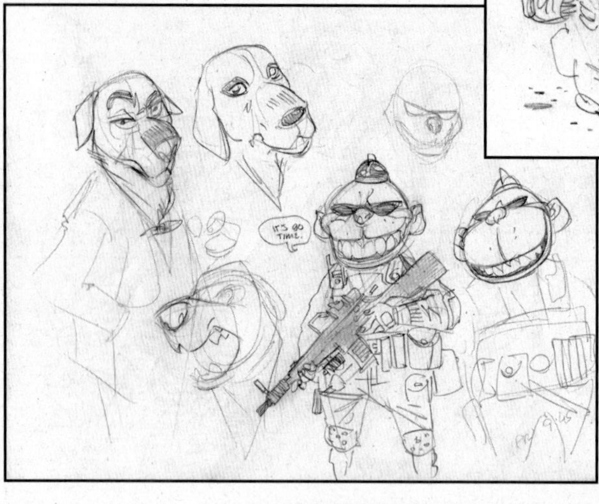
IT'S GO TIME.

SUICIDE SQUAD/BANANA SPLITS SPECIAL #1
sketches by **BEN CALDWELL**

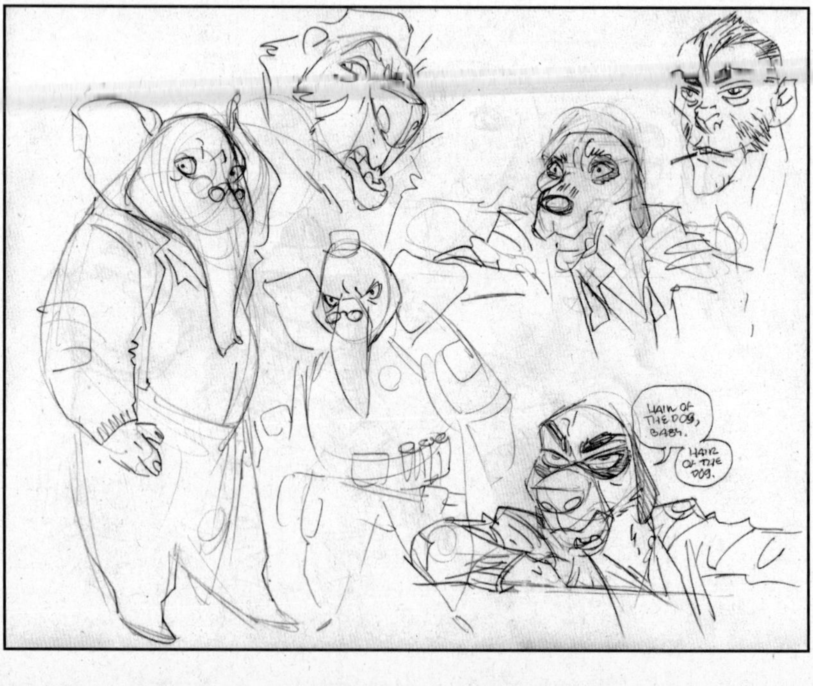
HAIR OF THE DOG, BABY.
HAIR OF THE DOG.